Autobiography

Autobiography
Narrative of Transformation

Carolyn A. Barros

Ann Arbor
The University of Michigan Press

2001   2000   1999   1998   4   3   2   1

A CIP catalog record for this book is available from the British Library.

Library of Congress Cataloging-in-Publication Data

Barros, Carolyn A.
    Autobiography : narrative of transformation / Carolyn A. Barros.
        p.   cm.
    Includes bibliographical references and index.
    ISBN 0-472-10786-0
    1. English prose literature—19th century—History and criticism.
2. Great Britain—History—Victoria, 1837–1901—Biography—History
and criticism.   3. Newman, John Henry, 1801–1890. Apologia pro vita
sua.   4. Oliphant, Mrs. (Margaret), 1828–1897.   Autobiography.
5. Mill, John Stuart, 1806–1873.   Autobiography.   6. Darwin,
Charles, 1809–1882.   Autobiography.   7. Narration (Rhetoric)
8. Autobiography.   I. Title.
PR788.A9B37   1997
828'.80809492—dc21   97-23875
                                                                CIP

Each unblinking eyelet linked now
to another in the shuttles of the loom.
"Thin rainbow-colored nets, like cobwebs,
all over my skin."
I affirm
all
of my transformations.

—Robin Morgan

Preface

This book is intended as a primer for the study of autobiography, one that attempts to make sense of what many consider the most problematic of discourses. It is not a study that focuses solely on the autobiographical *self*—lied about, murdered, written out of existence, reified, present, absent. It is not about what constitutes *truth* in autobiography. This study does not attempt to set definitive limits on what counts as autobiography. Rather, it introduces autobiography as a narrative of transformation: someone telling someone else "something happened to *me*."[1] This basic approach assumes transformation in the sense that "something happened" that is worth telling. It investigates how autobiography is rhetorically constituted and posits rhetorical perspectives from which traditional and nontraditional forms of autobiographical discourse can be studied.

Following an introductory chapter on autobiography as narrative of transformation, the second chapter investigates autobiography in terms of the functional elements or rhetorical perspectives that constitute transformation, elements I have termed *persona, figura,* and *dynamis.* The persona is the spoken or inscribed subject of the transformation, the "to me" while changing, being looked back on by the changed self; the figura is the mode or type of transformation, the "something" that happened; and the dynamis is the motive force or power to which the inscribed persona attributes the change, the "what" that changed the "me." The persona is constructed in sets of *before* and *after* qualities and characteristics that say, "I was not always as I now am; I have changed." The figura identifies and encapsulates the change that is implied by the before and after persona and frames the potential and limits of the change within its term or phrase. The dynamis specifies and elaborates the motive force to which the persona of autobiography attributes the transformation. Each of the aspects relies on and assumes the others. Also in this second chapter Thomas Carlyle's *Sartor Resartus,* not strictly an autobiography, provides a striking analogue and paradigm for the autobiographical narrative. *Sartor Resartus* self-consciously fictionalizes the composition of Diogenes Teufelsdröckh's life narrative; so it demonstrates how a textual persona is constructed and how transformation is dramatized through the figura and dynamis. As "emblematic autobiography," it is a *fictive* narrative of transformation.

This study looks at autobiographies from Victorian England, a rich period in autobiography's history.² Chapters 3 through 6 consider the autobiographies of John Henry Cardinal Newman, John Stuart Mill, Charles Darwin, and Margaret Oliphant in terms of persona, figura, and dynamis. Offering four very different types of transformation—religious, philosophical, scientific, and literary—they establish benchmarks for considering autobiographies from antiquity to the present.

Autobiographies are unique, idiosyncratic constructions of self and change; that is, perhaps, part of their attraction for us. These narratives also manifest the values, beliefs, and attitudes of the culture in which they are inscribed and to which they are addressed. Thus, autobiographies both conform to and speak against their cultures. The concluding chapter discusses autobiography's contribution to an individual writer's corpus, to a particular culture—in this case, Victorian England—and, finally, to the discourse overall. The study ends with a twist: autobiography, as narrative about change, shows us that "change itself is always changing"; written, spoken, or sung, the emplotted or bounded discourses of change have themselves changed across time. Surveying the persona, figura, and dynamis of Victorian narratives along with those that precede and follow them, autobiographical transformation shows its perversity over time. The transformation of a self, central to autobiographical discourse in earlier times, changes to a textual transformation—from the self speaking language to language speaking the self. Currently, more innovative autobiographers have refused to write the self out of existence and are constructing discourses that bring language and language users into new relationships. Finally, my major contention that autobiography is a narrative of transformation rests on the belief that it may be appropriate, from certain perspectives or for particular purposes, to contend that every narrative is autobiographical or, to take the other extreme, that every autobiography is fictive. If, however, the reader wishes to consider alternatives, reading autobiography as narrative of transformation offers new possibilities for interpretation of a complex and enigmatic genre.

I thank the National Endowment for the Humanities (NEH) for providing me with a Summer Seminar grant to work on this project. I also thank James Olney, Vorhees Professor of English at Louisiana State University and Director of the NEH seminar, for bringing together a group of scholars who added much to my understanding of autobiography. I thank George Simson, Editor of *biography*, who first published my work on autobiography.

I thank my colleagues at the University of Texas at Arlington: Thomas E. Porter, Johanna M. Smith, Simone Turbeville, Dabney Townsend, C. Jan Swearingen, and Judith McDowell, who gave me encouragement and their best criticism. I thank LeAnn Fields, Executive Editor, and Kristen M. Lare, Copyediting Coordinator, University of Michigan Press, for their astute suggestions and patient help. I thank my family for their loving support: my husband, David; my children, Wallace, Mark, and Timothy; and my mother, Katharine Paquato Carlton.

Contents

I

Narratives of Transformation

Someone Telling Someone Else
"Something happened to me"

" 'You must not tell anyone,' my mother said, 'what I am about to tell you.' " Then Maxine Hong Kingston, in *Woman Warrior: Memoirs of a Girlhood among Ghosts*, proceeds to tell what happened to her and her family. She tells of her aunt, the "No Name Woman," who drowns herself in grief and revenge. She tells of her mother, who sits on the heads of ghosts, and she tells of how she changes from a girl with a "dried duck" voice to a singing poetess. Whether it is Maxine Hong Kingston, Giambattista Vico, Saint Teresa, Jean-Jacques Rousseau, Vladimir Nabokov, or Wole Soyinka, whenever we pick up an autobiography, we expect to encounter a person, to "read a life." And we assume that this "life" will be an account that traces "what happened," the significant changes that this life experience entails. Autobiography is about change; it narrates a series of transformations. This is an expectation we bring to any autobiographical text.

As a text of a life, autobiography presents the "before" and "after" of individuals who have undergone transformations of some kind. These transformations may be slight—Ruskin in *Praeterita* changes from novice tourist to sophisticated traveler—or monumental—Bunyan in *Grace Abounding to the Chief of Sinners*, from sinner to saint; Harriet Jacobs in *Incidents in the Life of a Slave Girl Written by Herself*, from slave status to free woman. The transformations may be incremental—Montaigne changes each time he revises his *Essays;* his transformations can be read as *chaconne*, "variations on the theme of a sophisticated return to the world of artifice and appearance that was repudiated at the outset."[1] The transformation may entail a quantum leap: Bertrand Russell, the boy who learned his multiplication tables in tears, becomes the author of *Principia Mathematica* and wins a Nobel Prize. The transformation may be moebus like: Roland Barthes changes from self to text. Turning language on itself, Barthes's transformation is "zig-zag."

"Something Happened"

The change typical of autobiographies is not the product of nature or time. The metamorphoses are not just a matter of growing old, losing one's teeth or hair, developing aches and pains, misplacing one's memory. Change is presented as *transformative,* a significant mutation in the characteristic qualities and societal relationships of the principal persona. Autobiography offers these various metamorphoses emplotted, bounded, and framed by its language and inscribed in its configurations of words and images. Change is then the operative *metaphor* in autobiographical discourse.

Harriet Jacobs tells us that her narrative will be of her incredible "adventures" and "sufferings."[2] Edmund Gosse calls his autobiography "the record of a struggle between two temperaments," his father's and his own, "two consciences and almost two epochs," ending "as was inevitable, in disruption."[3] Harriet Martineau, in her two-volume *Autobiography,* precedes the narrative of her life with a table of contents, an "abbreviated" narrative of transformation, in which she gives a period-by-period listing of what happened to her, from her early "Tabulating Bible morals" to her "Fatal illness" and "Home and preparation" for death.[4]

Despite clear indications of change in the texts themselves, many critics pass over or fail to see transformation as the central metaphor in autobiography. I have discussed in an earlier essay how traditional critical approaches to the genre—historical, psychological, literary—in attempting to get at the nature of autobiography, have focused not on the issue of transformation, on how change is manifested in a text, but on other aspects: verifiability of data, analytical insights, aesthetic quality.[5] Obviously, each of these approaches presumes transformation in the text. The historian is attempting to verify the events of the life and, in so doing, looks at a dynamic series of events.[6] The psychologist looks at the continuum of behavior and thus projects some development in the personality.[7] The littérateur, viewing the autobiography in terms of a dramatic, or fictive, principle in the life, assumes progress in the narrative. Those writers who build their autobiographies on critical theory, like Sartre in *The Words* and Nietzsche in *Ecce Homo,* assume transformation, those of reading and the "reading other" ("the ear of the other," as Derrida characterizes it), respectively. Barthes's autobiography, *Roland Barthes by Roland Barthes,* draws on the permutations of language. Even those theorists who would deconstruct autobiography out of existence assume change: from presence to absence of self.

Additionally, critical works such as Janet Varner Gunn's *Autobiography: Toward a Poetics of Experience,* Susanna Egan's *Patterns of Experience,* and Gordon O. Taylor's *Chapters of Experience,* focus on experience, and thus imply that "things happen," or change. Stuart L. Charmi's *Meaning and Myth in the Study of Lives: A Sartrean Perspective,* Shirley C. Neuman's *Some One Myth: Yeats' Autobiographical Prose,* and James Olney's *Metaphors of Self: The Meaning of Autobiography,* in drawing analogies between the events or happenings in autobiographers' lives with those of myth, catalog transformation. Being less concerned with change and more concerned with the patterns of myth and experience, they focus on how meaning is made and enhanced by the invocation of such patterns.[8] There are, however, two notable exceptions: Jean Starobinski's *Montaigne in Motion,* an extraordinary work that shows Montaigne as "a spirited mind" that "never stops within itself," and Paul John Eakin's *Fictions in Autobiography,* which contends, with Sartre, that the "alternative to narrative motion is death."

All in all, it seems impossible to conceive of autobiography without considering that it entails change or of critiques of autobiographical works that do not, in one way or another, assume or speak to the centrality of transformation. In addressing the significance of transformation in an early essay, which he later develops more fully in his work on Montaigne, Starobinski remarks:

> If such a change had not affected the life of the narrator he could merely depict himself once and for all, and new developments would be treated as external (historical) events; . . . a narrator in the first person would hardly continue to be necessary. It is the internal transformation of the individual—and the exemplary character of this transformation—that furnishes a subject for a narrative discourse in which "I" is both subject and object.[9]

While we might disagree with Starobinski that all autobiographical transformations are internal (remembering Stein's preference for the external and Barthes's for the linguistic) or that they are necessarily exemplary (recalling Rousseau's *Confessions* and Genet's *The Thief's Journal*), we could agree that, where there are no significant developments or life-changing experiences, there is no narrative.

Tzvetan Todorov, in developing his theory of narrative, identifies transformation as the category that will make possible the specification of narrative theory, the elaboration of distinctions in narrative types, and the definition of narrative sequence.[10] He identifies narratives of transformation in terms of their predication, the simple or complex relationships between basic predicates and transformed predicates. Todorov then suggests the use of these transformation types to characterize texts by the "quantitative or qualitative predominance of one or another type of transformation."[11] He also suggests the application of transformation types to narrative sequence definition.

The transformation types implicit in Shklovsky's analysis of narrative Todorov makes explicit in *The Poetics of Prose:* "relation of characters inverted," "realization of prediction," "riddle solved," "accusation dismissed," "correct presentation of the facts," and "parallel motif," or, in Todorov's terms, transformations in: "status," "supposition," "knowledge," and "manner."[12] While Todorov admits that these formulations are very general, he sees their usefulness in proposing "a context for the study of all narrative." As for making finer distinctions in narrative types, he argues that the "very nature of the transformation already specifies the type of sequence."

> Finally, we might inquire if the notion of transformation is purely a descriptive artifice or if it allows us, more essentially, to understand the very nature of narrative. . . . Narrative is constituted in the tension of two formal categories, difference and resemblance; the exclusive presence of one of them brings us into a type of discourse which is not narrative. If the predicates do not change, we are not yet within narrative, but in the immobility of psittacism; yet if the predicates do not resemble each other, we find ourselves beyond narrative, in an ideal reportage entirely consisting of differences. . . . Now, transformation represents precisely a synthesis of differences and resemblance. . . . Rather than a "two-sided unit," it is an operation in two directions: it asserts both resemblance and difference; it engages and suspends time, in a single movement; it permits discourse to acquire a meaning without this meaning becoming pure information; in a word, it makes narrative possible and yields us its very definition.[13]

"Someone Telling Someone Else . . ."

Hayden White says that "it is a natural impulse to narrate" and suggests connections between narrative and knowing by laying out their etymological derivations: "the words 'narrative,' 'narration,' 'to narrate,' and so on derive via the Latin *gnarus* ('knowing,' 'acquainted with,' 'expert,' 'skillful,' and so forth) and *narro* ('relate,' 'tell') from the Sanskrit root *gna* ('know')." Calling on a remark from Roland Barthes that "narrative is 'simply there like life itself . . . international, transhistorical, transcultural,'" he suggests how narrative "might well be considered a solution to a problem of general human concern, namely, the problem of how to translate *knowing* into *telling*, the problem of fashioning human experience into a form assimilable to structures of meaning that are generally human rather than culture-specific."[14] White clarifies our understanding of narrative by contrasting it to the annal and chronicle, in which events are listed in a vertical order and terminate rather than conclude.[15] Gerard Genette further defines narrative:

> It is thus the narrative, and that alone, that informs us here both of the events that it recounts and of the activity that supposedly gave birth to it. In other words, our knowledge of the two (the events and the action of writing) must be indirect, unavoidably mediated by the narrative discourse. . . . But reciprocally the narrative (the narrated discourse) can only be such to the extent that it tells a story, without which it would not be narrative (like, let us say, Spinoza's *Ethics*), and to the extent that it is uttered by someone, without which (like, for example, a collection of archaeological documents) it would not in itself be a discourse. As narrative, it lives by its relationship to the story that it recounts; as discourse, it lives by its relationship to the narrating that utters it.[16]

While many narratologists stipulate that "a telling counts as a hardcore narrative only if it describes a transition from one state to an antithetical state or only if the something-that-happened comprises at least two temporally sequential and causally related events," Barbara Herrnstein Smith suggests that the conception of narrative discourse as "someone telling someone else that something happened" allows us "to make explicit the relation of narrative discourse to other forms of discourse and thereby, to verbal, symbolic and social behavior generally." She cautions, however, that "even in the narrow linguistic sense, narrative discourse may be composed of quite brief, bare, and banal utterances as well as such extensive and extraordinary tellings as might occupy 1,001 nights or pages." For Herrnstein Smith, if things are always happening, "it may be reasonably asked why, in any given instance of narrative discourse, someone has chosen (or agreed) to tell someone else that something happened and why the latter has chosen (or agreed) to listen."[17] Both Ricoeur's "story following"[18] and Herrnstein Smith's "someone choosing or agreeing to listen" assume readers (listeners) who ask "And then what happened?" as they move through the selected and arranged events related in the narrative.

". . . To Me*"*

If transformation is the "something happened" and narrative is "someone telling someone else that 'something happened,'" then my definition of autobiography as narrative of transformation becomes someone telling someone else "something happened to *me*." Montaigne tells us in the *Essays:*

> I cannot keep my subject still. . . . I do not portray being: I portray passing. . . . My history needs to be adapted to the moment. I may presently change, not only by chance, but also by intention. This is a record of various and changeable occurrences.[19]

The subject of Montaigne's discourse of transformation is himself.[20] He tells us that he is adapting both by chance and intention and that the *Essays* are a "record" of these "changeable occurrences." Lejune argues that Montaigne is practicing self-portraiture, not narrative.[21] He sees the *Essays* as nontemporal, thus not narrative. Yet the reader notes that Montaigne's editorial changes are not actually editorial. Initial text and additions (not deletions) constitute the text we read today. Versions A, B, and C of the *Essays,* along with Montaigne's comments on how these changes have changed him ("the book made me "), show us how the *Essays* can be considered narratives of transformation.

Unlike an "objective" history in which the events seem "to tell themselves," the something happened of autobiography always has reference to a *me*, but this me is not without its complexities. The inscribed me of the narrative must come into some kind of conflict with the culture and its values and laws if there is to be a transformation to narrate—a something happened worth telling. "The reality which lends itself to narrative representation," Hayden White suggests, "is the *conflict* between desire, on the one side, and the law, on the other. Where there is no rule of law, there can be neither a subject nor the kind of event which lends itself to narrative representation."[22]

To put it another way, autobiography mimics, as it constructs, a being *in* time and in conflict *with* the times. Change is the effect of emplotting or inscribing the "life." To inscribe the self as beginning, coming into conflict, and changing is to narrate. Thus, the title *Narrative of Transformation* suggests that the was and is self of autobiography can be charted in narrative, or, conversely, that the narrative requires a was and is configuration, a set of *before* and *after* traits of the autobiographical persona to serve as the termini of its inscription.

Augustine tells us that he recollects and narrates, "confessing not only what I have been but what I am."[23] Why does he choose to tell a story? It is not for God's edification. Augustine is telling the readers that the something that happened to *me*—God's transformation of his life—is nothing less than miraculous. Ordinary readers (ordinary sinners) may not require quite as much transforming as did he, but God's saving grace is there, nonetheless.

Chronological and factual problems in Rousseau's autobiography draw considerable interest. He tells us that "the succession of feelings have [*sic*] marked the development of my being. . . . I may omit or transpose facts, or make mistakes in dates; but I cannot go wrong about what I have felt, or about what my feelings have led me to do; and these are the chief subjects of my story."[24] As Rousseau's recollections slip into fantasy, his narrative grows more erratic. With the realization that things are breaking down, full-blown paranoia takes over; there is no single plot but *plots;* many conflicting or contradictory stories constitute Rousseau's narrative—his "me."

Nabokov recalls the something that happened to me in *Speak, Memory: An Autobiography Revisited.* Horizon shifts, in his case, are tied to language and memory shifts, "this re-Englishing of a Russian re-version of what had been an English re-telling of Russian memories in the first place."[25] Charles Darwin's *Autobiography* can be seen as a series of "me" anecdotes, short narratives from a humane scientist who may have feared that his personal story, like *The Origin of Species,* was too overwhelming, too big, for his English readers. Wole Soyinka's book *Aké: The Years of Childhood* is a narrative of a horizon shift from the personal me to a political me. It opens with Wole's childhood experiences of school, church, village, games, and mischief and concludes with his most memorable experience, the Nigerian Women's Union uprising. *Sartor Resartus,* as will be discussed in the next section, can be seen as a narrative *dramatization* of the process of composing a narrative of transformation; Carlyle calls it an "Auto-Biography." It is a fictive telling, narrated by a fictive, rather than an actual "me."

Autobiography's Many Forms

Reading autobiography as narrative of transformation allows us to make sense of its many and varied forms. John Henry Newman burned his journals, for instance, to ensure that we have only the story that he intended we have. His journals would have presented his narrative in a chronological, linear form. Instead, we are provided with an apologia, a reasoned defense, a history of Newman's religious opinions, a spiritual treatise that is a series of "convergences" between Newman and God—two luminous beings.[26]

Even if the narrative under consideration is a diary, a set of letters, an oral account, a collection of photographs, or a hymn, someone is telling someone else that something happened to *me*. While a single letter may be viewed as a minute fluctuation in the life of the writer, a set of letters over time from one person to another can be seen as an extended narrative of transformation. With letters, we know that a change has occurred from one letter to the next by a change in address, from change in tone—from terms of endearment to a more professional or distanced tone, or vice versa—or by a change in the usual closure. These changes are implicit; others are quite explicit. Keats often began his letters with, "Let me tell you what happened since last I wrote." Jane Carlyle's letters to Thomas (and his to her), a practice they continued from earliest acquaintance throughout their married lives, show Jane changing from a young woman awed by his writing ability to a mature and confident writer herself.[27] A published sequence of a writer's letters may be taken as a narrative of transformation, in which the writer's multiple voices, directed toward multiple recipients, change with receiver and time.

Letters are let go; they are social speech acts. Diaries are kept and acted upon and, at first, appear to be strictly inner directed. The "telling someone else" aspect of autobiographical narrative appears to be missing from the diary; however, in the Victorian period, for example, many diary writers (who were most often women and children) shared their diaries with one another. Female seminarians were required to keep diaries and to read them to a preceptress. Victorian wives and mothers shared medical information from their diaries. Victorian children wrote diaries that were read by their parents in which they completed exercises on proper behavior, a practice continued by Mormon children still.

While letters and diaries may be seen as forms of autobiography, a distinction between annals or chronicles and narratives might also apply to letters and diaries. Annals are comprised of a series of events listed in chronological order, while the chronicle "aspires to narrativity, but typically fails to achieve it." The chronicle does not come to closure; it simply "terminates . . . in the chronicler's own present." Like the annal and chronicle, the diary and the letter maintain the writer's own present. Like the chronicle, they terminate, rather than come to "narrative closure." They are what Hayden White calls *"unfinished* stories."[28] The reader is left to derive an "order of meaning."

Christian hymns, like other verbal religious performances, can be seen as formulaic autobiographies or narratives of transformation. John Newton, the English clergyman and hymn writer (who, coincidentally, authored an autobiography, *An Authentic Narrative of some Particulars in the Life of John Newton* [1764]), wrote, "I once was lost but now am found / Was blind but now I see"—the astonishing transformation of Christian conversion. Mary Dejong contends that in the singing of Newton's hymn, or others in this mode, the singer is *performing* autobiography. Thus, the transformation is twofold, Newton's and the singer's.[29] Additionally, the members of the congregation, in "following along" with the singer (and Newton), can be seen as potential performers of the narrative of transformation.

Perhaps one of the most unusual narratives of transformation has been suggested by Georges Gusdorf. He contends that when God asked Adam "where art thou?" He was asking Adam to write the first autobiography— the what happened between the time when God walked with Adam and Eve in the garden in the cool of the evening and the time when they hid themselves from His face![30]

A Rhetorical/Heuristic Approach to Autobiography

If we assume autobiography to be a narrative of transformation, how are we to approach it, to make sense of its various forms and its numerous appearances from antiquity to the present? Many contemporary scholars approach texts with the suspicion that a text is a screen behind which something is deliberately or unconsciously hidden. We are, perhaps, more suspicious of autobiography than of any other genre; witness the number of essays that focus on the fictive aspects of autobiography (Georges Gusdorf, of course, Timothy Dow Adams, Paul John Eakin, Jonathan Loesberg, and Herbert Leibowitz, to name but a few). Starobinski suggests (as does the autobiographer Montaigne) that we denounce suspicion and anxiety and shift to the interrogative mode.[31] My approach to autobiography is in that vein. It is a heuristic approach that explores the nature of autobiography by moving back and forth between the assumption that autobiography is a narrative of transformation and a set of functional perspectives or elements that account for this transformation. The rhetorical/heuristic approach attempts to examine the language, images, and structures of the text as they constitute the life change experience. If autobiography is to be viewed in terms of *what* it characterizes, transformation, and *how* it characterizes this life change experience, we cannot view it only as case study or as documentary evidence. We must examine it rhetorically; we must view it in terms of its contribution to the discourse. (Discourse is here understood "in its widest sense: every utterance assuming a speaker and a hearer, and in the speaker, the intention of influencing the other in some way.")[32] I propose, as a new approach to the genre, a heuristic or exploratory approach that is flexible enough to deal with the traditional or canonical forms of autobiography and the forms that most recently have been taken into the genre (or have enlarged our understanding of its boundaries) and the innovative forms that are emerging in the discourse. This heuristic approach is an attempt to find a workable, yet flexible, base out of which further critical study can proceed.[33]

Attempts to study texts in terms of functional elements can be problematic; this approach is often seen as absolutist, as setting out categories that require filling with *correct* content material and, thus, resulting in a single, prescriptive interpretation of the text. On the other hand, reading with suspicion, with a "terror of totalization," or with undue anxiety over definitions of language and reading may cause us to ignore functional perspectives and miss exciting complexities. More comprehensive readings of autobiography require that we take poststructuralist literary/critical issues into account as we attend to the elements that constitute the actual inscribed discourse. That is why I prefer to call the functional elements of this approach rhetorical/heuristic perspectives. Reading autobiography with an exploratory aim rather than from the mode of suspicion may allow us to examine the complexities of the genre and its historical and cultural contexts as we avoid some of the dead ends and reductive quagmires that attend suspicion and anxiety.

This study, then, takes autobiography as narrative of transformation. The what happened is "I have changed." The elements of that change, in the very simplest of terms, are the *who* of the change; the *type* or kind of change; and the *motive force* or cause to which the change is attributed. For purposes of this study I have identified these perspectives as persona, figura, and dynamis, respectively. Here I will give only a brief description of each. In the fuller treatment that follows I will show how these perspectives help us make sense of autobiography as narrative of transformation.

Persona, Figura, Dynamis

Autobiography's three rhetorical/heuristic perspectives—persona, figura, and dynamis—are each dependent upon and assume the others. They combine the characteristics of formal properties and contextual perspectives. They take into account Genette's (1) content of the (life)story, (2) the narrative or discourse, and (3) the telling or narrating,[34] as well as Herrnstein Smith's "multiple interacting conditions": (1) "such circumstantial variables as the particular context and material setting (cultural and social, as well as strictly 'physical') in which the tale is told, the particular listeners or readers addressed, and the nature of the narrator's relationship to them," and (2) "such psychological variables as the narrator's motives for telling the tale and all the particular interests, desires, expectations, memories, knowledge, and prior experiences (including his knowledge of various events, of course, but also of other narratives and of various conventions and traditions of storytelling) that elicited his telling it on that occasion, to that audience, and that shaped the particular way he told it."[35] And, while the approach of this study rejects the idea that all autobiographies have a peripeteia—a single, sudden change—the functional perspectives do take into account Hayden White's other narrative elements: connections between the events, a central subject, and an identifiable narrative voice.[36]

Persona, figura, and dynamis, as functional perspectives, are not just text-bound elements but, rather, are ways to analyze autobiography in terms of text and context and to account for both the reader and the writer's role in the interpretation of the life narrative. As a set of heuristic categories, they allow us to look at a narrative of transformation in local, cultural, and global terms. In terms of local characterizations of change they acknowledge the unique and idiosyncratic aspects of individual transformation: Charles Darwin's change is different from John Stuart Mill's (and my characterization of those changes is different from yours). In terms of cultural characterizations of change they allow us to see how both Mill and Darwin (and Carlyle, Newman, and Oliphant) shared in the sorts of transformations that were prevalent in their native England during the Victorian era; they appropriated metaphors that were shared by their culture to explain those changes (and we use our understanding of the beliefs, values, and institutions of that culture to understand those metaphors). Finally, the perspectives help us see transformation in more global terms, as persona, figura, and dynamis circumscribe the shared experiences of living and changing that connect autobiographical discourses across time.

The three rhetorical perspectives are beginning points for exploration; they are not intended as authoritative or definitive interpretations. They may be seen as converging places of writer, reader, and text as each participates in the autobiographical project. They are suggested as ways for opening up the potentialities of autobiography while providing a basis for examining some of its determining elements.

The "Who" of the Transformation: Narrative and the Persona
As the "who" of the transformation, the self of autobiography is the aspect most often studied, most maligned, most often erased. *Self* arouses suspicion and is open to charges of deceit and lying. It is tainted with vestiges of humanism and romanticism. To distinguish between the actual person who lived and wrote the autobiography and the self inscribed in the text (and who may or may not be purposely duplicitous), I have chosen the term *persona* to indicate the who of autobiography. *Narrator* seems a more obvious choice and is the one Genette employs. While *narrator* may imply a number of senses of the inscribed self of the discourse, it specifies only one of its elements. *Narrator* identifies the enunciator of the transformation, the reflective speaker looking back on the life, but *narrator* fails to specify the other elements of the who of the transformation, its subject and object. *Persona*, the larger term, as I use it, takes into account the two elements of the subjective me—the narrating me and the me of the action—and the objective me, the me transformed. *Persona,* then, is a "reinscription" of the self "within a textual system."[37]

By way of contrast, Genette tells us that Marcel, recounting his past, is the narrator who produces the narrative and is not to be confused with "the act of Proust writing the *Recherche du temps perdu.*"[38] Without digressing to a discussion of the fictive elements of autobiography,[39] I would like to clarify, from the standpoint of autobiography as narrative of transformation, that, unlike fictive discourse, in which the narrating situation—the act of telling—is simulated, with autobiography the narrating situation is actual.

While the actual narrating situation is one of the elements that distinguishes autobiography from other narratives, autobiographers, both ancient and contemporary, have attempted to subvert this distinction. Isocrates creates a fictive narrating situation, a court defense modeled on Socrates' *Apology,* to reveal his true character to those he believes are mistaken about his virtue. Gertrude Stein creates a fictive narrating situation when she presents her life narrative in the guise of *The Autobiography of*

Alice B. Toklas. The term *persona* allows us to make sense of the many voices that speak Gertrude Stein or Isocrates.

Persona serves to account for all the elements of the inscribed self of the text. It locates the narrator in the actual narrating situation; it specifies the subject of the narrative and identifies the object of the transformation. The nature of the persona is detailed in chapter 2 and is elaborated more fully in the critical discussions on Newman, Mill, Darwin, and Oliphant.

The Something That Happened: Narrative and the Figura
Figura is the image or metaphor for the type of change described in the autobiography. As the mode of explanation, it figures or suggests the dominant interpretive strategy of the autobiographer's change in the narrative. Figura is a metaphor for the emplotted narrative of transformation as "whole."

Figura names the particular human story inside the history of the age. The figura that would identify Rousseau's type of transformation would need to account for the confession of feelings in an Enlightenment culture. The figura that might encapsulate Gertrude Stein's transformation would need to account for her many changing faces, faces that Stein turns to us through the eyes of those who lived in Paris during the Cubist movement— Pablo Picasso's Stein, Henri Matisse's Stein, Alice B. Toklas's Stein. A figura that might name Roland Barthes's transformation would need to account for a textual transformation in an age of deconstruction.

The figura encapsulates the transformation. It stands as the term for the narrative of transformation, as it is particular *and* universal. Its function can be seen as analogous to a story's title or a poem's ordering metaphor. It is totality and potentiality. In reading autobiography from the perspective of the persona, we come to understand the "before" and "after" qualities and characteristics of the inscribed self of the transformation. From the perspective of the figura we can see the transformation as whole. *Figura* identifies this transformation in a term or phrase that accommodates the many twists and turns, complexities, contraries, and contradictions of a life inscribed. While terms like *plot* or *action* only deal with events in the story line, *figura* assumes the narrating situation, the "was" and "is" configurations of the persona, and the motive for the transformation.

One possible metaphor or figura for Augustine's transformation is confession. "To *meditate in Thy law* and to confess to you both my knowledge and my lack of skill in it, the first beginnings of the light you shed on me and the remnants of my darkness, until my weakness be swallowed up in strength."[40] It is in the act of confessing that Augustine is transformed from sinner to saint. "Magic Lantern" can be seen as the figura of Ingmar Bergman's transformation. Bergman's first toy movie projector, when he turned its handle forward and backward, illuminated still frame upon still frame. Like his movie projector, Bergman's autobiography is a playing and replaying of the Bergman life in interplay with the scenes of his films—a "magic lantern" view.[41] A figura that might describe Sor Juana Inés de la Cruz's transformation in all its complexities is "self-education," a very complex one, acquired through her own study and writing, through her discussions with the wise men of the Royal Court of seventeenth-century Mexico City, and through prayer. She learns deference to her religious and political superiors; she learns theology, law, philosophy, logic, rhetoric, physics, arithmetic, geometry, history, and music. She also learns that women have a right to a formal education and that it has been denied her.

Rather than providing a single interpretation of a narrative of transformation, figura possesses the potential for further explanation and interpretation of the transformation and the possibility for overturning itself with new meanings. Sor Juana's transformation as education, in addition to its aspects of learning, might also be characterized as "torment."

> With this I confess how interminable has been my labor; and how I am unable to say what I have with envy heard others state—that they have not been plagued by the thirst for knowledge: blessed are they. For me, not the knowing (for still I do not know), merely the desiring to know, has been such torment that I can say, as has my Father Saint Jerome. . . *how often I have ceased my labors and turned to them again, driven by the hunger for knowledge.*[42]

The potential and limits of the figura are detailed in chapter 2 and elaborated in the critical sections.

The Motive Force of the Transformation: Narrative and Dynamis
If autobiography can be read as narrative of transformation, the "something happened" characterized as the figura, and the "to me" identified as the persona, then in terms of the narrative the dynamis can be understood as the motive force to which the narrative persona attributes the change. It is the construct in the text that provides explanation for the force or forces that transform the persona from was to is. Saint Augustine attributes his transformation to God ("And Thou knowest how far Thou hast already changed me . . ."). Historians and contemporary readers may be able to

identify other forces that bring about change in Augustine's life: changes in the culture, in economic or political situations, or in family circumstances. The dynamis is that force to which the autobiographer attributes the change. This attribution is not always explicit; many times it is merely implied by the persona and figura. Even when the dynamis is explicit (as is often the case in religious conversions like Augustine's, in which God is described as force for change), the attributes of God may be different for each of those writers who inscribe him as motive. John Bunyan and Richard Baxter attribute their salvation to a Puritan God, while Saint Teresa's God is a god of visions and raptures.

The rhetorical elements of persona, figura, and dynamis constitute auto-biography as narrative of transformation and provide an alternative approach to the study of the genre. Focusing the investigation on Victorian autobiography illuminates the way in which a rhetorical/heuristic approach illuminates not only a genre but also a culture's manifold complexities.

Only Three? Autobiography and Time and Order

Does focusing on persona, figura, and dynamis get at all the constitutive elements of autobiography? For many narrative theorists such as Genette, Ricoeur, Kermode, and Goodman, "time" and "order" are the aspects of greatest concern. It is worth pointing out here that autobiographies do not always, as the reader might expect, proceed chronologically. The ability to "follow" an autobiography, as Ricoeur would put it, is based on a general understanding of a life: a person is born, things happen—minute by minute or year to year—and then the person dies. If these narratives are presented in nonchronological order, if the time of the life narrative is changed in any way, we will want explanations about why our expectations of the life order have not been met.

We might see the deterioration of the narrative order in Rousseau as unconscious, but for other writers there may be good reasons for a nonlinear ordering of the events of the life narrative. Nonliterary autobiographers, such as scientists or public figures, may see the events themselves as sufficiently interesting and arrange them into something close to a chronological order. Literary autobiographers, on the other hand, may choose to subvert chronology or thwart time to serve literary purposes. Maxine Hong Kingston moves back and forth between the time of her mother's life in China and her own in America; she shifts to mythic time when she presents her "talk-story" of the Woman Warrior. Ingmar Bergman has us at one moment riding with him on the handlebars of his father's bicycle as they are on their way to Amsberg, where his father is to preach. The next moment he is making preparations for the filming of *Winter Light*. He is at one moment filming the Dance of Death scene from *The Seventh Seal,* and the next he is fighting with another minister's son over the existence of God. "I can still roam through the landscape of my childhood and again experience lights, smells, people, rooms, moments, gestures, tones of voice and objects," he tells us. "These memories seldom have any particular meaning, but are like short or longer films with no point, shot at random."[43] For Sartre, as he relates in *The Words,* once he learns to read, his world is books, and time belongs to cardboard, paper, and ink.

> In vain would I seek within me the prickly memories and sweet unreason of a country childhood. I never tilled the soil or hunted for nests. I did not gather herbs or throw stones at birds. But books were my birds and my nests, my household pets, my barn and my countryside. The library was the world caught in a mirror. . . . the Larousse Encyclopedia took the place of everything.[44]

For Gertrude Stein the time of the autobiography is recursive, not in the circular sense but as moments cut across and back through other moments in what we might call "Cubist" time. Stein is in the atelier in Paris talking with Picasso; she is the military zone of World War I; she is in the atelier in Paris hanging Frances Rose's paintings. Time and order for Kingston, Bergman, Sartre, and Stein is narration time, rather than narrative time, thwarted and subverted versions of the time of the life.

As readers, in following any narrative, we at first assume that the order of occurrence and the narrative order are the same.[45] In comparing the narrative order of visual narratives—paintings and films—with inscribed narratives, we as readers make necessary adjustments in our understanding when we discern discrepancies between the two orders of occurrence and telling. In contrast to the Bayeux Tapestry that depicts William the Conquerer's invasion of England in the fairly straightforward left-to-right narrative order of its seventy-nine embroidered panels, Goodman describes a Japanese "picture biography" of Shotoku Taishi, a Japanese Buddhist prince. Although it was painted in 1069, around the time that the Bayeux Tapestry was embroidered, the relationship between the order of telling and the order of occurrence in this "picture biography" is much more complex. Five large screens with the Nara countryside and surrounding regions as background landscape hold sixty scenes from the prince's life—or "lives."

Scenes from all periods of the prince's career appear on each screen: on screen one the incidents date from conception to age twenty-seven; on two, from age six to forty-three; on three, from seventeen to forty-nine; on four, from sixteen to fifty, when Shotoku died; and on the right half of five, from nine to thirty-seven. Furthermore, the scenes on each screen are not arranged in any simple chronological order. . . . At the end—on the left side of the leftmost screen—are scenes from the prince's previous incarnations.[46]

Goodman concludes that, if there is some ordering factor in the principles that govern the complex arrangement of Prince Shotoku's life, he has not as yet discovered it. This picture biography, at least for Western critics, makes the narrative difficult to follow.

To follow autobiography, in contrast, readers, if they care enough, can always construct a "rough" chronology of the life out of the selected and arranged events of the life narrative.[47] Readers will generally make order out of nonchronological autobiographies by a process that employs understandings of temporal sequence and of how discourse conventions work, in other words, out of understandings of life and life narratives. Thus, the notions of time and order are not absent from this study altogether. The relationships of persona, figura, and dynamis to time and order are assumed. Persona assumes order as it presents a "was" and "is" configuration of qualities and characteristics. Figura allows us to deal with events in time and out of time and see them as whole. The dynamis, as motive force for transformation, assumes a time shift as it drives the discourse from beginning to conclusion.

One further point needs to be made about time and order in this brief discussion of time and autobiography: time and order in an inscribed narrative, both (imperfect) chronology and nonchronology, are constructs. There is no absolute chronological order in any narrative.

> By virtue of the very nature of discourse, nonlinearity is the rule rather than the exception in narrative accounts. . . . to the extent that *perfect* chronological order may be said to occur at all, it is likely to be found only in acutely conscious, "artful," or "literary" texts."[48]

These constructs may be conscious—"artful"—or unconscious. Autobiographers who claim a chronological order for their narratives, because of the nature of discourse in general, and of autobiographical discourse in particular, often pause in their carefully ordered narratives to reflect on past behaviors or make pronouncements on past actions. One would imagine that Camara Laye's autobiography, *The Dark Child,* written at the young age of twenty about his childhood in Africa, would have few of the sort of interruptions or digressions that are often present in more mature narratives, but the flow of his childhood recall is often broken by the voice of a reflective young adult. Laye's ordering of the past is disturbed by the present. Time in the autobiography of Mary McCawley is subverted by memories, as memories are blurred or exaggerated with the passage of time. Nabokov's autobiographical "revisitations" of the various language versions of his life cause him to ask which events are "real"? Which happened in actual time and which only in memory time? Nabokov's questions point to the complexities of time and order in autobiography and warrant further exploration at another *time* and place.

2

Persona, Figura, Dynamis

A Rhetorical/Heuristic Approach to Autobiography

This chapter defines and details a rhetorical/heuristic approach to autobiography. The methods of the approach are first applied to Thomas Carlyle's *Sartor Resartus,* read as fictive "Auto-Biography." Because the construction of the fictive autobiography is clearly a conscious act—*Sartor Resartus* relates how Diogenes Teufelsdröckh and his English Editor work together to construct a narrative of Teufelsdröckh's transformation—it serves well to illustrate the approach. The first section of the chapter defines the nature of the autobiographical persona. This is followed by an analysis of the persona in *Sartor Resartus:* Teufelsdröckh's transformation from "Professor of Things in General" to a "Philosopher of Clothes in Particular." The second section details the nature of the figura and discusses how retailoring serves as figure for Teufelsdröckh's "thaumaturgic transformation," as it identifies and encapsulates the type of transformation inscribed in the text. The final section of chapter 2 offers an extended definition of the motive force, or dynamis, of autobiographical transformation. Carlyle constructs a fictive dynamis to which his fictive autobiographer ascribes his transformation. *Sartor Resartus* again serves to show how motive force, like persona and figura, is a rhetorical construction. Teufelsdröckh's "whole Me" serves as image for the power of the "romantic and wild-eyed" German philosopher to transform himself.

Sartor Resartus, read as fictive autobiography across the rhetorical/functional elements of persona, figura, and dynamis, attempts a definition of the genre and clarifies the nature of the autobiographical project. More than a way to investigate a genre, however, the chapter lays out a method for examining the autobiographical discourse of a particular people at a specific time and place in their history, in this case, Victorian England. The persona types that populate a certain segment of Victorian society—the educated, professional class—along with the metaphors, figures, and images that describe Victorian transformation for this group and the sorts of motive forces to which these Victorians attributed their changes, are introduced in Carlyle's fictive autobiography, *Sartor Resartus*, and expanded in the autobiographies of Newman, Mill, Darwin, and Oliphant.

Persona: The Who of the Transformation

As rhetorical concept, persona is the subject of the action. The personae or characters in an inscribed text are generally thought of as agents or actors, that is, as forces for movement. We speak about character development, the growth of the persona, the fall of the hero. With autobiography it is not so simple; much of contemporary autobiographical criticism centers around concerns with the persona, or self, of the text—"which 'I' is the 'I' of the autobiography?" Problems of referentiality have led to various and provocative descriptions and characterizations of the autobiographical subject: "fictions of the self," "eye for I," the "disappearing I," the "recounting I," and "dummy ego."[1] Jerome Buckley is concerned with the subjective impulse in *The Turning Key*, Robert Sayre with *The Examined Self*, Paul Jay with *Being in the Text*, Robert Elbaz with the *Changing Nature of the Self*, Heather Henderson with *The Victorian Self*. Patricia Spacks's *Imagining a Self*, James Olney's *Metaphors of Self*, and John Morris's *Versions of the Self* are also concerned with explaining this aspect of autobiography.[2] These works have increased substantially our understanding of autobiography by pointing out that the self of autobiography is a construct, a persona, not the person. For example, when Morris speaks of a "version" of the self, he is assuming that the self of autobiography is a form, a rendering, an account of the self that can take many shapes, or versions. When Spacks posits the self as "imagined," or "imaged," she is indicating, again, that the self appears in autobiography as a creation. When Olney contends that Carl Jung's "metaphor of self" is myth, he is arguing that Jung both saw his life and inscribed that life in *Memories, Dreams, and Reflections* as myth. When Sprinker speaks of "fictions of the self," he is explaining how the self of a text is an "articulation of an intersubjectivity structured within and around the discourses available to it at any moment in time."[3]

While these perspectives of the self as construct have advanced our understanding of the genre, they have also limited our analyses. This limiting derives from the collapsing of all of autobiography's images and metaphors into those of the self. Preoccupation with the self of autobiography, because of a seemingly privileged relationship to an actual self, has caused many to ignore autobiography's other important aspects. *Self* is often used interchangeably with *autobiography* as if there were no other functional elements to be considered. We would not study a novel or a play solely in terms of its protagonist, nor would we be satisfied with analyses of texts that focus solely on the author.

The opposite extreme, preoccupation with the "absent self," is just as limiting. While this position enlarges our understanding of the relationship between the self and language, as we acknowledge that the present speaking "I" of discourse disappears with the saying, it tends to shut down further discussion, once the point is made. The end of the subject becomes the end of autobiography. In either case, as a beginning point for moving beyond preoccupation (and, for some, total absorption) with the self of the text, I introduce some exploratory categories that separate the metaphors of self, the persona, from the what happens, the figura, and from the how, the dynamis, or motive force.

There is no argument that an autobiography's persona, figura, and dynamis share a network of images and metaphors that make for its coherence. In positing a set of rhetorical elements for analyzing the genre, I am assuming (1) that a single element does not serve to fully explain autobiography, (2) that from inside a text we can "see from" or talk about only one element at a time, (3) that once autobiography has been analyzed from the perspectives of each of these elements such an analysis may untangle the critical confusion, relieve the self of bearing total responsibility for defining the genre, provide explanations of what and how autobiography speaks its life narratives, and lead to interpretations of its meanings—its contributions to the discourse. And a reminder, the elements are exploratory; they are *ways* of seeing autobiography; they do not render absolutes. They are maps for reading or misreading autobiography.

So, back to persona. While Rousseau, like many autobiographers after him, may have suffered from anxiety over being "fixed" in a text, the self of an inscribed discourse inevitably exists in the text as persona. The metaphorical nature of the term *persona* itself should not be overlooked. The *mask* equivalent from the Latin has quite different connotations from *persona* as it is used here. *Mask* implies that there is a real identity hidden behind the appearance. *Persona,* on the other hand, implies a medium of transmission that does not assume the reality-appearance dichotomy. In the dramatic context the persona/mask *is* the reality (the voiced words that constitute the character). With autobiography it is the same. Persona is metaphor for the inscribed self of the text; it is neither guise nor facade.[4] In autobiography we have, on the one hand, the *before* persona and, on the other, the *after*, or transformed, persona. The two aspects of the persona, before and after, differ in that they represent two different sets of psychic qualities. These roles or aspects represent the *termina* of the transformation—*a quo* and *ad quem*. The before is not prior to the text. It is the first name the persona gives itself. The after is not the end of the persona; rather, it is the name to which the narrating persona presently subscribes. Taken together, the before and after also provide the *continuity* demanded by the action of transformation. These sets of characteristics or qualities of the persona are static, not dynamic; they proclaim that the persona has been transformed but not how or why. They function, then, as the subject of the narrative action and object of transformation. The two aspects of the persona, old and new, affirm that (1) transformation happened and (2) that the new persona is the same as the old; that is, the persona is a continuum; it is the old persona who is transformed into the new. In this characterization of the persona "the 'I' is not *fixed* in relationship to its author," and its identity is generated less in relationship to the author than in relationship to the "specific code" of discourse. "The subject in autobiography is defined less by its history (i.e., its author's past) than by its status as a linguistic referent, a trope."[5] The self in this tropological status, however, does in fact reside in autobiography, suggesting a valuing of the "life lived" while acknowledging that the self exists as text.

This is not to suggest that the before and after aspects force a coherence or unity on the persona. Rather, while the state of the persona may range from psychic unity to fragmentation and disjunction, it remains, throughout the multitude of life-change experiences, the self-same "I" of the text. The persona, as the enunciating or narrating "I," is constructed to give voice to the *was* and *is* qualities and characteristics. We note that Margery Kempe exchanges her before persona, "bride of man," for her after persona, "bride of God." Abelard, in the *Story of My Misfortunes,* was an afflicted master teacher; he is a persecuted and calumniated cleric. In *Father and Son* Edmund Gosse depicts his before persona as dutiful son, his after persona as skeptical agnostic. Gertrude Stein is first "Alice B. Toklas's Gertrude Stein" and, last, a collage of all those artists who constitute her existence, "everybody's" Gertrude Stein. In the discussion of *Sartor Resartus* that follows, the before persona is "tailor," and the after is "retailored tailor." These simple terms illustrate the complex nature of the autobiographical persona.

Tailor Retailored: The Transformation of Diogenes Teufelsdröckh

One of literature's more famous narratives of transformation, *Sartor Resartus*,[6] first published in 1833–34 in serial form in *Fraser's Magazine*, dramatizes the autobiographical project, the transformation of a self and the construction of a text of the self. From this perspective *Sartor Resartus* becomes a "caricature" of life writing[7] and the tailor/professor a comic persona. *Sartor Resartus* works well as analogue precisely because it is not an autobiography, strictly so called, but, rather, fictive discourse in which the rhetorical aspects and functions of autobiography are developed clearly and consciously. Carlyle uses the devices of autobiography to create a fictional narrative and introduces the elements of the genre absent of the central personage, "I," that is characteristic of autobiography. Since autobiographies identify the narrator persona with the actual author, *Sartor Resartus* serves to highlight the persona as a rhetorical construct.

In *Sartor Resartus* a German professor wishes to change the world with his latest work, *A Philosophy of Clothes*, a philosophy that claims that "Society is built on Cloth." An English editor, on receipt of the manuscript, determines that this exceptional plan for society's reconstruction can only be carried forward if the designer is himself publicly acclaimed and accepted. An autobiography of the Professor must be written immediately, and the project of *Sartor Resartus* becomes that of "Auto-Biography." It is the "putting forward, in the best light possible," of a certain romantic and "wild-eyed" German philosopher, Professor Diogenes Teufelsdröckh of Weissnichtwo ("born of God" and "Devil's dung," from "Know-not-where").

Readers note that in the city of Weissnichtwo the "whole conversation is little or nothing else but Biography or Auto-Biography; ever humano-anecdotical" (*SR* 93) and are immediately struck with the sense of the centrality of the autobiographical project. It is a project that is to be "philosophico-poetically written" and "philosophico-poetically read." Before our very eyes a tailor will be retailored from "snips and shreds."

Professor Teufelsdröckh promises to send to his English Editor "not a Biography only, but an Autobiography: at least the materials for such; wherefrom, if I misreckon not, your perspicacity will draw fullest insight" (*SR* 94). The Editor is incredulous when,

> In the place of this same Autobiography with 'fullest insight,' we find—Six considerable PAPER-BAGS, carefully sealed, and marked successively, in gilt

China-ink, with the symbols of the Six southern Zodiacal Signs, beginning at Libra; in the inside of which sealed Bags lie miscellaneous masses of Sheets, and oftener Shreds and Snips. (*SR* 95)

The Professor's "Auto-Biography" is nothing more than "masses of Sheets" that fly around the room "like Sibylline leaves," incomprehensible, "without connection, without recognizable coherence." Our "Most respected Editor," Herr Herausgeber, must "evolve printed Creation" out of the Professor's "German printed and written Chaos." The Editor assumes responsibility for bringing order to the leaves and attempts to plot the various stages of Teufelsdröckh's transformations: "Genesis, Growth, Entanglement, Unbelief, Reprobation, and Conversion," these editorial captions indicating the tortuous route the soon-to-be emplotted life has taken.

Yet, before the reader ever opens the book or takes note of the narrative captions, Carlyle's title, *Sartor Resartus* (literally translated "tailor retailored"), suggests an unusual kind of conversion or transformation—retailoring—and poses an interesting set of questions: "Why a tailor?" and "How retailored?" In the first instance "tailor and retailored" necessarily imply retailoring. That is, the past participle requires a present participle: the tailor is retailored by a process of retailoring. This understanding raises other questions: "If the tailor is a craftsman who works on clothes, are the clothes for the tailor or for another?" "If the retailoring applies specifically to the tailor, does the tailor retailor himself or is he being retailored by other agencies?" "Who is the tailor?"

While the title suggests, at first glance, that the same persona is both retailored and tailor, the grammatical forms are ambiguous. The title would be less puzzling, for example, if it were made clear that someone other than the tailor were either doing the retailoring or being retailored by him. But then we would need another title—for example, *Sartor Resartiens* (tailor retailoring) or *Sartor Se Resartiens* (tailor retailoring himself). The designation *tailor,* however, insists that the acted upon, the tailored, is also the one whose work is retailoring. The tailor here is both the transforming subject and the object transformed. Thus, the phrase includes the following senses: (1) the tailor is retailored by virtue of his own retailoring, (2) the tailor is retailored by someone or something else, and (3) the tailor is retailored by his own retailoring *and* by someone or something else. There is no ground in the text for excluding any of these meanings, and the third carries the richest sense: the retailored tailor has remade himself and has been remade by some other agency. If we take the title *Sartor Resartus* in this third sense, we observe that an extraordinary change is implied—a very unusual retailoring. The title, then, encapsulates the narrative of Teufelsdröckh's transformation and introduces the before and after aspects of the persona—tailor and retailored tailor.

Who Is the Tailor?

If we read *Sartor Resartus* as a narrative of transformation and as a fictionalization of the autobiographical project, in asking the question "Who is the tailor?" we are asking "Who is transformed?" "Who is transforming?" This is not a question we generally put to autobiography. We understand that Wole Soyinka is the child in *Ake: The Years of Childhood,* that Montaigne is the essayist in the *Essays,* and that Genet is the thief in *The Thief's Journal.* In asking the question "Who is the tailor?" we can, because *Sartor Resartus* is a fictive work about constructing an autobiography and an autobiographical self, get at the rhetorical aspects of the persona more directly. Not only are the before and after aspects of the persona clearly set out for the reader, tailor and retailored tailor, but another aspect of the persona, not immediately accessible, but always problematic to the study of autobiography—the "enunciating "I," the"ordering I," the "writing self," the "narrator"—is made directly available for scrutiny in the persona of the Editor. In posing the question "Who is the tailor?" we are tackling autobiography in one of its most troublesome spots and using the "caricature self" (the tailor) to help us make sense of the multiperspectival persona of autobiography.

Is the tailor the Professor? The Professor is an anomaly; he is "like a man dropped thither from the Moon" (*SR* 55). He is a "kind of Melchizedek" without father or mother. He is a man of "boundless Learning," familiar with "Talmuds, Korans, Laplace, *Robinson Crusoe,* and the Belfast Town and Country Almanack" (*SR* 55, 45). From time to time "gleams of ethereal love burst forth from him" and "soft wailings of infinite pity." He is "self-secluded" and "enigmatic." The Professor is also speculative; he is a philosopher by discipline, an "indomitable Inquirer" (*SR* 57–58, 53). He asks: "Who am I; What is this Me?" The Professor is also a "Wander"; they call him "Everlasting or Wandering Jew." He reminisces:

> My breakfast of tea has been cooked by a Tartar woman, with water of the Amur, who wiped her earthen kettle with a horse-tail. I have roasted wild-eggs in the sand of the Sahara; I have awakened in Paris *Estrapades*

and Vienna *Malzleins,* with no prospect of breakfast beyond elemental liquid. That I had my Living to seek saved me from Dying,—by suicide. (*SR* 158)

The Professor of Things in General is radical, mystical, unrestrained, and poetic, the experiencer. He is the before aspect of the Teufelsdröckh persona—a "Chaos." The Philosopher of Clothes in Particular is a "Worldkin."

> I too could now say to myself: Be no longer a Chaos, but a World, or even Worldkin. Produce! Produce! were it but the pitifullest infinitesimal fraction of a Product, produce it, in God's name! 'Tis the utmost thou hast in thee: out with it, then. (*SR* 188)

Productive, committed to duty, and dedicated to pure reason, the Philosopher of Clothes is the after, or transformed, Teufelsdröckh of *Sartor Resartus.*

Is the Editor the tailor? The Editor, in contrast to the Professor, is clearly not a Wanderer. His very title, Editor, suggests that he is anything but a "roving reporter." Like a "Chinese Shopkeeper," he is ensconced in his study; mole-like, he ferrets out "puffery" and "quackery."

> Daily and nightly does the Editor sit (with green spectacles) deciphering these unimaginable Documents from their perplexed *cursiv-schrift;* collating them with the almost equally unimaginable Volume, which stands in legible print. . . . the materials are to be fished-up from the weltering deep, and down from the simmering air, here one mass, there another, and cunningly cemented, while the elements boil beneath: nor is there any supernatural force to do it with; but simply the Diligence and feeble thinking Faculty of an English Editor, endeavouring to evolve printed Creation out of a German printed and written Chaos. (*SR* 96)

Out of this chaos an autobiography will emerge; where there is fragmentation, a unity will evolve, where there are only "leaves," a narrative of transformation. But the Editor, while convinced that the autobiographical project is a worthy one, has some doubts about the enterprise and acknowledges that the form has some serious limitations. On discovering Teufelsdröckh's words (on a small slip, with ink barely visible): "Wilt thou know a Man, above all a Mankind, by stringing-together beadrolls of what thou namest Facts? The Man is the spirit he worked in; not what he did, but what he became" (*SR* 192); he wonders if there is any need to keep tracing the "complex gyrations (flights or involuntary waftings)" and closes the Paper-bags. Since all that constitutes a life cannot be told by the listing of facts and events, where does the essence of the life show up? the coherence? Can transformation be caught in the web of the text? Must the Editor fall back on the listing of events as they fly loose and unconnected in the atmosphere? Teufelsdröckh has his own problems with the autobiographical project:

> Pity that all Metaphysics had hitherto proved so inexpressibly unproductive! The secret of Man's Being is still like the Sphinx's secret: a riddle that he cannot rede; and for ignorance of which he suffers death, the worst death, a spiritual. What are your Axioms, and Categories, and Systems, and Aphorisms? Words, words. High Air-castles are cunningly built of Words, the Words well bedded also in good Logic-mortar; wherein, however, no Knowledge will come to lodge. (*SR* 76)

The autobiographical task is a difficult one. Can reducing the welter of facts or the ordering of experiences reveal the depths of the spirit of man or only chronicle his wanderings? What seems to be required is that the Editor help Teufelsdröckh recognize his experiences as more than vain wanderings or "pools and plashes," that he see them as potent and significant and as prefatory to a larger task—that of writing the "Philosophy of Clothes." The Professor as professor cannot accomplish this task alone. He needs the reflective and discriminating intelligence of the Editor. In the process of interacting with the Editor, Teufelsdröckh is transformed into the Philosopher of Clothes.

The professorial aspect of the persona needs the editorial, but the Editor would have no autobiography to revise without the Professor. Professor Teufelsdröckh is a radical who sees beyond the material world. Possessing a sense of the divine, he sees spirit everywhere. His is a vision of a new social system that draws on traditional systems but reaches far beyond them. Prior to his transformation, however, the mystical ideas are only a vision. Working with the Editor to make them a reality, Teufelsdröckh is transformed. He *was* whimsical, creative, poetic, fragmented, a mystic, a Romantic German Professor. Having lost none of his creative imagination, and with the help of the English Editor, he *is* now contributing and productive, committed to duty—an acknowledged and acclaimed Philosopher of Clothes. The attributes of the Philosopher of Clothes combine the best of the attributes of both the Professor and the Editor. And the Editor and Philosopher finally come to "speak" as one. The struggle for authorship is at an end. The tailor, as the title implies, is retailored or transformed. The mystical, imaginative verbal ramblings of the Professor as they are shaped and ordered by the Editor cohere into an "Auto-Biography" and a "Philosophy of Clothes" and serve to create and propagate a new self-tailor and a new philosophical system. The system the two design together outdistances what either could have created working in isolation. The Professor would never have completed the task; the Editor would never have begun.

A tailor is responsible to the community as he engages in the activities of the material world; he is common man. Concerned with order and service, he upholds those values deemed critical to daily existence: mending and fixing. A retailored tailor assumes responsibility for inciting "Wonder" in the community with his designs for making divinity apparent, the invisible visible. He calls upon citizens to utilize all their faculties—emotional, ethical, and rational—in the realization of the divinity within. The retailored tailor believes that change is possible and that the word brings about change in the citizen and the society. In this new role the tailor/citizen is transformed finally to prophet or poet:

> A Hierarch, therefore, and Pontiff of the World will we call him, the Poet and inspired Maker; who, Prometheus-like, can shape new Symbols, and bring new Fire from Heaven to fix it there. (*SR* 210)

As the rhetorically and poetically constituted personae of *Sartor Resartus*, the Professor and Editor make manifest the aspects of the autobiographical persona. Teufelsdröckh serves as referent for the before and after aspects of the persona; the Professor of Things in General is transformed into the Philosopher of Clothes in Particular. The Editor is referent for the reflexive aspect of the self of the text. He is like Darwin's reflexive self, the "dead man in another world looking back at my own life." The Editor is comparable to Harriet Jacobs's "poor Slave Mother" and to Roland Barthes's "hand that writes." With Darwin, Jacobs, and Barthes we discern, on careful study, that the "dead man," the "Slave Mother," and the "writing hand" are the rhetorically constituted, reflexive, narrating selves of the autobiographies. The tailors of *Sartor Resartus*—Teufelsdröckh, before and after, and Editor—facilitate the study of the characteristics, roles, and functions of the autobiographical persona. And, as an aside, the comic image of tailor retailored adds a touch of humor to the somewhat humorless discussions of absence of the self and the disappearing "I," when we conceive of the autobiographical project as Carlyle did, as humano-anecdotical—as the weaving of a philosophy of affirmation and the tailoring of a "Poet of Cloth."

To summarize: reading *Sartor Resartus* in terms of a was and is configuration of the persona—tailor and retailored tailor—prepares us to examine the autobiographical personae of John Henry Cardinal Newman, John Stuart Mill, Charles Darwin, and Margaret Oliphant. Their before and after qualities and characteristics, unique and individual, also share in the values, beliefs, and customs of the cultures to which they address their narratives of transformation. Newman is first Anglican then Catholic; Mill is first "school-boy logician" then "philosopher of feeling"; Darwin is first "beetle collector" then "acclaimed naturalist." Oliphant is first "breadwinner" then "a bigger me." Newman's religious persona is different from Darwin's scientific one, and neither Newman nor Darwin are particularly interested in politics, as are Mill and Oliphant. Newman's "children" are religious adherents; Oliphant's children are her own as well as her two brothers, various nieces and nephews, and family retainers whom she supports by her literary endeavors. Yet the Newman, Mill, Darwin, and Oliphant personae share concerns that are crucial to citizens in Victorian England.

The persona (comprised by its several characteristics) is a set of attributes that define and describe; while they imply transformation, they do not themselves change; rather, the persona represents the subject that undergoes change and the object that results from it. Aristotle reminds us in *The Poetics* that the dramatis personae are constituted by qualities, not action. In summary, to view the autobiography as narrative of transformation from the perspective of the persona is to understand that:

1. Persona is a functional aspect of autobiography as narrative of transformation.

2. Persona exists in the text as sets of imaged characteristics, traits, and qualities that may be either explicit or implicit.

3. Persona identifies the terminal aspects of transformation through a was and is configuration that circumscribes the narrative self.

4. Persona serves as subject of the narrative action and object of the transformation.

5. In relation to the figura the was and is configuration of the persona marks out or implies the transformation type.

6. In relation to the dynamis the persona is the recipient of the attributed motive force.

7. Persona identifies an idiosyncratic set of qualities and characteristics that are distinctive to the self inscribed in the text: a local configuration.

Persona is also shaped by a particular people, place, and time: a cultural configuration. Finally, persona shares in a general or global configuration of self as it moves from birth to death, what might be termed as "life shape."

Given that these sets of before and after characteristics mark out and affirm that the persona has changed from "old" to "new," we are now at a point where we can investigate transformation from a second rhetorical element, that of the figura or mode of transformation, as it is implied by the persona and configurated by the words, images, and events of the text. Since both the persona and the figura of transformation share a network of words, images, and metaphors, it is easy to see how discussions of the inscribed self of the text can blur into discussions of the mode of transformation. Taking care to keep them distinct for the moment, we can now ask, "How does autobiography construct, describe, and explain the life change experience?" "How does autobiography speak transformation through the figura?"

Figura: The Configured Mode, Ground, and Limits of the Transformation

Distinctive in that each narrative is about a different life, autobiographies are also distinctive in the way that each life change experience is configured. If all narratives of transformation were configured in the same way, we would hardly trouble to read them: Rousseau's *Confessions* characterize his transformation quite differently from the way that Augustine's *Confessions* characterize his. Black Elk "speaks" a different sort of life experience from the one that Fanny Crosby "sings" through her hymns of a saved life.[8] Yet we are aware that many autobiographers, particularly the earlier ones, employed universal patterns or models—quest, journey, initiation, redemption, gnosis—to make sense of their life experiences and to inscribe their lives for others to read. A familiar configuration, for example, is John Bunyan's transformation from sinner to saint. Bunyan shapes his narrative in terms of a pilgrimage, a long, lonely journey (with his wife and children crying after him to return), where "I could not rest content until I did now come to some certain knowledge whether I had faith or no."[9]

While many autobiographers have adopted these models and many critics have used pattern or myth to study autobiography productively, these approaches tend to focus less on the uniquely emplotted individual narrative and to herd the self, text, and reader into a pattern of action in which signification is predetermined. Seeing autobiography, from the perspective of writer *or* reader, solely in terms of pattern or myth severely limits the scope of the critical enterprise. In contrast, viewing autobiography from the perspective of the figura, or ground and mode of transformation, allows us to read each life narrative as both idiosyncratic and historical (in terms of what Peter Brooks calls the inner and outer narrative or "case history within history"),[10] as the singular (not single) transformation of a self in a time and place and as it is voiced, figurated, or emplotted.

Jean Starobinski wants to account for the uniqueness of each autobiography by focusing on the personal relationship between the narrator and style. By employing the concept of figura—the metaphor for the type, mode, and ground of the configured transformation—in the stead of style, I separate the discussions of persona and figura, show how they rest on and assume the other, and avoid psychologizing about style and its relationship to the author.[11]

Several contemporary concepts may promote an understanding of how the figura functions: Barbara Herrnstein Smith's "frames," Kenneth Burke's representative anecdote, Heidegger's forestructure, Haydn White's trope, and M. Katherine Hayles chaos, or orderly disorder, among them.

We might first consider figura in somewhat the same way that Herrnstein Smith speaks of the enclosures, frames, stages, versification, and "pedestals" that keep us from mistaking art for nature. She suggests that it is not actual experience that surrounds a fictive work but, rather a frame, which, like the painting, is itself created. With regard to her own work on poetry, she concludes that it is "by virtue of the enclosure that the poem achieves its amplitude and infinitude." Both the poem and versification are constituted objects.[12] The figura of autobiography, in Herrnstein Smith's terms, would be the constituted boundary for the text. Figura is that and more. It not only provides the structure within which the other aspects of the text reside; it is also ground for the explanation of the transformation in the text.

Figura may be understood to function somewhat like Burke's representative anecdote in that it both summarizes the terms of the transformation and implies the process. Similar to the first musical statement in a baroque piece,

the informative [representative] anecdote, we would say, contains *in nuce* the terminological structure that is evolved in conformity with it. Such a terminology is a "conclusion" that follows from the selection of a given anecdote. Thus the anecdote is in a sense a summation containing implicitly what the system that is developed from it contains explicitly.[13]

Here Burke is saying that the representative anecdote is both instigation and summation. As instigation, a meaning system and terminology are developed from the anecdote; at the same time, the anecdote stands as summation of the very system it has initiated. Like the representative anecdote, the figura implies a unity, serves as a metaphor of that unity, and invites and makes possible participation in its vision. The figura contains all the elements of the system that it represents; unlike the representative anecdote, however, these elements are not explicit in the figura. The anecdote is representative and, as such, can function at a literal and representative level. A grammar, in Burke's terms, can be developed from it. The figura, on the other hand, does not function at a literal level; it is metaphorical; its resonances are multivalent. It would be difficult to extract or evolve a system out of such ambiguity, but it is just that ambiguity that makes for the potential of the figura.

Figura may also be thought of as forestructure, Heidegger's mental structure (*vorstructur*), which he contends each interpreter brings to the object being interpreted. In terms of autobiography the forestructure is constituted as forehaving (*vorhabe*), foresight (*vorsicht*), and foreconception (*vorgriff*). *Forehave* can be seen as a grasp or hold on the life as totality; *foresight* as the view of the image through which the unity is understood and preserved; *foreconception* as an awareness of the figura's "structural manifoldness."

We could also think of the figura as a trope, in Hayden White's sense of an inaugurating gesture toward interpretation. In the case of autobiography the figura is a trope that allows for the configuration of the narrative in metaphorical, metonymic, synecdochic, and ironic terms.[14] As the encapsulating image for a specific type of discourse, "autobiography" is itself a trope.

We can also see the figura or metaphor for transformation as chaotic, in Hayles's sense of "orderly disorder."[15] Like a Mandelbrot fern or a Lorenz butterfly, the figura encapsulates transformation, holding within its boundaries the contraries and contradictories of the transformation. It accounts for the complexities of the transformation of a unique individual within his or her culture in a sort of "feedback loop," between local and global sites.[16] Within the figural there is always a surplus of meaning, but there are also boundaries. Lorenz's nonlinear weather conditions never move outside the butterfly. Narrated history as well as lived history are always bounded by the actual events in some way. Columbus did not sail to the Americas aboard the *Acile Laro*. Darwin was not a French scientist.

The figura, like the representative anecdote, frame, enclosure, forestructure, trope, or chaos, can be seen as the term that encapsulates a particular narrative of transformation; it is the says-it-all of the narrative. For Vladimir Nabokov's *Speak, Memory,* the figura may be seen as "metamorphosis"; for Harriett Jacob's *Narrative of a Slave Girl,* as "freedom"; for filmmaker Ingmar Bergman's autobiography, as magic lantern. Metamorphosis, freedom, magic lantern—these figurae aid in the general validation or understanding of the transformation experience, while this general understanding is aided, in turn, by those individual images, metaphors, events and actions (events and actions being both the "what happens" in the autobiography [Augustine's stealing the pears] and linguistic events [Augustine's speaking to God]) as they constitute the figura. The figura is not to be understood as a pattern superimposed on the work by the reader nor as literary device consciously applied by the autobiographer to give the work its coherence; it is neither myth nor tool.[17] What I am suggesting, to the contrary, is that the figura, like the life change experience itself, is both idiosyncratic and shares some common features with other life inscriptions. Relying solely on myth to explain or interpret the life makes the autobiography little more than a retelling of the same old story and makes the autobiographer little more than a carbon copy.

Tool, pattern, and myth imply that each of the elements of the work fits together neatly at both a literal and a mythical level. The figura, on the other hand, is specific to the unique transformation of a particular autobiography in a given culture. It is, as Mikhail Bakhtin would say, heteroglossic, dialogical—in "the language of the everyday" and of the author.[18] Within the boundary of the figura its many voicings, words, images, and metaphors may well be at odds, since it is locus for the contraries and tensions of the text and since it is enclosure and potential for the transformation. This is the value of exploring the autobiography from the perspective of figura. In mirroring the hermeneutic process, the figura requires that we move back and forth continually between the whole and the parts that constitute and are bounded by it as we come to understand the transformation experiences.

In our fictive or comedic autobiography, *Sartor Resartus,* the figura must be a metaphor that names a transformation that is implied by tailor and retailored tailor (the "was" and "is" persona) and that encompasses the construction of an "Auto-Biography" and a "Philosophy of Clothes." The philosophico-poetical figura of retailoring works to explain these transformations and illuminates the rhetorical elements of the figura.

Retailoring: The Figura of Teufelsdröckh's Thaumaturgic Transformation

Literally translated, the title of our fictive "Auto-Biography," "Tailor Retailored," creates a visual image of a tailor-tailoring-retailored. It has more power than a single visual image, however, since it has the potential for incorporating the internal *and* external aspects of change (the implied action of retailoring that remakes the tailor) within the boundaries—text and context—of its two terms. Given its reflexive and extended applications, the title prepares the reader for the process that will be described in the text. The title contains implicitly the elements, potential, and boundaries of the tailor's transformation. The two elements of the title (tailor and retailored) serve as metaphor for the process of transformation in the text and in this way stand as meaning of the text as whole. It is as if Carlyle designed an icon, an engraving, or a logo and inserted it at the beginning of the text to prefigure what was to follow. By encapsulating the notion of transformation within the title's image, the possibility of change is established from the beginning.

Since the mode and ground of the tailor's transformation is readily accessible in title and text as retailoring, the problem in this fictive "Auto-Biography" is not to discern what the figura might be but, rather, how it functions to "speak" the change in the tailor.

Retailoring, the encapsulated figura emblematically revealed in the title, reappears in extended form throughout the text. Tailoring is the project that engages a tailor; to "tailor" is to make clothes by tailor's work; to cut, form, produce clothes. *Retailoring* would be to "remake" clothes. *To remake* suggests transformation through reconstruction. It is to take the garment at hand and, using the deftness and creativity of the tailor, make new clothes from old, and in the case of *Sartor Resartus,* to remake a self, a text, and a world. Teufelsdröckh's "pattern," or figura, for the retailoring of self and society is a thaumaturgic system based on clothes:

> Aprons are Defences; against injury to cleanliness, to safety, to modesty, sometimes to roguery. From the thin slip of notched silk (as it were, the emblem and beatified ghost of an Apron), which some highest-bred house-

wife, sitting at Nurnberg Workboxes and Toyboxes, has gracefully fastened on; to the thick-tanned hide, girt round him with thongs, wherein the Builder builds, and at evening sticks his trowel. . . . How much has been concealed, how much has been defended in Aprons! Nay, rightly considered, what is your whole Military and Police Establishment, charged at uncalculated millions, but a huge scarlet-coloured, iron-fastened Apron, wherein Society works (uneasily enough); guarding itself from some soil and stithy-sparks, in this Devil-smithy (Teufelsschmiede) of a world: But of all Aprons the most puzzling to me hitherto has been the Episcopal or Cassock. Wherein consists the usefulness of this Apron? The Overseer (Episcopus) of Souls, I notice, has tucked in the corner of it, as if his day's work were done: what does he shadow forth thereby? (*SR* 67)

The apron, one of the many garments appearing in the Professor's "Clothes Philosophy," is elevated from the simplest and most unassuming of nineteenth-century garments to the status of metaphor. As emblematic of social roles, professions, guardianship, rebellion, and hypocrisy, aprons and royal raiment alike are woven into a curious system that is postulated as corrective for society and as a means for retailoring the tailor. Constructed by a "Thinking Man" (the "worst enemy the Prince of Darkness can have" [*SR* 129]), the "Philosophy of Clothes" challenges the darkness of ignorance and shatters the void of a mechanized universe with a view of the Divine. As a system of symbols, it is thaumaturgic, transforming, miraculous, a cause for wonder. As the poet's inspired message, it "makes and unmakes whole worlds."

Teufelsdröckh speaks of how clothes at first gave identity. They were role bound: the thick-tanned leather apron identified the builder; the thin, silk-slip apron characterized the wealthy housewife; the cassock labeled the Episcopal. But clothes led to sham and abuse. The king was paid homage because of his royal raiment, while his subjects understood little about the importance of his function in society. Nor were they able to discern guilt or innocence; they were clothes blind. The beggar in the threadbare blue coat was automatically hanged, while the man in the fine red coat, because of his superior dress, escaped punishment. Be they wool rags or swallowtail coats, clothes had become, for Teufelsdröckh's contemporaries, more important than the individuals beneath them. He warns against a society of "Dandies":

A Dandy is a Clothes-wearing Man, a Man whose trade, office, and existence consists in the wearing of Clothes. Every faculty of his soul, spirit, purse, and person is heroically consecrated to this one object, the wearing of Clothes wisely and well: so that as others dress to live, he lives to dress. (*SR* 248)

Clothes have "tailorise[d]" and "demoralise[d]" the members of the society. If clothes make society clothes blind, then one solution is to remove the problematic garments; to undress before redressing. The Professor strips his fellowmen of their "outmost wrappage," "vestural Tissue" (*SR* 34).

> Often in my atribiliar moods, when I read of pompous ceremonials, Frankfort Coronations, Royal Drawing-rooms, . . . how Duke this is presented by Archduke that, and Colonel A by General B, and innumerable Bishops, Admirals, and miscellaneous Functionaries, and advancing gallantly to the Anointed Presence; and I strive, in my remote privacy, to form a clear picture of that solemnity,—on a sudden, as by some enchanter's wand, the—shall I speak it?—the Clothes fly-off the whole dramatic corps; and Dukes, Grandees, Bishops, Generals, Anointed Presence itself, every mother's son of them stand straddling there, not a shirt on them; and I know not whether to laugh or weep. (*SR* 81–82)

Teufelsdröckh quickly redresses his society in retailored apparel. Clothes are required for participation in the society and for the orderly functioning of its institutions. Each individual has a task to perform; each contribution is necessary; each role is symbolized by the appropriate adornment. The Professor's system both reveals and conceals a mystery: the divine order is manifested in a system of clothes roles through which the nature of the hierarchical structure of rule and the maintenance of a productive order are revealed emblematically; the mystery of participation in the divine order is concealed (made to be held in reverence) by the garments of office. The Professor borrows on the sense, from the Greek, that the person is both the "living body of a human being as distinct from clothing" and "the body with its clothing and adornment." He places society under the necessity of both states in the process of retailoring. Here, then, the tailor is not only retailored by himself and by his clothes, as was suggested earlier; he is also responsible for retailoring the society, for weaving garments, for emblem making, for constructing a system to live by.

The "Philosophy of Clothes" both exists as a system of symbols and utilizes symbols to articulate its meanings.

> Whatsoever sensibly exists, whatsoever represents Spirit to Spirit, is properly a Clothing, a suit of Raiment. . . . the whole External Universe and what it holds is but Clothing; and the essence of all Science lies in the PHILOSOPHY OF CLOTHES. (*SR* 92)

Teufelsdröckh points to other ideal symbol systems: the Magna Carta, the authority of the law, the sacredness of rulers, the *Thirty-nine Articles*—each functioning, he believes, as verbal embodiments of the Spirit. The "Philosophy of Clothes" is, similarly, a representation of the Ideal. It is a constructed system that stands for the reality of the divine order. The imagination as it weaves garments, or visible symbols of the invisible, is thus engaged so as to reveal the Spirit.

> All visible things are emblems; what thou seest is not there on its own account; strictly taken, is not there at all: Matter exists only spiritually, and to represent some Idea, and *body* it forth. Hence Clothes, as despicable as we think them, are so unspeakably significant. Clothes, from the King's mantle downwards, are emblematic, not of want only, but of a manifold cunning Victory over Want. On the other hand, all Emblematic things are properly Clothes, thought-woven or hand-woven: must not the Imagination weave Garments, visible Bodies, wherein the else invisible creations and inspirations of our Reason are, like spirits, revealed, and first become all-powerful. (*SR* 91)

This excerpt is a summation of the "Philosophy of Clothes"; all clothes are emblematic; emblematic things are clothes. Put another way, matter exists to express the spiritual and to represent the Ideal. The society can be remade by participating in and operating out of this system. The tailor can be retailored through the construction of a clothes philosophy. And, finally, the acquisition (understanding, integration) of a "Philosophy of Clothes" will result in an understanding of symbol systems and, in turn—in the Professor's scheme of things—an idea of the divine.

> Neither say that thou has now no Symbol of the Godlike. Is not God's Universe a symbol of the Godlike; is not Immensity a Temple; is not Man's History, and Men's History, a perpetual Evangel? Listen, and for organ-music thou wilt ever, as of old, hear the Morning Stars sing together. (*SR* 233)

Retailoring, the figura of transformation, is specified and explicated in the "Philosophy of Clothes." It summarizes emblematically the action (transformation) that it describes. As a figural element, it is a symbolic (composed of symbols, words) representation of the larger meaning of the text, a constructed perspective that serves as structure for the discourse and as ground for the assumption of transformation.

What is the nature of the transformation in *Sartor Resartus*? It is retailoring—society and self—but for our purposes it is also a rhetorical retailoring. *Sartor Resartus* is a narrative of textual (re)construction, the making of a book. The Professor tells us that it is "words about words." Rhetorical retailoring is to make new texts from old. Professor and Editor are making and remaking texts; they are ordering language to new purposes. The Professor is attempting to reconstruct the universe through his "Philosophy of Clothes," and the Editor is attempting to collate this manuscript with the Professor's "Auto-Biography" for the purpose of promoting the larger work, the *Life and Opinions of Herr Teufelsdröckh*. In designing the retailoring project, they are "reseeing" the world through a tailor's eyes, and, in publishing the document(s), they are "resaying" the world in a tailor's language.

Reseeing through tailor's eyes is to have already seen and to look again, to "revision" through a set of figures or images that imply retailoring. To resee the world through the tailor's eyes is to see that "all that men have thought, dreamed, done, and been . . . is but Clothing." It is to see "the Cut betoken Intellect and Talent"; "Colour betoken Temper and Heart" (*SR* 61). It is to see history as "a view of the costumes of all mankind, in all countries, in all times" (*SR* 62). To resee the world as tailor is to know that "Society is founded on Cloth" (*SR* 81) but that "no fashion will continue" (*SR* 70). In reseeing the world, the tailor discovers that under the "Charlemagne Mantle" and the "Gipsy Blanket" are to be found both "Contemptibility" and "reverend Worth." The tailor recognizes that "the beginning of all wisdom is to look fixedly on clothes . . . till they become transparent" (*SR* 86).

> Happy he who can look through the Clothes of a Man . . . into the Man himself; and discern in this or the other Dread Potentate, a more or less incompetent Digestive-apparatus; yet also an inscrutable venerable Mystery, in the meanest Tinker that sees with eyes. (*SR* 87)

To resee the world is the beginning of rhetorical retailoring. It is to take an old worldview and an old text and see them through new sets of images. These images transform the vision; they initiate new insights and new designs.

Rhetorical retailoring is also resaying. To resay the world in a tailor's language is to dramatize or inscribe the images of the reseeing or, conversely, to allow language to bring about a new reseeing (our third sense of the meaning of the title applies here; the tailor is tailored by himself and by another agency), so as to bring the reader into the writer's new vision (version). The meaning the Professor makes of his life experiences are unavailable to anyone but himself until he jots them down—scraps and snips. They make sense only to the Editor (and then only with difficulty) when they are ordered and arranged by the Editor in the "Auto-Biography." There is no philosophy until, as text of a new worldview, it is presented to readers for their consideration. The Professor says with Goethe, " 'Tis thus at the roaring loom of Time I ply and weave for God the Garment thou seest Him by" (Faust, 1.1). "Ply and weave," "loom," and "Garment" are a collection of images that cluster around the notion of the retailoring enterprise. At the literal level they suggest process toward a product, weaving a garment. At a figurative level the Editor, surrounded by confounding textual versions of the Professor's experience, reweaves the text so as to explain its insights, using the metaphors of retailoring to make sense of experiences that might otherwise be obscured.

The qualities of the rhetorical retailoring process imply revision, redesign—reseeing and resaying through a collection of images that result in a retailored product: garment, apron, vestures, a "Philosophy of Clothes." Rhetorical reconstruction is to engage in those sorts of transformation *Sartor Resartus* endorses as retailoring. Retailoring works as figure or image for the act of rhetorical transformation because it is rooted in life. At some commonsense level we recognize that to see anew and say anew is to engage in analysis and invention. Understanding retailoring as characteristic of rhetorical transformation requires that we see texts like clothes, as constructs ever available for redesign or revision. Retailoring in *Sartor Resartus*, then, is the "Science of affirmation and reconstruction."

Sartor Resartus *as Transformative*

Sartor Resartus, "these sheets," as the Editor calls his narrative about the project of making Professor Teufelsdröckh's life and philosophy known to English readers, is the text that encompasses three other texts: the "Auto-Biography," the "Philosophy of Clothes," and the potential *Life and Opinions of Herr Teufelsdröckh*. *Sartor Resartus* is not itself retailored but, rather, serves as locus for the retailoring narrative. It is the place in which the experiences described in the "Auto-Biography" are evaluated, interpreted, and related to the philosophical stance of the Professor. It is the place in which the philosophical implications made in the "Philosophy of Clothes" are drawn out and examined.

The nature of the transformation in *Sartor Resartus* is rhetorical.

Through the figura of retailoring the text demonstrates that change is possible and that speaking brings change. Language is the "Wonder" of *Sartor Resartus* as the "Auto-Biography" and "Philosophy" are transformed into *The Life and Opinions of Herr Teufelsdröckh*. Employing image, figure, and metaphor to speak across realities, the tailors use the language of the material world—tailor, retailoring, and clothes—to "call for" a new order. This call for change takes the form of an inscribed text. Language viewed in this way becomes a means of transformation, creating a new worldview and a retailored society: "tailors speak language." But the language users are themselves changed by language: two rhetorical *tailors,* an English Editor and a German Philosopher, come to speak as *tailor.* They have been transformed by the retailoring figura. Language viewed in this way is transformative, "retailoring language speaks tailor."

The figura, then, as it encapsulates, summarizes, and grounds the narrative of transformation, must be a metaphor that "names" the transformation. Just as retailoring serves as figura in *Sartor Resartus,* in the following sections we will examine how "economy" works as a suitable figura for John Henry Newman's transformation from Anglican to Catholic in the *Apologia.* The figura of economy is only implied by the persona; however, it is not specified. Viewing the *Apologia* from the perspective of the figura allows for an examination of the nature of the change itself.

We will also examine the images and events that characterize and explain John Stuart Mill's transformation from reasoning machine to humanistic political philosopher and how they suggest a conversion experience. Unlike Bunyan's religious transformation, however, Mill's conversion is the conversion of "reeducation" as it is implied in the transformation from "school-boy logician" to "philosopher of feeling." From logician to poet, from Utilitarian to Romantic, the qualities and characteristics of Mill's persona imply, but do not specify, the nature of his political transformation. It is to the figura that we turn for this specificity.

The limits of Darwin's development are circumscribed by the figura of evolution as it incorporates or assumes the characteristics of naive scientist and mature scientist in the terminal aspects of the persona. Darwin's transformation from beetle collector to acclaimed naturalist within the figura of evolution is implied and assumed but not specified by the terminal aspects of the Darwin persona. A study of the figura of Darwin's transformation will specify the nature of the transformation of a scientist.

A figura that works to illustrate Margaret Oliphant's transformation is "production." *Production* encompasses the notions of the literary marketplace and the competition among Victorian writers to create literary works for profit. The need to produce is implied in Oliphant's before and after attributes—"breadwinner" and "a bigger me"; the way in which production functions as the ground, limits, and mode of her transformation is detailed in chapter 6.

We derive the figura, then, from the general type of transformation as it is implied by the two terms of the persona. This general type, when placed within the network of metaphors, images, and events of a particular autobiography, suggests a specific or unique transformation metaphor: retailoring, economy, reeducation, evolution, and production. The concept of figura encompasses both the figure of speech and the visual image that stands behind it as generative and aggregate. Engaging the autobiography from the perspective of the figura in the following sections will allow us to make sense of Newman's, Darwin's, Mill's, and Oliphant's transformations as they emplot unique, individual narratives and as they share common social and cultural concerns. To summarize the figura's nature and functions:

1. Figura is a functional aspect of autobiography as narrative of transformation.

2. Figura consists of images, words, not abstractions, that function as tropes: metaphor, metonymy, synecdoche, or irony. (The figura may *seem* to be an abstraction; I am here calling attention to the image under the word; evolution [to roll on], conversion [to turn around], economy [to set in order].)

3. It involves the notions of reduction and representation; it is what the text is about. It summarizes emblematically the action or events it describes. It is the idea of the text drawn small and so is a part/whole relationship. Conversely, it is the idea of the text drawn large; it is the place of signification and so is a whole/part relationship.

4. It provides definition; that is, it sets the boundaries of the text by providing a context for the elements of the work.

5. As extended through the text, it serves as structure or design for the discourse, establishing relations between the several elements of the work. It is the locus of the assumptions and contraries of the text.

6. In relation to the persona, figura specifies the type of transformation implied by the before and after configurations of the persona.

7. In relation to the dynamis, figura assumes a motive force specific to its type.

8. Figura identifies a local transformation that is unique and specific to the persona. Figura is also shaped by a particular people, place, and time—a cultural configuration. Finally, figura shares in a general or global configuration of transformation as it encapsulates a "life shape."

Given that we have taken care to distinguish between the configuration of metaphors and images that constitute the transformation type retailoring, from the qualities and characteristics or names of the persona—tailor and retailored tailor—we are able to see how autobiography speaks transformation from two different functional perspectives. We may conclude that, while it is inappropriate here to ask (as do the historians), "Did the actual personage go through a change exactly as the autobiography describes it?" or "Is there really such a thing as personality change?" (as perhaps the psychological critic might), we have answered the question of how the autobiography characterizes the transformation, or life change experience, of the persona within the rhetorically constructed context of the figura. Having answered this question, we are led, quite naturally, to a related one: "How does the persona, within the surround of the figura, change from 'was' to 'is'?" In other words, what is the dynamis, the motive force or power, that accounts for transformation in autobiography? Answering this question will require that we investigate autobiography from a third rhetorical element, that of its dynamis.

Dynamis: The Motive Force of Transformation

Any change assumes a force or motive for that change. The blistering sun changes green lawns to dried and cracked earth. The gods breathe life into the mythic hero. Good nurturing facilitates growth in children. These changes are dramatic and dynamic. With autobiography, to look at the dynamic aspect of the process of transformation is to understand and account for the transforming action between the old persona and the new. It is to view the text from the perspective of dynamis. To attribute transformation to the dynamis is to recognize that "something happened to me" in autobiography and that happening assumes the operation of motive forces on the persona, or me. Barrett Mandel uses the word *dynamis* to describe that aspect of a work that shapes the choice of personae and the form of autobiography. For Mandel the dynamis is the "governing focus," the "organizing principle," the "synthesizing purpose" of the autobiography.

Mandel collapses *mode,* or type, of transformation (what I call figura) with the *motive force,* or power, of transformation into a single aspect, dynamis. "Governing focus" and "organizing principle" seem to suggest the mode of the narrative, while "purpose" may suggest its power. Given his use of the term, the critic's job would be to examine to what extent the narrative voice is consonant or dissonant with this dynamis.[19]

The term *dynamis* has, etymologically, a wider sense. The Greeks gave the word at least seven senses: (1) dynamis is power of might, bodily strength, both of one's own and outward power; (2) dynamis is faculty, capacity, agency, art or craft, potency; (3) dynamis is the power, force, or meaning of a work; (4) it is capability; it is the opposite of actuality; (5) it is mathematical power, exponential; (6) it is the actuation of divine power; (7) it is manifestation of divine power, miracle. In Latin *dynamis* was used in the mathematical sense as exponential power and to mean "store," "plenty." These definitions offer an astounding range; I borrow something from all of them to characterize the motive force that accounts for transformation in autobiography. The persona, within the surround of the figura, is transformed through the potential, capacity, agency, or power of the dynamis. If we see the persona as the was and is of the changed self of autobiography and the figura as the mode of that change, then we could say that the dynamis is the what that changed the *me* of the autobiography. For example, John Henry Newman gives himself many names in the *Apologia:* Christian, Anglican, Evangelical, Noetic, Tractarian, Layman, Catholic. These names tell us that at each juncture in his doctrinal development, at each convergence of new opinion, Newman has changed and that each change requires a new name. It is the dynamis that causes Newman's renaming. In rhetorical terms we could say that the name changes in each of the autobiographies (as they imply transformation) result from the power of the dynamis. With regard to the figura, to use Newman as example again, while the figura of his transformation, economy, implies the dynamis of the transformation, the figura, in turn, relies upon it for its transforming power. This is what is meant by the earlier statement with regard to persona, figura, and dynamis: "each of the rhetorical perspectives rests on and assumes the other."

As imaged construct, the dynamis is the power to which each autobiographer attributes change. For Newman the dynamis for his religious transformation may be seen as "living intelligence," for John Stuart Mill's political change as "thought coloured by feeling," for Charles Darwin's scientific change "zeal and environment." Margaret Oliphant problematizes the concepts of motivation and causation by asking whether her productivity can be attributed to "economic necessity" or "artistic fervour." In each case the identifying terms for the dynamis are text specific; they are among several images or metaphors that may characterize the motive force for change in the autobiographies. As metaphors, they hold the potential for conveying the many senses of dynamis that are imaged in the texts and that allow us to explore their range and scope. In the discussions that follow we will look at how these terms work to explain dynamis, first, in the philosophico-poetical dynamis of our fictive autobiography, *Sartor Resartus*, then in the autobiographies of the Victorians.

The Dynamis of the "Whole Me"

In *Sartor Resartus* the dynamis for retailoring is implied in the title. "Tailor Retailored" implies that there is the *possibility* and *potential* for the tailor's retailoring. In the text itself the agency, or motive power, is specified. It resides in the agent, in the individual will and imagination of the Romantic Professor as he voices the "Everlasting No" and the "Everlasting Yea" that are required for retailoring the tailor.

Teufelsdröckh, as a "kind of Melchizedek," you will recall, sets out on his pilgrimage in sorrow. At the loss of his love, Blumine, he wanders "as if that curse of the Prophet had fallen on him, and he were 'made like unto a wheel'" (*SR* 152). The pilgrimage continues in doubt and loneliness. *Wanderings, temptations, buffetted and foiled, cowering and trembling* engender images of emotional states prefatory to conversion. They signal an expected change, but the pilgrim must undergo numerous trials before the crisis is past. Teufelsdröckh, "plagued by the spirit of Inquiry" and with a genuine love of Truth, searches for answers to his misery and finds none.

> Thus has the bewildered Wanderer to stand, as so many have done, shouting question after question into the Sibyl-cave of Destiny, and receive no Answer but an Echo. . . . The speculative Mystery of Life grew ever more mysterious to me: neither in the practical Mystery had I made the slightest progress, but been everywhere buffeted, foiled, and contemptuously cast out. A feeble unit in the middle of a threatening Infinitude. (*SR* 162–64)

The Philosopher is at a major turning point; he is searching for his sense of self and his place in the world. Overwhelmed by the seeming insignificance of his being, he gets no help from the traditional sources of self-definition: his fellowmen, his society, or his religion. Human resources are but "Figures" and seem to be automatic. His God has become an "absentee God, sitting idle, ever since the first Sabbath, at the outside of his Universe, and *see*ing it go" (*SR* 161). He cannot even blame his misery on the Devil; he has been "pulled down by disbelief." The Professor's society is threatened by a "Profit and Loss Philosophy" fashioned on the needs of stomach rather than the soul, on the passions rather than virtue. Teufelsdröckh's universe is "void of all Life, of Purpose, of Volition, even of Hostility: it is one huge, dead, immeasurable Steam-engine, rolling on, in its dead indifference, to grind me limb from limb" (*SR* 164).

This materialistic, dehumanized, and mechanical universe is finally too much. Along the Rue Saint-Thomas de l'Enfer one sultry Dogday Teufelsdröckh walks

> among civic rubbish enough, in a close atmosphere, and over pavements hot as Nebuchadnezzar's Furnace; whereby doubtless my spirits were little cheered; when, all at once, there rose a Thought in me, and I asked myself: "What *art* thou afraid of? Wherefore, like a coward, dost thou forever pip and whimper, and go cowering and trembling? Despicable biped! what is the sum-total of the worst that lies before thee? Death? Well, Death; and say the pangs of Tophet too, and all that the Devil and Man may, will or can do against thee! Hast thou not a heart; canst thou not suffer whatsoever it be; and, as a Child of Freedom, though outcast, trample Tophet itself under thy feet, while it consumes thee?"

Teufelsdröckh rejects everlasting nothingness:

> "Let it come, then; I will meet it and defy it!" And as I so thought, there rushed like a stream of fire over my whole soul; and I shook base Fear away from me forever. I was strong, of unknown strength; a spirit, almost a god. Ever from that time, the temper of my misery was changed: not Fear or whining Sorrow was it, but Indignation and grim fire-eyed Defiance. Thus had the Everlasting No *(das ewige Nein)* pealed authoritatively through all the recesses of my Being, of my ME. . . . My whole Me now made answer: "I am not thine, but Free." (*SR* 166–67)

With the Everlasting No pealing through his being, Teufelsdröckh is free. He realizes that he need not be the victim of the grinding and indifferent steam engine universe. As a "Child of Freedom," he has strength to defy hell itself. The conversion of the Professor is not as yet an affirmation, but it is a first step toward that affirmation; it is a rejection of fear, death, hell—nothingness. The Child of Freedom throws aside whining sorrow and takes up indignation and defiance.

> So that, for Teufelsdröckh also, there has been a 'glorious revolution': these mad shadow-hunting and shadow-hunted Pilgrimings of his were but some purifying 'Temptation in the Wilderness,' before his apostolic work (such as it was) could begin. (*SR* 179)

The Professor has initiated the process of transformation through the dynamis of the "whole Me." This transformation or retailoring of the tailor reads in many ways like a religious conversion: pilgrimage, wanderings, sense of loss, and crisis, or turning point, but with one notable difference—the power to which the transformation is attributed. There is no breath of God; there is no grace abounding. Teufelsdröckh is not an unworthy receptacle of a manifest power from above. God is "absentee" and "idle." The god of the Professor's conversion is the whole Me, grim, fire-eyed, and defiant. The converted Teufelsdröckh is now "strong, of unknown strength; a spirit, almost a god." The miserable biped is transformed to "Child of Freedom"; the tailor has retailored himself.

The whole Me stands as image for the potential, power, and capacity of the tailor to transform himself. It is through the dynamis of the whole Me that the Professor can shout an Everlasting No into the abyss, and it is the dynamis of the whole Me that brings the Professor to the point of the Everlasting Yea.

> Love not Pleasure; love God. This is the EVERLASTING YEA, wherein all contradiction is solved: wherein whoso walks and works, it is well with him. (*SR* 185)

The Everlasting No has been a cleansing prelude that precedes the affirmation of the Everlasting Yea. With this affirmation the conversion is complete. In the Everlasting Yea the "mad primeval Discourse" is hushed, the exhilaration of full freedom is experienced, and Teufelsdröckh's unlimited potential is revealed. In the Everlasting Yea the new, or retailored, tailor now has more "tailoring" work to do. The injunction is to shape the Ideal; to say Yea to "walk" and "work." The work of the Everlasting Yea is an acceptance of duty. "Do the duty which lies nearest thee" (*SR* 187) is not a call to duty for duty's sake but, rather, a challenge to the individual of freedom to realize his full potential through purposeful action. It is a call to move out of the isolation of self-aggrandizement into the responsibility of community.

O thou that pinest in the imprisonment of the Actual, and criest bitterly to the gods for a kingdom wherein to rule and create, know this of a truth: the thing thou seekest is already with thee, "here or nowhere," couldst thou only see! (*SR* 187)

Through the power of the dynamis of the whole Me Teufelsdröckh discovers that he houses in himself a kingdom. He is now able to respond to a call to duty, one that requires him to work, believe, live, and be free. Teufelsdröckh's Editor urges him to understand the experiences of the Everlasting No and the Everlasting Yea as preparation for the writing of the "Philosophy of Clothes." It is the writing and publication of this document that will manifest the triumph of community responsibility over self-indulgence, whimpering, and wandering ("mad shadow-hunting" and "Pilgrimings").

Taking up this challenge, the Professor of Things in General has changed to a Philosopher of Clothes in Particular, through the dynamis of the whole Me, the unlimited capacity and potential of the individual. Yet this dynamis is more than Romantic in character; it is Victorian. The dynamis of the whole Me is individual power and potential within the context of social responsibility. Teufelsdröckh is ready to begin retailoring the society. Committed to using his imaginative powers in a concerted effort toward mending the torn garment of traditional institutions and offices, his task is to remind society's members of the purposes of their garments—their social roles and functions. He is dedicated to the alteration of those garments that are poorly constructed, those institutions that are crumbling. Saying Yea to the construction of new garments that will fit new traditions, he calls for an enlarged view of the Spirit, "a torch for burning" *and* a "hammer for building" (*SR* 186). He speaks for a new mythos that values both the speculative and the practical aspects of the Divine.

Teufelsdröckh is no longer a dreamer who weaves fantastic garments solely for his own pleasure and amusement; in contemporary language he is now the "locally owned and operated" public tailor who is always open for the business of the imagination. He is actively involved in making the Spirit manifest through the reclothed members of the society and its reclothed institutions. The dynamis that permeates *Sartor Resartus* is evident enough; it is the power of the individual, the whole Me, asserting itself in the face of a materialistic, dehumanized, and mechanical universe and turning its creative power to the task at hand. *Sartor Resartus* insists that retailoring is within the reach of the little tailor and everyone.

In summary: at the level of the events as they are figured as retailoring, *Sartor Resartus* is about a tailor who is changed from private to public tailor through the dynamis of the whole Me. At the level of the text, however, it is about constructing an "Auto-Biography" out of the snips and shreds of a life. In this second sense figura can be seen as retailoring a text and dynamis as the revisionary power of the writing persona characterized in the aspects of Professor and Editor. Thus, the dynamis of autobiography has a dual power; it is the motive force as imaged construct to which the transformation of the self is attributed, and it is also the motive force for the construction of the text—the writing.

Sartor Resartus, as fictive autobiography, assumes that change is possible and characterizes the dynamic quality of that change through a unique construct that is rhetorically constituted within the boundaries implied by its figura and persona. Because it is not about actual events and personages, it provides a fictive example of dynamis as both attributed power for the transformation of the persona, or tailor, and motive power for the construction of the "Auto-Biography." In viewing autobiography from the perspective of the dynamis, we might summarize its nature and function in the following ways:

1. Dynamis is a functional property of autobiography as it is a narrative of transformation.
2. Dynamis, an abstraction, a relationship, or an image, is the motive force, power, and potency to which the transformation of the persona is attributed in the text.
3. It is the dynamic aspect of the autobiography; as such, it is its creative force; it is the power to which the construction of the autobiography can be attributed.
4. Dynamis "exists" in the text as a construct of the relationships established by the persona and figura as those relationships imply action, movement, change. (I use *exists* metaphorically here. As with the perspectives of persona and figura, perceiving the autobiography as dynamis is an interpretive act between writer and reader that converges in the text.)
5. In relation to the persona, dynamis is involved in the choice of the first name the autobiographer gives the self and in the renaming of the persona from was to is.

6. In relation to the figura, while the figura, or type of change, implies the motive power for change, the attributed dynamis helps to identify the type of change and its foundation and limits.

7. Dynamis moves the text by reflection and extension. Turned in on itself, the dynamis twice convinces: first by the "memory" as it is rhetorically constituted in the was persona, and again through "reflection" as it is rhetorically constituted in the is persona. As extended, the dynamis specifies and elaborates the power for change.

8. Dynamis identifies a local motive force that is unique and specific to the persona. Dynamis is also shaped by attributions that are shared by a particular people, place, and time—a cultural attribution. Finally, dynamis shares in a general or global attribution as it is tied to universal notions of life change.

3

From Anglican to Catholic

The Transformation of John Henry Cardinal Newman (1801–90)

The conversion of John Henry Cardinal Newman from Anglican to Catholic in 1845 shook his entire nation. "Gladstone compared it to a storm which left a wreck on every shore." Disraeli long afterward called it "a blow from which the Church [of England] still reeled."[1] Oxford was riddled with strife; families were divided; the nation was in shock. Newman's conversion was considered a national disaster; he was branded a traitor to his country and to his church.

> In every part of the country and every class of society, through every organ and opportunity of opinion, in newspapers, in periodicals, at meetings, in pulpits, at dinner-tables, in coffee-rooms, in railway carriages, I was denounced as a traitor.[2]

Under other circumstances Newman's change to Catholicism might have been seen as a private matter of individual conscience, but, given that he was involved so intensely in the reform movement of the Church of England, his abandonment of the Anglican Church was nothing less than traitorous in the eyes of his countrymen.

In the *Apologia Pro Vita Sua* (literally, A Defense of His Life), subtitled *A History of His Religious Opinions,* Newman attempts to explain and defend a transformation so unforeseen that it broke the hearts of many young followers and scandalized an entire nation, from Oxford to Parliament, from the prime minister to country pastor. Having for many years after his conversion accepted the "imputations which have been so freely cast upon me" as a "portion of the penalty which I naturally and justly incurred by my change of religion" (*Apol.* 1), Newman, on the occasion of the second challenge to the integrity of his decision nearly twenty years later, finds himself "publicly put on my defense." Published in 1864 as a response to Charles Kingsley's charges that he was "teaching and practising deceit and dishonesty," the *Apologia* recounts Newman's transformation from Anglican to Catholic. Newman's religious transformation is quite unlike those of Saint Paul or John Bunyan, which are characterized by sudden, onetime conversions, with personae that are defined in terms of sinner and saint, lost and saved, cast away and redeemed. Newman's conversion is slow and gradual, and the various aspects of the persona of the *Apologia* are progressively defined by the religious opinions adopted through each new revelation, or, as Newman would say, through each successive manifestation of God's divine economy.

When various aspects of the Newman persona are discussed here, for example, "the Evangelical persona . . . places Newman in the religious community," what is meant is that Newman, in a reflexive act, characterized himself as Evangelical so as to identify the inscribed self of the *Apologia* at a particular juncture in his transformation. We, as Newman's readers, are able to identify (the rhetorical) him by those qualities and characteristics that are embodied in each of the names he gives himself throughout the autobiography. At any juncture, when I make the statement Newman as Noetic says or Darwin as beetle collector says, I am assuming that my readers understand me (and Newman or Darwin) to mean the rhetorically constituted and named self of the text. I am reflecting on Newman's Cardinal persona reflecting on his Evangelical persona. It is in this way that Newman, through the medium of the persona, becomes *myself* to himself and *himself* to his readers.

In the *Apologia* Newman characterizes the before aspect of his persona as Anglican, and the after aspect as Catholic. The Anglican aspect is itself multiple—Evangelical, Noetic, Tractarian, and Layman—and functions to give definition, or name, Newman at each of the progressive stages of his transformation. The Catholic aspect of the persona functions as the terminus of his religious development. It is the resting place for Newman's religious opinions. In addition to Anglican and Catholic, "Christian" functions for Newman as continuum, the narrating persona that appears throughout the text. It is diacritical and synthetic; it reflects and evaluates.

Christian

When I was fifteen, (in the autumn of 1816), a great change of thought took place in me. I fell under the influences of a definite Creed, and received into my intellect impressions of dogma, which, through God's mercy, have never been effaced or obscured. (*Apol.* 16)

Newman here sets out his first formal religious experience. It is not the agonizing struggle with the sins of the flesh that Augustine describes nor that of the "vilest sinner returning like a dog to its vomit" that Jonathan Edwards recounts.[3] It is a "great change of thought." Readers note that the emphasis here is on thought, the intellectual apperception of the creed leading to commitment, itself a "Catholic" notion of belief. The reception of creed and dogma identify the persona of the *Apologia* as Christian. Throughout the text Christian is that aspect of persona out of which all others are engendered. As repository, or "depositum fidei," Christian functions as continuity, allowing for the transformation of Newman's persona through the gradual revelation of the Divine. For Newman there can be no transformation of religious opinion outside a religious (Christian) persona, nor can Christian dogma reside in any other but Christian. Christian provides "antecedent plausibility" for Newman's transformation from Anglican to Catholic.

> To the pure all things are pure, and have a self-correcting virtue and a power of germinating. And though I have no right at all to assume that this mercy is granted to me, yet the fact, that a person in my situation *may* have it granted to him, seems to me to remove the perplexity which my change of opinion may occasion. (*Apol.* 162)

The relationship that is established between Christian Newman and God at this time serves to ground and justify Newman's subsequent religious experiences. Though he comes to understand more and more of God's activity as disclosed through the dispensations of the church and the fathers, Newman never loses the sense that he has an unusual relationship with God—the relationship of two "luminously self-evident beings"—begun in the autumn of 1816.

As Christian, Newman chooses to "lead a single life," takes little notice of the material world (except as manifestation of spiritual reality), and chooses the priesthood as profession. As Christian, Newman recalls the past experiences of "doubt" and "certitude" and struggles with the pain consequent on his dedication to truth. As Christian, Newman makes inquiry into theology, examines the Anglican and Catholic positions, and prepares *Tract 90*. Both the "recounting I" and the "I" recounted of the autobiography are Christian. It is the Christian aspect of the persona that dismantles the "scarecrow" (the false persona that Newman is accused of being), extinguishes the "phantom" (the ghostly persona that "gibbers" lies "instead of me"), and is the "heart" out of which Newman "speaketh to heart." The Christian aspect of the persona, then, is the voice of Newman's past convictions and of his present heart, and, finally, Anglican Christian becomes Catholic Christian.

Anglican

As Christian, the Anglican aspect of Newman's persona is, as noted earlier, multiple: Evangelical, Noetic, Tractarian, Layman. *Anglican* is the broad, general term for the Newman persona from his admission into the Church of England at the age of fifteen up to his reception into the Roman Catholic Church in 1845. *Anglican* encompasses four of the major transformations of Newman's religious opinion and the innumerable instances of divine revelation. Each of these aspects serves a particular function in the economy of Newman's transformation: the Evangelical aspect of the persona serves a pietistic function, the Noetic serves a systemizing function, the Tractarian serves a mediating function, and the Layman serves a meditative function. Each of the four is defined by a unique set of religious opinions and occupies a particular position in the economy of Newman's transformation. They serve to identify, or name, Newman at the various intervals in the working out of his religious opinions that precede the transformation to his Roman Catholic persona.

Anglican Evangelical

It is as Evangelical that Newman enters the realm of the spiritual for the first time. Newman's Evangelical persona is characterized as devoted, holy, "unworldly," "enamoured with the Early Fathers," existing on the "milk of the word." In this Evangelical persona Newman attends meetings of the Missionary Society and takes "great delight in reading the Bible." The youthful Evangelical reads books of Calvinist bent and follows the teachings of Mayers, Wilson, Scott, and Milner. He holds to the religious doctrines of final perseverance, the Holy Trinity, and Christian warfare. He opposes Antinomianism (the belief that Christians, because of grace, have no need to observe moral law), and he expresses a confirmed "mistrust of the reality of material phenomena." The Evangelical persona exemplifies piety and establishes the place of intimate, personal, and emotional religious practice in Newman's spiritual transformation. The language of the Evangelical Newman, highly colored by affect, places emphasis on the emotions. In this elevated state Newman considers making a "pilgrimage" to his mentor:

> The writer who made a deeper impression on my mind than any other, and to whom (humanly speaking) I almost owe my soul,—Thomas Scott

of Aston Sanford. I so admired and delighted in his writings, that, when I was an undergraduate, I thought of making a visit to his Parsonage, in order to see a man whom I so deeply revered.

The Evangelical Newman is obsessed with religious zeal:

> I hung upon the lips of Daniel Wilson, afterwards Bishop of Calcutta. . . .
> I had been possessed of his "Force of Truth" and Essays from a boy; his
> Commentary I bought when I was an under-graduate. (*Apol.* 17)

The Evangelical persona "exists" in the "first Dispensation" of Newman's religious transformation and, for all its emotionality, places Newman in a religious community. Awakened spiritually, if at first the Evangelical sees "Angels everywhere disguised" because he is "looking," Newman will later come to recognize and understand other less spectacular manifestations of the spiritual world. The Evangelical persona serves to characterize those pietistic aspects—emotional, zealous, and unworldly—that identify Newman at this point in the history of his religious opinions.

Anglican Noetic

Emotionally centered faith has its problems, and thus Newman begins to desire a more substantial religion. The autobiography records that, having obtained his B.A. degree from Trinity College, he is elected fellow of Oriel in 1822. It is here that he comes under the influence of the Noetics. This group of theologians "sought to increase the comprehensiveness of the Church of England" by approving all forms of worship, the Protestant as well as the High Church. Because of their liberalism, they were to become the "inevitable opponents of the Tractarians" (*Apol.* 50). The Noetics, as serious scholars in their approach to Christian doctrine, rejected the emotionalism of the Methodists and other dissenters and insisted on intellectual (noetic) adherence to Anglican dogma.

Newman, now as Noetic, is at first "awkward and timid"; he is developing a new devotion—the Noetic devotion to the intellect. He is ready for the "strong meat" of the Gospel, "beginning to prefer intellectual excellence to moral" (*Apol.* 24). At Oriel the Noetic Newman comes under the influence of Edward Hawkins and Richard Whatley. It is Hawkins who teaches him to

> weigh my words, and to be cautious in my statements. He led me to that
> mode of limiting and clearing my sense in discussion and in controversy,

and of distinguishing between cognate ideas, and of obviating mistakes by anticipation.

Hawkins also brings the Noetic to see the Bible in a new way.

> He lays down a proposition . . . that the sacred text was never intended to teach doctrine, but only to prove it, and that, if we would learn doctrine, we must have recourse to the formularies of the Church; for instance to the Catechism, and to the Creeds. (*Apol.* 20–21)

Under Hawkins's influence, as well, the Noetic Newman is "led to give up my remaining Calvinism, and to receive the doctrine of Baptismal Regeneration" in 1822 (*Apol.* 20). From Whatley Newman comes to see the church as a "substantive body or corporation; next to fix in me those anti-Erastian views of Church polity" (*Apol.* 23). Newman comes to view church rulers, through Apostolic Succession, as having ascendancy over rulers of state. It is about this time that Newman also reads Bishop Butler's *Analogy of Religion, Natural and Revealed, to the Constitution and Course of Nature* (1736), "the study of which has been to so many, as it was to me, an era in their religious opinion." Newman is led to believe that the proof of God's existence is revealed in the material world, that a "system which is of less importance is economically or sacramentally connected with the more momentous system" (*Apol.* 21).

From other Noetics Newman learns doctrines that would be drawn upon much later: from Rev. William James he learns the doctrine of Apostolic Succession; from Hurrell Froude, another Oriel fellow, Newman is encouraged to "look with admiration towards the Church of Rome, and in the same degree to dislike the Reformation." Froude also teaches the Noetic Newman to "believe in the Real Presence" and "fixed in me the idea of devotion to the Blessed Virgin" (*Apol.* 3). From John Keble, also an Oriel fellow and friend, Newman learns of the sacramental system:

> Keble struck an original note and woke up in the hearts of thousands a new music, the music of a school, long unknown in England. Nor can I pretend to analyze, in my own instance, the effect of religious teaching so deep, so pure, so beautiful. . . . The first of these was what may be called, in a large sense of the word, the Sacramental system; that is, the doctrine that material phenomena are both the types and the instruments of real things unseen. (*Apol.* 27–28)

If Newman is devoted to Keble and his belief in the sacramental system, he is dissatisfied with Keble on "Probability." He feels that Keble's view is "beautiful and religious," but it is not logical. Newman endeavors to complete the view himself. Where Keble ascribed assent to "the living power of faith and love which accepted it," Newman demonstrates that assent is the result of "an assemblage of concurring and converging possibilities, and that, both according to the constitution of the human mind and the will of its Maker" (*Apol.* 29). The Noetic Newman is beginning to "see with my own eyes and to walk with my own feet." While he is learning, inquiring, and being influenced by others, he is influencing them and "cooperat[ing] rather than merely concurr[ing] with them" (*Apol.* 22).

In this mind-set Newman begins, on his own, a study of the church fathers and later accepts a proposal to work on a "History of the Principal Councils." While engaged in this enterprise he comes to believe in the "Economies or Dispensations of the Eternal."

> The process of change had been slow; it had been done not rashly, but by rule and measure, "at sundry times and in diverse manners," first one disclosure then another, till the whole evangelical doctrine was brought into full manifestation. (*Apol.* 34)

The church fathers also teach the inquiring Noetic that antiquity is the basis of the Church of England. The teachings of Origen and Clement "carried me away." From the Alexandrian fathers Newman constructs his Doctrine of Angels: "Every breath of air and ray of light and heat, every beautiful prospect, is, as it were, the skirts of their garments, the waving of the robes of those whose faces see God" (*Apol.* 35)." Newman's Noetic persona is a mixture of intellection and emotion, with the intellect, at this point, dominating. The Noetic persona functions as inquirer, systematizer, and analyzer, occupying a place of conjunction between Butler's *Analogy,* Keble's *Christian Year,* and the opinions derived from the church fathers.

The Noetic persona, then, exists in the second major dispensation of Newman's religious transformation, a period marked by unusual activity, intellectual inquiry, learning, and teaching. During this period the Noetic is ordained a priest and appointed vicar at St. Mary's. As Noetic, Newman begins his own inquiry into religious opinion. His language has a "zeal and freshness, but with the partiality, of a neophyte" (*Apol.* 34). If at times he still speaks of Angels disguised and hosts of evil spirits, he also, at other times, speaks of certitude and assent. The Noetic is still a neophyte, no doubt, but he is systematically making preparation for an ever more serious work: "a work to do in England" (*Apol.* 40). The discoveries that the neophyte makes follow one after another—collecting, colliding, modifying, combining—until they thrust Newman into the center of a major religious movement and the persona of the Tractarian emerges from the mix.

Anglican Tractarian

When does Newman actually begin to take on the Tractarian persona? Is it while he is finishing up his work on the *Arians of the Fourth Century,* in 1832? Is it while he is writing of "the 'vision' which haunted me" in the *Lyra Apostlica?* Is it while he is vacationing away from Oxford and "think[ing] that some inward changes, as well as some larger course of action, were coming upon me"? Is it in Castro-Giovanni where he sobs to his servant that "I have a work to do in England"? Is it while the "Bill for the Suppression of the Irish Sees . . . filled my mind. I had fierce thoughts against the Liberals"? Is it as he writes the words to the hymn "Lead, Kindly Light" on board an orange boat bound for Marseilles? Is it when he returns to Oxford to hear Keble preach the Assize Sermon on National Apostasy in July 1833?

While historians can cite Keble's sermon as the signal beginning of the Tractarian movement, it is difficult to mark the exact point at which Newman is transformed from Noetic to Tractarian, since his transformation is the consequence of a gradual revelation. It is the case, however, that in September 1833 the Tractarians (Keble, Froude, Palmer, Perceval, Rose, Newman, and, later, Pusey) publish their first *Tracts for the Times.* They are united in defending Apostolic Succession and the integrity of the Prayer Book; they are determined to answer the question "How were we to keep the Church from becoming liberalized?"

> The true principles of Churchmanship seemed so radically decayed, and there was such distraction in the councils of the Clergy. Blomfield, the Bishop of London of the day, an active and open-hearted man, had been for years engaged in diluting the high orthodoxy of the Church by the introduction of members of the Evangelical body into places of influence and trust. . . . I thought little of the Evangelicals as a class. I thought they played into the hands of the Liberals. (*Apol.* 37)

Here the Tractarian Newman compares the Liberal state of the Anglican Church to the "fresh vigorous power" of the early church and feels "dismay at her prospects, anger and scorn at her do-nothing perplexity" (*Apol.* 38). He concludes that it is time to take action: "Now it was that I repeated to myself the words, which had been dear to me from my school days, 'Exoriare aliquis!'" The Tractarian is repeating Aeneas' ancient challenge, loosely translated, "Rise, Avenger" (*Apol.* 40).

Newman's Evangelical persona had manifested principally the passive characteristics of piety, emotive responses, and receptivity, while his Noetic persona, though less passive, was, nevertheless, more receptive than active and had manifested the neophyte qualities of systematic inquiry and investigation. By contrast, the Tractarian Newman is fully active, with "high energy," "supreme confidence," and a "mixture of fierceness and sport" (*Apol.* 48). The Tractarian at times manifests "recklessness," "negligence," and "wantonness" and is aggressively hostile toward the Liberals, that segment of the Anglican Church that sought to congregate all its variant denominational practices within the established church. (By liberalism Newman himself meant "the antidogmatic principle and its developments" [*Apol.* 50].) This hostility toward the Liberals shows up in a number of ways: he refuses, because of the success of the Liberals in France, to look at the French flag when in Algiers and "kept indoors" to avoid the French for the twenty-four hours he is forced to spend in Paris in 1833; he declines a "Whitehall preachership," because of the liberal stance of the bishop even before the bishop formally offers it to him, and, finally, he questions Dr. Thomas Arnold's Christianity because of the illustrious educator's opposition to a tax-supported church (*Apol.* 39). Anything that tends to suggest liberalism, political or religious, Newman openly rejects.

Newman, as Tractarian, also foolishly stops seeing his own brother. He bases his conduct toward his brother "upon a syllogism. . . . St. Paul bids us avoid those who cause divisions; you cause divisions: therefore I must avoid you." He dissuades "a lady from attending the marriage of a sister who had seceded from the Anglican Church" (*Apol.* 50). The Tractarian recklessly proceeds to develop further his doctrine of "The Angels of the Seven Churches." He feels he has found a solution to the presence of intelligence or inspiration in nations, institutions, and certain leaders. The Tractarian Newman's behavior is often careless and whimsical. Reflecting on these cavalier actions and his highly personalized views at this time, he characterizes them as "doing credit to my imagination at the expense of my judgement—'Hippoclides doesn't care.' I am not setting myself up as a pattern of good sense or of anything else: I am but giving a history of my opinions" (*Apol.* 36).

Contrast these decidedly immature behaviors to the Tractarian's more serious work as he becomes involved in a "second reformation" of the Anglican Church.

I thought that if Liberalism once got a footing within her, it was sure of the victory in the event. . . . I ever kept before me that there was something greater than the Established Church, and that that was the Church Catholic and Apostolic, set up from the beginning, of which she was but the local presence and the organ. She was nothing, unless she was this. She must be dealt with strongly, or she would be lost. There was need of a second reformation. (*Apol.* 38)

This is to be Newman's work, then, the second reformation. The corrective for the threat of liberalism is to show how the Anglican Church is part of the Catholic (world) Church but does not partake in the Roman Errors: Invocation of Mary and the Saints and popery, the doctrine of papal infallibility. As Tractarian, Newman will seek to articulate an Anglican theology that will make of Anglicanism more than a "paper religion," more than a "mere modification or transition-state of either Romanism or popular Protestantism" (*Apol.* 65).

The *Tracts for the Times,* begun ("out of my own head") and edited by Newman, are a first attempt at a corrective to liberalism and an argument for dogma.

The main principle of the movement is as dear to me now, as it ever was. I have changed in many things: in this I have not. From the age of fifteen, dogma has been the fundamental principle of my religion: I know no other religion; I cannot enter into the idea of any other sort of religion; religion, as a mere sentiment, is to me a dream and a mockery. (*Apol.* 51)

In the midst of his reactionary Tractarianism Newman retains his Christian persona. His adherence to dogmatic principle never waivers. For Newman Christian is equivalent to dogmatist, and the later *Tracts* give evidence of that adherence, while the early *Tracts* are "short, hasty, and some of them ineffective; and at the end of the year, when collected into a volume, they had a slovenly appearance" (*Apol.* 59). The Tractarian Newman, with regard to his editorship of the *Tracts,* is "lounging, free and easy" and "exercises no sufficient censorship" on them (*Apol.* 58). When Edward Pusey joins the group in 1835, he influences Newman to publish "larger and more careful works in defence of the principles of the Movement" (*Apol.* 61). It is at this time that Newman becomes convinced that reform can proceed no further until the relationship between the Anglican and Roman systems is "brought out with precision." This came to be the "work" that occupied Newman as Tractarian for the next few years, and this was to be the work that moved him closer and closer to the Catholic Church. *The*

Prophetical Office of the Church Viewed Relatively to Romanism and Popular Protestantism and the infamous *Tract 90* were attempts to articulate a via media, an Anglican position midway between Rome and Geneva.

> A *Via Media* was but a receding from extremes,—therefore it needed to be drawn out into a definite shape and character: before it could have claims on our respect, it must first be shown to be one, intelligible, and consistent. . . . Even if the *Via Media* were ever so positive a religious system, it was not as yet objective and real; it had no original any where of which it was the representative. It was at present a paper religion. (*Apol.* 64)

Preparation of these documents, the *Prophetical Office* and *Tract 90,* thrusts the Tractarian Newman into new investigations. They bring new information and insights to bear on his present understandings. In the attempt to discover the "true Church" in the Anglican writings, Newman draws ever closer to the Church of Rome. With the writing of the *Prophetical Office,* the Tractarian wishes to build up an Anglican theology out of the "past toil of the great divines." The theology is "not so gentle to the Church of Rome," since Newman wants to avoid the charges of popery that are being leveled at the Tractarians and to show that "the Anglican can be as little said to tend to the Roman, as the Roman to the Anglican." So he deals with Romanism, not in the sense of its formal decrees but in terms of its "traditional action and its authorized teaching" (*Apol.* 62). The *Prophetical Office* emphasizes the differences between the Anglican and the Roman systems; what becomes more obvious to the Tractarian, as he proceeds with his work on a via media is that (1) he must consider the similarities of the two systems more fully, and (2) when he does so he discovers that he must correct his misunderstanding about the "dominant errors" of the Roman Church.

In *Tract 90* Newman explores the "limits of elasticity" in the Anglican Creed. He shows just how far the *Thirty-nine Articles* and the *Homilies* are tolerant of a Roman interpretation.

> In the minds of the men who wrote the Homilies, and who thus incorporated them into the Anglican system of doctrine, there was no such nice discrimination between the Catholic and the Protestant faith, no such clear recognition of formal Protestant principles and tenets, no such accurate definition of "Roman doctrine," as is received at the present day:— hence great probability accrued to my presentment, that the Articles were tolerant, not only of what I called "Catholic teaching," but of much that was "Roman." (*Apol.* 75)

Newman tells us that it was only the supremacy of the Holy See that the *Articles* denied, nothing more. He insists that Popery "in any other shape" could and did find sanction in the *Articles* (*Apol.* 73).

The *Prophetical Office* attempts to "benefit the Church of England, at the expense of Rome." *Tract 90* seeks to "benefit the Church of England *without* prejudice to the Church of Rome" (*Apol.* 148; my emphasis). Both are the Tractarian's attempt at a via media, but they are more than that. They are the "working out" of Newman's own spiritual certitude. As Tractarian, Newman's mediating persona explores the Anglican and Roman systems (through their dogmata, their actions, and their writings), so as to derive a middle ground for his own religious opinions. They are opinions, however, that are constantly "under correction."

Existing in the third dispensation of Newman's religious transformation, the Tractarian is at first hostile to Rome. Further disclosure ("correction," "collision," "modification," "convergence") brings him to "look with admiration towards the Church of Rome" as the visible manifestation of invisible certitude, "Holy Church in her sacraments and hierarchical appointments . . . but a symbol of those heavenly facts which fill eternity," the "One Fold and under One Shepherd" (*Apol.* 34, 216). This "longing look towards Rome," articulated in *Tract 90,* costs Newman his place in the movement and forces him to relinquish his clerical status and take up the persona of Layman. When he declares, "It is a duty which we owe both to the Catholic Church, and to our own, to take our reformed confessions in the most Catholic sense they will admit" (*Apol.* 108), he is sounding the death knell for his Anglican priesthood and his mediating, Tractarian persona.

Layman

From the end of 1841 Newman is, in reality, "on my death-bed, as regards my membership with the Anglican Church" (*Apol.* 121). He is "shaken," "in a state of unsettlement," and in doubt "too strong to suppress with propriety" (*Apol.* 168). The furor over *Tract 90,* from the church and from the countryside, has caused him such anguish that he wants nothing more than to "fall back into Lay Communion" and "be allowed to die in peace" (*Apol.* 121). Where once Newman, as Noetic and Tractarian, had existed on the "strong meat of the gospel" in the rarefied air of Oxford, Newman now wants only to take on the persona of Layman and subsist on prayer, meditation, and reflection in the quiet surroundings of Littlemore—"door closed and curtains drawn."

Newman wishes to gain no more converts but to "keep simply to my
own case." He hopes to hold back the young men who were desirous of
going over to Rome with him—he feels he has an obligation to their Anglican parents and a duty to his bishop and the Anglican Church—but he is
reluctant to do more. He sees his responsibility: "in my case it was, 'Physician, heal thyself.'"

> My own soul was my first concern, and it seemed an absurdity to my rea-
> son to be converted in partnership. I wished to go to my Lord by myself,
> and in my own way, or rather His way. I had neither wish, nor, I may say,
> thought of taking a number with me. (*Apol.* 170)

At this point Newman is in despair over his young followers and in despair
over his own spiritual condition. He needs time to recover from the "three
blows which broke me" (*Apol.* 114) and to find a way to "go to my Lord by
myself." As Layman he could do what he could not do as Anglican priest.
A priest must function as minister, shepherd, guide; a Layman could "say
[his] prayers" and clear up "a certain doubt about the Anglican system"
(*Apol.* 138).

In 1841 Newman gives up his place in the movement; in early 1842 he
moves permanently to Littlemore. During the fall of 1843 he resigns his vic-
arage at St. Mary's and becomes laicized. But he is not to be left alone to
pray and meditate. The "sudden storm of indignation with which *Tract* 90
was received" continues to build and Newman is accused of being "insidi-
ous," "sly," and "dishonest" by the English bishops (*Apol.* 138). He is
charged with being a "concealed Romanist" and reproached for not
"leav[ing] the Anglican Church sooner" (*Apol.* 147). The newspapers
accuse him of establishing a monastery:

> A so-called Anglo-Catholic Monastery is in the process of erection at Lit-
> tlemore, and that the cells of dormitories, the chapel, the refectory, the
> cloisters all may be seen advancing to perfection, under the eye of a Parish
> Priest of the Diocese of Oxford. (*Apol.* 139)

The bishops, of all persons, would not leave him alone to pray and meditate. They wanted to know, like the reporters, "Why did I go up to Littlemore?" (*Apol.* 138). Newman had taken in some of his young followers in
an effort to dissuade them from Rome, but the bishops "one after another
began to charge against me." In response Newman warns:

> If conversions to Rome take place in consequence of the Tracts for the
> Times, I do not impute blame to them, but to those who, instead of

acknowledging such Anglican principles of theology and ecclesiastical polity as they contain, set themselves to oppose them. Whatever be the influence of the Tracts, great or small, they may become just as powerful for Rome, if our Church refuses them . . . it is plain that our members may easily be persuaded either to give up those principles, or to give up the Church. If this state of things goes on, I mournfully prophesy, not one or two, but many secessions to the Church of Rome. (*Apol.* 115)

The bishops, in refusing to accept the catholicity of his views in *Tract 90,* ignore his warning and become more abusive, "directing charges against me for three whole years." They consider Newman a "concealed Romanist" and keep him constantly under watch. Newman describes such a scene:

One day when I entered my house, I found a flight of Under-graduates inside. Heads of Houses, as mounted patrols, walked their horses round those poor cottages. Doctors of Divinity dived into the hidden recesses of that private tenement uninvited, and drew domestic conclusions from what they saw there. I had thought that an Englishman's house was his castle. (*Apol.* 138)

The experience with the bishops is a "blow" to Newman's religious opinions as Anglican. The "blows that broke me" were the Layman's way of describing the final events that were to bring Newman to Rome. Earlier transformations, from Evangelical to Noetic and from Noetic to Tractarian, came, in the main, of gentle impressions; the transformation from Tractarian Layman to Catholic came of "blows." Previous revelation had been more gradual and certainly less dramatic. These painful experiences, more rapid and severe, hastened the transformation of the Anglican to Catholicism.

Though my Tract was an experiment, it was, as I said at the time, "no feeler"; the event showed this; for, when my principle was not granted, I did not draw back, but gave up. I would not hold office in a Church which would not allow my sense of the Articles. My tone was, "This is necessary for us, and have it we must and will, and, if it tends to bring men to look less bitterly on the Church of Rome, so much the better." (*Apol.* 108)

Prior to this setback Newman had experienced an earlier "blow" to his religious opinions when "I set myself down to my translation of Saint Athanasius" (*Apol.* 114). As Newman is working, he discovers a heresy "far bolder" than the Monophysite heresy he had encountered in his earlier readings. Two years before he had been studying the Monophysite heresy and Saint Augustine's warning, "Securus judicat orbis terrarum" (The world judges with assurance that they are not good men who, in whatever part of the world, separate themselves from the rest of the world [*Apol.* 98 n. 5]). At that time he concluded that the Anglican Church was guilty of schism. Now, upon discovering the Arian heresy, Newman sees a parallel to his present concerns: "the pure Arians were the Protestants, the semi-Arians were the Anglicans," and "Rome now is what it was then" (*Apol.* 114–15). The Layman concludes that not only is the Anglican Church in schism; but, if the Arians are heretics, the Anglicans are heretics. There is no middle course. With the discovery of the Monophysite heresy in 1839, "Down had come the Via Media. . . . My 'Prophetical Office' had come to pieces" (*Apol.* 100). With the blow of the Arian heresy in 1841 the via media was pulverized; there is no plea to be made for Anglicanism. The Layman Newman now believes that Rome may have "added to the Creed" but that the Anglican is "estranged from the great body of Christians over the World" and should look for providential direction on "how to comport themselves toward the Church of Rome" (*Apol.* 95).

Newman, as Layman, might well have been content to retire to Littlemore to "advance again within the Anglican Church" at a later date and to support a union of the Anglican and the Roman—"Church with Church" (*Apol.* 121)—had it not been for the affair of the Jerusalem bishopric. This third and final incident deals the deathblow to Newman's Anglicanism. Newman discovers that the Prussian Court and the Anglican Church plan an experiment to join Evangelism and Episcopacy in the Prussian Church. To save embarrassment if the project fails, the experiment is to be conducted in Jerusalem. British citizens would be consecrated bishops and would exercise spiritual jurisdiction over "the ministers of British congregations of the United Church of England and Ireland, and over such other Protestant Congregations, as may be desirous of placing themselves under his or their authority" (*Apol.* 117). The Layman Newman is severely distressed over the Jerusalem affair and makes solemn protest both to the archbishop of Canterbury and to his own bishop. They refuse to reverse their decisions. This final blow to his Anglican loyalties is seen by many of Newman's friends to be a "great misfortune"; in contrast, Newman looks upon the incident as merciful:

> As to the project of the Jerusalem Bishopric, I never heard of any good or harm it has ever done, except what it has done for me; which many think a great misfortune, and I one of the greatest of mercies. It brought me on to the beginning of the end. (*Apol.* 120)

The "three blows that broke me" are severe; they are "shocks" to New-man's Anglican persona, but in light of his religious transformation they are the "greatest of mercies."

As Layman, Newman is in a state of meditation in terms of his transfor-mation, a very special sort of meditation, with hope of *solus cum solo*. In this state there is "no cloud interposed between the creature and the Object of his faith and love" (*Apol.* 154). In the meditative persona of Layman, Newman tries to find a way to "go to my Lord" through the dogma of the Anglican Church, but that hope is not to be realized; the blows are too severe. The Anglican Church has been "a place of refuge and temporary rest" (*Apol.* 176), a place of belief preceding a "positive doubt," but that place can no longer serve. While Newman remains certain that through God's ordered process of self-disclosure he will come to "believe as if I saw" (*Apol.* 51), yet the Layman wonders, "I had been deceived greatly once; how could I be sure that I was not deceived a second time?" (*Apol.* 176). To resolve the matter of any lingering doubts Newman, still as Layman, deter-mines to work out the *Essay on the Development of Christian Doctrine,* "and then, if, at the end of it, my convictions in favor of the Roman Church were not weaker, of taking the necessary steps for admission into her fold" (*Apol.* 177).

Catholic

The Anglican Tractarian, six years before his reception into the Catholic Church, had proclaimed, quietly and to himself, that "the Church of Rome will be found right after all" (*Apol.* 99). The Evangelical Anglican had related instances of crossing "myself on going into the dark" (*Apol.* 14) and of drawing "a set of beads suspended, with a little cross attached" in his childhood *Ealing Verse Book* (*Apol.* 15). The Noetic Anglican had learned from Hurrell Froude "to look with admiration toward the Church of Rome" (*Apol.* 33). The Anglican Layman had confessed a longing love of Rome, "in spite of my old friends, in spite of my old life-long prejudices. In spite of my ingrained fears of Rome . . . in spite of my affection for Oxford and Oriel, yet I had a secret longing love of Rome the Mother of English Christianity" (*Apol.* 133).

Throughout the *Apologia* Catholic characteristics infuse the Anglican persona. They forecast the Catholic in the Christian and prepare the reader for the eventuality of the conversion from Anglican to Catholic. If the church "by her step . . . reveal[s] herself a goddess (Incessu patuit Dea)," Newman, as Christian, places his feet in her every footprint. As Evangelical, he was awed by her "mystery"; as Noetic, he had admired her; as Tractarian, he argued for her; as Layman, he longs for her.

It is no wonder, then, that in October 1845, the "tangled and manifold controversy" comes to an end. Newman asks Father Dominic, the Passionist, to receive him into the Church of Rome.

> He is a simple, holy man; and withal gifted with remarkable powers. He does not know of my intention; but I mean to ask of him admission into the One Fold of Christ. (*Apol.* 181)

The Catholic Newman does not go over to Rome out of "resentment, or disgust, at any thing that has happened to me." He is convinced that "my one paramount reason for contemplating a change is my deep, unvarying conviction that our Church is in schism, and that my salvation depends on my joining the Church of Rome" (*Apol.* 177); "the Anglican Church was formally in the wrong" (in schism), and "the Church of Rome was formally in the right" (*Apol.* 157). Newman's decision has nothing to do with how he feels personally; "I have no existing sympathies with Roman Catholics; I hardly ever, even abroad, was at one of their services; I know none of them, I do not like what I hear of them" (*Apol.* 177). Newman's conversion has everything to do with the assurance of his salvation in the One Church. The Anglican Evangelical, characterized by emotional attachment to the Church of England, is transformed to Catholic Newman, characterized by conviction that his salvation is with Rome.

Newman, as Catholic, has "no further history of my religious opinions to narrate," no further "variations to record." He has "no anxiety of heart whatever" and finds himself "in perfect peace and contentment." His doubt is gone, but otherwise his convictions remain the same as they have been.

> I was not conscious to myself, on my conversion, of any change, intellectual or moral, wrought in my mind. I was not conscious of firmer faith in the fundamental truths of Revelation, or of more self-command; I had not more fervour; but it was like coming into port after a rough sea; and my happiness on that score remains to this day without interruption. (*Apol.* 184)

The Catholic Newman speaks as one who has experienced the gradual revelation of the Holy Church. There is no momentous change, only that those beliefs that were erroneous have suffered a "gradual decay and extinction" rather than a "violent death." He now adopts with ease those additional articles not found in the Anglican Creed.

> Nor had I any trouble about receiving those additional articles. . . . Some of them I believed already, but not any one of them was a trial to me. I made a profession of them upon my reception with the greatest ease. (*Apol.* 184)

"A thousand difficulties do not make a doubt." Newman as Catholic distinguishes between the doubting of doctrine and those points of faith that cause difficulty. He works out his previous conflicts concerning the services and devotions to Saint Mary and the infallibility of the church in this way. He comes to recognize that the church is a living system and that its infallibility is "a provision, adapted by the mercy of the Creator, to preserve religion in the world, and to restrain that freedom of thought, which of course in itself is one of the greatest of our natural gifts, and to rescue it from its own suicidal excesses" (*Apol.* 189).

In the "safety of port" all previous difficulties take on their proper perspective. In the church the Catholic Newman locates his salvation and the "provision" for dealing with all difficulties of belief. He is, indeed, in the state of *solus cum solo.*

> For here again, in a matter consisting in the purest and most direct acts of religion,—in the intercourse between God and the soul, during a season of recollection, of repentance, of good resolution, of inquiry into vocation,— the soul was "sola cum solo;" there was no cloud interposed between the creature and the Object of his faith and love. The command practically enforced was, "My son, give Me thy heart." (*Apol.* 154)

In reading the *Apologia* from the perspective of the persona, we have discovered, in addition to the obvious fact that Newman is transformed from Anglican to Catholic, that the self (rhetorically constituted and transformed) of the *Apologia* is quite complex. This self is not *I* but, rather, the *myself,* constituted as a mature Catholic cardinal reflecting on the Evangelical, Noetic, Tractarian, and Layman characteristics of the self and infusing them with Catholic attributes. Has this rhetorical Newman ever been anything but Catholic, then? The answer is not a simple one. The Newman of the *Apologia* has been constituted to defend what seems to many a radical and traitorous change in Newman's religious opinions. Thus, it is necessary for reader and writer to conceive of "Newman" in at least two ways: first, as changing names or identities so as to mark out each new spiritual revelation and, second, as incorporating into each of the identities some aspect of the Catholic persona that will gradually emerge full-blown in the cardinal. We can have it no other way: both Newman and his readers knew (or know) the outcome and "see" Catholic traits in the Anglican, but a narrative of transformation, rhetorically constituted, requires that readers and writers construct personae that convey the notion of transformation through a set of before and after qualities and characteristics. Evangelical, Noetic, Tractarian, Layman, Catholic, say that "Newman has changed."

Economy: The Figura of a Religious Transformation

The before and after aspects of the persona mark out and affirm that a change has occurred in the life of John Henry Newman: he was Anglican; now he is Catholic. In general terms we could say that the type of Newman's transformation is spiritual. But this general or global type does not specify its unique character. It is the figura of "economy" that holds the potential for explaining the nature of a spiritual transformation that was so unusual that it "shook an entire nation."

Newman's transformation from Anglican to Catholic can be said to span thirty years, if one includes the whole of Newman's life as Anglican until the time when he became Catholic (1814 to 1845). Or, if we consider only that period from 1835 to 1845, when Newman was heavily engaged in the development of his religious opinions, the conversion spanned a ten-year period. Either way, the inordinate length of this conversion process, as implied by the before and after characteristics of the persona, suggests that Newman's transformation is anything but a precipitous event. The direct opposite of a sudden, onetime conversion, it is, rather, the result of a long and arduous search for spiritual truth through historical documents, the writings of the fathers, and the actions of the Councils of the church.[4]

If other than a sudden, emotional conversion, what is the nature of Newman's astounding transformation from Anglican to Catholic? How is Newman moved to leave " 'my kindred and my father's house' for a Church from which once I turned away with dread?" More specifically, what is the nature of Newman's religious transformation as presented in the text of the *Apologia Pro Vita Sua?* He has

> no autobiographical notes to consult, no written explanations of particular treaties or of tracts which at the time gave offence, hardly any minutes of definite transactions, or conversations, and few contemporary

memoranda, I fear, of the feelings or motives under which from time to time I acted. I have an abundance of letters from friends with some copies or drafts of my answers to them, but they are for the most part unsorted. . . . Then, as to the volumes which I have published, they would in many ways serve me, were I well up in them: but though I took great pains in their composition, I have thought little about them, when they were once out of my hands. (*Apol.* 12–13)

The problem for Newman is how to "reveal myself," how to "draw out . . . the history of my mind." Newman chooses to reveal himself and his religious opinions through an *apology*. *Apologia,* the form used by Plato to present Socrates' defense at his trial before the Athenians, was appropriated by the early Christians to defend themselves against paganism or government reprisals. It set forth a history of Christian experience and an explication of Christian doctrine. The apologies of Justin Martyr, Clement, Tertullian, and Origen are some of the more famous examples. *Apo* was originally a separation word; it meant "over against, from." Here, used with *logos,* it means a "word" over against, in opposition to, and so, "defense." This etymology is infected by the derived English meaning, which is not supported directly by the Greek. Newman has chosen to persuade us of the truth of his transformation through the form of apology. He has chosen to "speak off" the charge of traitor, liar, "concealed Roman," by providing a "History of His Religious Opinions."

This subtitle reinforces the notion of apology by suggesting the mode of defense—a "history." For Newman this is a very different sort of history; it is not a list of facts, events, or dates; it is a dramatic, living history. It is a record of a gradual revelation *to* himself, a history of the religious opinions that "grew, were modified, were combined, were in collision with each other, and were changed." It is also a gradual revelation *of* himself and his dramatic transformation: of the "Religion which I profess," for the "Priesthood in which I am unworthily included," for "my friends," and "my foes," and for the "general public" (*Apol.* 11).

The title and subtitle, then, encapsulate the transformation of John Henry Newman. They suggest that his change is historical, not in the usual sense of history in which one event seems to follow another, the previous one appearing to cause the successive one, but history in the sense of the dramatic and the evolutionary. Like the action in a story or drama, each event is a convergence of numerous other events, experiences, and influences; in turn, each "new" event influences future events. Ever burgeoning, this sort of narrative is neither linear nor cyclical but organic; each new disclosure makes sense of previous occurrences and forecasts events yet to be revealed. The title and subtitle, taken in this manner, prepare the reader for Newman's defense of his conversion from Anglican to Catholic.

Keywords and phrases from the *Apologia* support this notion of transformation as it is characterized in the title and subtitle: gradual revelation or dramatic history. Words like *gradual assent, probabilities, certitude, change, modified, collision, converging, cumulative, economies, history* (*Apol.* 30, 157, 12, 29, 34) appear repeatedly throughout the text. Other references, more extended, point to this same type of transformation: "things are wonderfully linked together," "limit of that elasticity," "slow course of change," "gradual decay and extinction," "antecedent plausibility," "wrote . . . under correction," "I was in misery of this new unsettlement," "to know that one knows," "doubt is a progress," "first one disclosure and then another," "*assemblage* of concurring and converging possibilities," "Economies or Dispensations of the Eternal," "keen and vivid realizing of the Divine Depositum of Faith" (*Apol.* 137, 72, 173, 19, 137, 63, 115, 168, 34, 29, 34, 163).

Such phrases reinforce the notion that Newman's conversion involves a gradual revelation, or disclosure, of God's divine plan, one that encompasses both the intelligence and the heart.[5] Newman speaks of a theology that is elastic; it could accommodate changing times and circumstances. He points to the way that ideas are "linked" to one another, how each is dependent on the other by "antecedent plausibility." He characterizes the whole as "Economies or Dispensations of the Eternal." The assimilation of new information converges with previous knowledge to shape larger views and greater understanding. When certain previous opinions will not fit into the enlarged system, they are not discarded immediately, nor are they tossed aside carelessly. They experience a "gradual decay and extinction," leaving Newman with a new "assemblage" of possibilities.

The operative metaphors of gradual change in the life of John Henry Newman cluster around the idea of economy. Taken together with Newman's definition of history from the subtitle, they communicate a sense of spiritual transformation that is brought on by the slow but steady disclosure of God's lively working in history. As Newman partakes of and participates in this divine economy, he is transformed from Anglican apologist to Catholic cardinal. The remainder of this section explores the nature of economy, how it functions as figura for the process of transformation in the *Apologia Pro Vita Sua,* and how the autobiography itself illustrates the notion of economy, as each new personal disclosure "makes sense of previous occurrences and forecasts events yet to be revealed" for Newman's readers.

Economy is defined by J. N. D. Kelly in *Early Christian Doctrines*. Kelly tells us that the early fathers of the second century "approached God from two directions, envisaging Him both as He exists in His intrinsic being, and also as He manifests Himself in the 'economy.'" Kelly defines the nature of economy as the "ordered process of His self-disclosure."[6] At first *economy* held only the concept of "divine plan or God's secret purpose" and the ideas of "distribution" *(dispensatio)*, "organization," and "the arrangement of a number of factors in regular order." It was later extended in Christian theology to include "self-disclosure through the Incarnation."

Economy stands as figura of the *Apologia* as it characterizes the gradual revelation of God's purpose in history *and* the development of Newman's religious opinions. It is dispensation and incarnation, in their widest senses: first, God disclosed in His Son the "Word" and, second, disclosed to a human, Newman. Economy circumscribes all the events in Newman's life as they are emplotted in the *Apologia*. The text provides no other explanation from Newman. Hayden White would say that Newman cannot "escape the trope" of economy. Within this figura each new exploration of religious doctrine results in a new disclosure of the "divine plan or God's secret purpose." This disclosure, in turn, leads Newman back to the doctrinal discourses that he will explore for further disclosures or dispensations. Newman, in making himself a "patron of Economy," believes that he is drawing closer and closer to God and the One Church.

It is within the figura of God's economy that Newman comes to realize that the Anglican perspective is completely out of phase with the Catholic.

> We [Newman, speaking here still as Anglican] have a vast inheritance, but no inventory of our treasures. All is given us in profusion; it remains for us to catalogue, sort, distribute, select, harmonize, and complete. (*Apol.* 64)

For the Anglican there is no dynamic history; everything has already happened. There is no new revelation; all has been given. It is only after Newman confronts the dynamic history of the development of Catholic dogma that he is able to critique the Anglican tradition. Within the figura of economy Newman gets a sense of the stages of his religious opinion as necessary and appropriate to God's continuing revelation, as being "wonderfully linked together," each "antecedent plausibility" for the successive opinion. Within the figura of economy Newman can always write "under correction"; he can be assured that, while there are times when he is under "the misery of this new unsettlement" (new revelation), he can see that "doubt is a progress." For Newman's own understanding and transformation the figura of economy functions to keep him moving toward Rome. Newman is assured that if he allows himself to operate within God's economy, he will obtain religious certitude, which he characterizes as a "keen and vivid realization of the Divine Depositum of Faith."

As the figura of economy functions to ground, circumscribe, and encapsulate Newman's own transformation from Anglican to Catholic, it also functions to explain the ground and mode of his transformation to the readers of his day.

> The Principle of the economy is familiarly acted upon among us every day. When we would persuade others, we do not begin by treading on their toes. Men would be thought rude who introduced their own religious notions into mixed society, and were devotional in a drawing-room. Have we never thought lawyers tiresome who did *not* observe this polite rule, who came down for the assizes and talked law all through dinner?[7]

While many of Newman's educated contemporaries understood *economy* in its religious sense, others were more familiar with its practical and general senses: *political economy,* proper production, distribution, and consumption of resources (via Malthus, Adam Smith, and Harriet Martineau), and *household economy,* taking care with one's domestic resources." Attuned to his "lawyer joke," they also viewed the principle of economy as simply good manners. In its religious sense, its general and practical senses, and its prudent sense the figura of economy has the potential for sounding all these resonances in Newman's readers. He "dispenses" gradually what he wants to reveal of himself to them:

> Now, as to the Economy itself, it is founded upon the words of our Lord, "Cast not your pearls before swine;" and it was observed by the early Christians more or less, in their intercourse with the heathen populations among whom they lived. In the midst of the abominable idolatries and impurities of that fearful time, the Rule of the Economy was an imperative duty. (*Apol.* 206)

Here Newman is speaking directly to Kingsley's charges of "liar" and "deceiver." He reminds his readers that "stating it [the truth] only partially and representing it under the nearest form possible to a learner or inquirer, when he could not possibly understand it exactly" (as the early fathers had done among the "heathen populations"), was the sense in which he was to be understood as a "patron of the Economy" (*Apol.* 206–7). Newman goes on to warn against abuse of the economy and to plead his own cause with his readers through a "cautious dispensation of the truth."

> The *abuse of the Economy in the hands of unscrupulous reasoners,* is obvious. *Even the honest* controversialist or teacher will find it very difficult to represent, *without misrepresenting,* what it is yet his duty to present to his hearers with caution or reserve. Here the obvious rule to guide our practice is, to be careful ever to maintain *substantial truth* in our use of the economical method.[8]

Newman expresses real bitterness over abuse of economy in the teachings of the Anglican Divines. He recalls being in a humor to "bite off their ears." Reliance on their authority had led him to be careless in his own understanding and in the teaching of his followers. He had "read the Fathers through their [the Anglican Divine's] eyes" and had placed too much faith in Ussher, Taylor, and Barrow (*Apol.* 159). Now believing that dispensations of the Eternal "are not to be taken lightly," Newman wants to make certain that there are no questions about his own commitment to the truth nor any questions about his duty in making divine truth accessible to his readers. In other words, Newman does not want to be guilty of the same sins he lays at the feet of the Anglican Divines.

> The principle of the Economy is this; that out of various courses, in religious conduct or statement, all and each *allowable antecedently and in themselves,* that ought to be taken which is most expedient and most suitable at the time for the object in hand. . . . Here the obvious rule to guide our practice is, to be careful even to maintain substantial truth in our use of the economical method.[9]

Economy's function is to reveal God to human beings. It serves its best purposes as an expedient of God's self-disclosure. As such, economy was not instituted for the theologian. It is a dispensation for the confessor. Economy, Newman tells us, is "a way of winning men from greater sins by winking for the time at the less"; God allows Himself to be "represented as having eyes, ears, and hands, as having wrath, jealousy, grief, and repentance." Newman reminds his readers that "Joseph made himself strange to his brethren" and that "St. Paul circumcised Timothy, while he cried out 'Circumcision availeth not.'" Newman insists that "Nature was a parable: Scripture was an allegory: pagan literature, philosophy, and mythology, properly understood, were but a preparation for the Gospel" (*Apol.* 212, 257, 34). Newman is reminding his readers that what Joseph can do, what Saint Paul can do, what God himself has done in gradually revealing Himself, Newman can do. He can make himself known to his readers through means of the economy. What justification—centuries of tradition and God's own example!

Within the *figura* of economy, then, Newman discovers the way that God has revealed Himself to him, and, conversely, he finds a way to reveal himself to his readers. We could say that Newman's *History of His Religious Opinions* mirrors the process of transformation that Newman describes. Newman is reluctant to drag the history of his conversion before the public once again. He is also reluctant to

> practice on himself a cruel operation, the ripping up of old griefs, and the venturing again upon the "infandum dolorem" [grief beyond words] of years, in which the stars of this lower heaven were one by one going out. (*Apol.* 81)

But Newman feels that this is his duty.

> It may easily be conceived how great a trial it is to me to write the following history of myself; but I must not shrink from the task. The words, '*Secretum meum mihi*' [My secret is my own], keep ringing in my ears. (*Apol.* 14)

Newman realizes that a religious leader cannot allow the charge of deception to go unchallenged, nor can insults to the priests of the church he has come to love go unanswered. His faith has been too hard-won.

Newman attempts to answer the critics who reproach him for not leaving the Anglican Church sooner, for waiting to say what he believed, for publishing his views: "Why, however, did you *publish?* had you waited quietly, you would have changed your opinion without any of the misery, which now is involved in the change, of disappointing and distressing people" (*Apol.* 162). In response to these and other charges of untruthfulness, Newman presents his defense. He has not proceeded from "weakness," "mysteriousness," or "shuffling and underhanded dealing" (*Apol.* 134). He has proceeded under the "protection" of the divine economy. God has made himself known to Newman through gradual disclosure; who can fault him for acceding to each revelation as it is given him? Be it his Evangelical conversion or his admiration of the beautiful Catholic churches he visited in 1832 and 1833, be it his hatred of popery and Invocation of the

Saints, be it his reading of the Arian heresies or Augustine's injunction against schism, be it his attempts at a via media or his *Essay on the Development of Christian Doctrine,* Newman's defense is economy. He pleads for "justice" by invoking the *figura* of economy.

The *Apologia,* then, is "economical." It is the history of Newman's gradual transformation, and it is his defense. It is an *"assemblage* of concurring and converging possibilities": Newman's own ability to "throw himself generously" into spiritual inquiry, his faithful obedience to the revealed knowledge of God, and his willingness to reveal himself to his readers.

John Henry Newman would have been most happy to keep the "secret" of his conversion as a matter between himself and his God—the "two only absolute and luminously self-evident beings, myself and my Creator" (*Apol.* 16), but that was not to be. As a patron of God's economy, he was obliged to reveal himself and his conversion to his readers. Newman's narrative of transformation, the *History of His Religious Opinions,* is a vital and lively document that stands in sharp contrast to the guilt-ridden and emotionally charged writings of Dissenters' conversions and parts company with the unreflective and dutiful commitment of the adherents to the Anglican Creed. It takes the form of a *"divine call"* like that from his sermon by the same name, written on reading Augustine's *Centra epistolain Parmeniana.*

> O that we could take the simple view of things, as to feel that the one thing which lies before us is to please God! . . . What gain is it to be applauded, admired, courted, followed, — compared with this one aim, of 'not being disobedient to a heavenly vision?' . . . Let us beg and pray Him day by day to reveal Himself to our souls more fully. (*Apol.* 99)

As Newman reveals himself to his readers, he is being obedient to the heavenly vision and is revealing God's work of economy in him.

"What Can Have Made Him?"
The Dynamis of the Living Intelligence

He who made us has so willed, that in mathematics indeed we should arrive at certitude by rigid demonstration, but in religious inquiry we should arrive at certitude by accumulated probabilities;— He has willed, I say, that we should so act, and, as willing it, He co-operates with us in our acting, and thereby enables us to do that which He wills us to do, and carries us on, if our will does but co-operate with His, to a certitude which rises higher than the logical force of our conclusions. (*Apol.* 157)

The transformation that John Henry Newman describes in the *Apologia* is, in essence, a change from doubt to certitude. Stated another way, it is from changeable opinion to the "clearness and firmness of intellectual conviction." The Anglican Newman held the opinion of Apostolicity from antiquity; the Catholic Newman is convinced of the certainty of Unity in the One Church. How did Newman get from doubt to certitude? The dynamic question raises itself in yet another form, and in Newman's own words, "What *can* have made him?" (*Apol.* 179). What is the motive force of his transformation? What sort of dynamis is operative in Newman's spiritual economy that made him continue to search for a truth he loved more than "dear friends"?

Reading Newman's *Apologia* from the perspective of the persona has revealed the characteristics of the Anglican transformed to Catholic; viewing it from the perspective of figura has specified the type and ground of Newman's transformation as economy. Examining the *Apologia* from the perspective of the dynamis provides yet another way of exploring this text and of understanding the power of Newman's transformation. A statement from the latter part of the *Apologia* is indicative of this dynamis.

> You see then that the various ecclesiastical and quasi-ecclesiastical acts, which have taken place in the course of the last two years and a half, are not the *cause* of my state of opinion, but are keen stimulants and weighty confirmations of a conviction forced upon me, while engaged in the *course of duty,* viz. that theological reading to which I have given myself. (*Apol.* 172)

Newman's transformation comes in the "course of duty"—*course* negating by implication a onetime instantaneous conversion and *duty* suggesting that Newman was "working" at his own transformation (through "theological reading" and doctrinal development). Other phrases that suggest attribution, motive, or dynamis for change show that Newman's mind was open to God's instruction as it came to him in his study and work: "my change of opinion arose, not from foreign influences, but from the working of my own mind, and the accidents around me" (*Apol.* 68); "in what external suggestion or accident each opinion had its rise" (*Apol.* 12); "I was not proceeding on any secondary or isolated grounds of reason, or by controversial points in detail, but was protected and justified . . . by a great and broad principle" (*Apol.* 157); "in the intercourse between God and the

Soul" (*Apol.* 154); "according to the constitution of the human mind and the will of its Maker" (*Apol.* 29); "that living intelligence, by which I write, and argue, and act" (*Apol.* 11); "our will does but co-operate with his" (*Apol.* 157); and, finally, "I was led on to examine more attentively . . . the concatenation of argument by which the mind ascends from its first to its final religious idea" (*Apol.* 156). These textual images point to a dynamis that embraces both the mind of Newman and the will of God. The dynamis, or motive for change, in the *Apologia* may be summed up in Newman's phrase *living intelligence.* Living intelligence is the power to which Newman attributes his "first" and his "final religious idea" and the transit from the one to the other. The living intelligence is Newman's way of defining the interaction between his own mind and God's divine revelation.

Newman believes that it is God's will that he should arrive at certitude: "He who made us has so willed . . . in religious inquiry we should arrive at certitude" (*Apol.* 157), through the "cautious dispensation of the Truth."[10] The dynamis we see at work in the *Apologia,* then, is the mind of Newman, his intelligence working in conjunction with God's dispensations, the gradual revelations of the truth (economy). The divine revelations of God's economy include "life situations," the "three blows," the influence of other theologians (Whatley, Hawkins, Keble, Froude, Russell, Pusey), and the inspired theological treatises that Newman reads. These are the lively substances on which Newman's intelligence works to bring about his transformation. So long as the revelation continues, Newman's inquiring and believing mind sees God's will manifested in the divine economy. Newman relates that he becomes a Catholic

> by virtue of my believing in God; and if I am asked why I believe in God, I answer that it is because I believe in my self, for I feel it impossible to believe in my own existence (and of that fact I am quite sure) without believing also in the existence of Him, who lives as a Personal, All-seeing, All-judging Being in my conscience. (*Apol.* 156)

Newman's transformation of religious opinion is possible because Newman equates belief in himself with belief in God. The underlying security of this belief, coupled with reasonable belief in the power of his own mind, provide the motive for transformation. Newman's search does not begin with the presumption that, if God's existence could be proved, then he would seek the true abode for worship of him. Rather, he begins at the point of belief in One God; what then remains for his transformation is his coming to certitude about the One Church.

In coming to certitude, the dynamis of living intelligence precludes intuitive apprehension of the truth. It proceeds, instead, on the basis of gradual consent to continuous revelation. The living intelligence moves Newman toward certitude by what he calls a "graduated scale of assent": (1) reject, denounce, (2) tolerate, (3) opine, (4) believe, be sure (*Apol. 30*).

Reject, Denounce. In the first stage of assent toward certitude—reject, denounce—the dynamis of the living intelligence causes Newman, as Evangelical and Noetic, to reject the Catholic Church. He denounces Her errors in his treatises and identifies the pope as the Antichrist. When, after his reception into the Catholic Church, Newman is criticized for having earlier denounced the Roman Church, he maintains the stance implied by his adherence to the principle of the living intelligence.

> Therefore, though I believed what I said against the Roman Church, nevertheless I could not religiously speak it out, unless I was really justified . . . I did believe what I said on what I thought to be good reasons; but had I also a just cause for saying out what I believed? I thought I had, and it was this, viz. that to say out what I believed was simply necessary in the controversy for self-defence. It was impossible to let it alone: the Anglican position could not be satisfactorily maintained, without assailing the Roman. (*Apol.* 158–59)

Newman assails the Catholic Church so as to maintain the Anglican. This is "just cause for saying," but what are the "good reasons" for believing? He believes *against* the Catholic Church because of the tradition in which he was reared and the divine revelation that he has received up to this point.

> But, not only did I think such language necessary for my Church's religious position, but I recollected that all the great Anglican divines had thought so before me. . . . I had not used strong language simply out of my own head, but that in doing so I was following the track, or rather reproducing the teaching of those who had proceeded me. . . . I had read the Fathers with their eyes. (*Apol.* 159)

Rejection of the Roman was the consequence of Newman's own mind interacting with the knowledge that was available to him at that moment. While in this stage of rejection or denouncing, however, Newman is not without faith: "I had thought myself safe, while I had their warrant (the Anglican fathers) for what I said. I had exercised more faith than criticism in the matter." The living intelligence allows Newman to examine this faith throughout the entirety of his Christian development, yet there were never "broad misstatements" made, rather, "carelessness in matters of detail" (*Apol.* 159). Newman is indicating that, while he, in his faith, may have made some careless errors in small matters, that same faith would never allow him to make the larger, more serious errors of interpretation.

Tolerate. The force of the living intelligence operates to bring Newman from denunciation to tolerance, the second stage in his gradual scale of assent toward certitude in the One Church. The mature Tractarian, using more rigorous methods, becomes more careful in his study and writings; he shows "more sobriety, more gravity, more careful pains, more sense of responsibility" in the publication of the *Tracts* (*Apol.* 60). This more exacting examination, when directed toward the *Thirty-nine Articles* and the *Homilies,* results in a significant difference in Newman's attitude toward the Catholic Church and the Catholic system. The denunciation of earlier days is replaced by tolerance. Newman comes to acknowledge that there is as much of the Catholic as Anglican in the major creeds of the Anglican Church. This tolerance for the Catholic shows itself in all his writing from this period.

In "The Prophetical Office of the Church viewed relatively to Romanism and Popular Protestantism," written prior to *Tract 90,* Newman brings out with "precision the relation in which we stood to the Church of Rome" (*Apol.* 61). The "Prophetical Office," however, has a "larger scope than that of opposing the Roman system" (*Apol.* 62). The living intelligence, directed away from the failures of the Roman system and applied to the creation of an Anglican theology, results in a tolerance for the Catholic. His intelligence is employed to "catalogue, sort, distribute, select, harmonize, and complete" the "vast inheritance" of Anglicanism (*Apol.* 64). Newman hopes to restore "doctrinal purity and unity" to the Anglican system. In the "Prophetical Office" he calls on Anglicans to "Look at home; let us first (or at least let us the while,) supply our own shortcomings, before we attempt to be physicians to anyone else" (*Apol.* 66).

The Tractarians are encouraged to tend to reformation in their own church and to tolerate the Church of Rome rather than attack it. Tolerance of this sort can only mean for Newman that it is but a short step from the "Prophetical Office" to *Tract 90* and the acknowldgment that the Anglican *Articles* are as much Catholic as they are Anglican; "that the Articles were tolerant, not only of what I called 'Catholic teaching,' but of much that was 'Roman' " (*Apol.* 75). Newman's tolerance matches that of the *Articles.* The insights of the living intelligence move Newman from rejection to tolerance regarding the Church of Rome and lead him to desire cooperation with Rome "in all lawful things."

Opine. In this third stage toward religious certitude Newman shows how the power of the living intelligence moves him from mere tolerance of the Catholic to "opine" for Rome. The "three blow that broke me" (mentioned earlier) cause Newman to doubt the Anglican system and to opine, or begin to have stronger opinions, in favor of Rome. The blows—the reading of the heresies and seeing parallels in the Anglican system, the harassment and accusations by the Anglican bishops over the *Tract 90,* and the incident of the Jerusalem bishoprics—present Newman's intelligence with its most serious challenge and force him to come to several new opinions at this juncture: (1) the Anglican Church is in greater error; the church passes "final sentence against such portions of it as protest and secede" (*Apol.* 98); (2) there is "no longer a distinctive plea for Anglicanism" (*Apol.* 100–101); a via media is impossible; Anglicanism is dying "by degrees"; (3) the Anglican Church "had no claim on me, except on condition of its being a portion of the One Catholic Communion, and that that condition . . . had to be distinctly proved" (*Apol.* 123). Newman's loyalty has been to the Anglican Church because he believes it part of the One Church: if it is in schism, it has no claim on him at all.

Believe, Be Sure. For Newman tolerance is closer to conviction than rejection and denunciation. Opinion is nearer certitude than tolerance. Within the figura of the divine economy and through the dynamis of the living intelligence Newman is approaching the "One Fold." Newman makes no apology for his gradual transformation. He does not hold himself guilty of treason as he moves toward Rome.

> Nor surely is it a thing I need be sorry for, that I defended the system in which I found myself. . . . For is it not one's duty, instead of beginning with criticism, to throw oneself generously into that form of religion which is providentially put before one? . . . May we not, on the other hand, look for blessing *through* obedience even to an erroneous system, and a guidance even by means of it out of it? (*Apol.* 161–62).

Throughout all the stages of his progress toward certitude Newman proceeds in good faith and with "previous zeal." Thus, while in Lay Communion the living intelligence brings him to the final stage in his search for religious certitude: "believe," "be sure." It is here that he determines to resolve his remaining doubts. Empowered by the living intelligence, he embarks on the final assignment he has set for himself, that of completing a critical appraisal that will formalize his position in relation to the Church of Rome:

> On the one hand I came gradually to see that the Anglican Church was formally in the wrong, on the other that the Church of Rome was formally in the right. . . .Then, I had nothing more to learn; what still remained for my conversion, was, not further change of opinion, but to change opinion itself into the clearness and firmness of intellectual conviction. (*Apol.* 157)

Newman determines to write the *Essay on the Development of Christian Doctrine,* and, if his "convictions in favour of the Roman Church were not weaker," he would ask to be accepted into her Communion (*Apol.* 177). In October 1845 the living intelligence brings Newman to certitude, to belief; John Henry Newman is received into the Roman Catholic Church. He relates that from this time on "I never had one doubt" (*Apol.* 184). The dynamis of living intelligence has brought Newman to certitude through the divine economy as it was revealed in the Catholic Church. He reviews the process:

> For the first four years of the ten (up to Michaelmas, 1839,) I honestly wished to benefit the Church of England, at the expense of the Church of Rome [denounce, reject].
> For the second four years I wished to benefit the Church of England without prejudice to the Church of Rome [tolerate].
> At the beginning of the ninth year (Michaelmas, 1843) I began to despair of the Church of England, and gave up all clerical duty; and then, what I wrote and did was influenced by a mere wish not to injure it, and not by the wish to benefit it [opine].
> At the beginning of the tenth year I distinctly contemplated leaving it, but I also distinctly told my friends that it was in my contemplation.
> Lastly, during the last half of that tenth year I was engaged in writing a book (Essay on Development) in favour of the Roman Church, and indirectly against the English: [believe, be sure]. (*Apol.* 148)

Newman now believes "as if I saw." He insists that "certitude is a reflex action; it is to know that one knows. Of that [certitude] I believe I was not possessed, till close upon my reception into the Catholic Church" (*Apol.* 168).

It is the living intelligence, not "paper logic," that has illuminated the development of Newman's religious opinion through its gradual scale of assent toward religious certitude; it is the power of Newman's transformation from Anglican to Catholic, from denunciation of Rome to fullest surety.

I had a great dislike of paper logic. For myself, it was not logic that carried me on; as well might one say that the quicksilver in the barometer changes the weather. It is the concrete being that reasons; pass a number of years, and I find my mind in a new place; how? the whole man moves; paper logic is but the record of it. All the logic in the world would not have made me move faster towards Rome than I did; as well might you say that I have arrived at the end of my journey, because I see the village church before me, as venture to assert that the miles, over which my soul had to pass before it got to Rome, could be annihilated, even though I had been in possession of some far clearer view than I then had, that Rome was my ultimate destination. Great acts take time. At least this is what I felt in my own case. (*Apol.* 136).

Within the figura of the economy, or gradual revelation, Newman is changed from Anglican to Catholic by the dynamis of the living intelligence. He sees his transformation as a "great act." The dynamis of the living intelligence, like the "whole Me" of *Sartor Resartus,* may also be seen as the dynamis, or motive power, for the construction of the *Apologia.* While writing for Newman is but "paper logic," a mere record of what has conspired between "two luminous beings" in secret and over time, it is the power of the living intelligence that empowers the writing. "In the Economy, the representation is secondary to the thing represented, whose 'substantial truth' is nevertheless preserved and conveyed in its re-presentation which Newman calls a 'shadow' . . . economical; necessarily imperfect."[11] The *Apologia,* as record, is an imperfect inscription of Newman's transformation, but, as that transformation is empowered by the dynamis of the living intelligence, the inscription, Newman's words—the *Apologia*—take on God's authority. They move from the realm of "scarecrows" to those of spiritual signification. "Logical mazes" did not bring Newman closer to certitude and the "perfect peace and contentment" of the Catholic Church. Nor does Newman's autobiography convince through formal logic or argument. The "whole man moves" and moves us to consider the authenticity of the transformation of his religious opinion through gradual revelation. The living intelligence is the authority that guarantees Newman's truthfulness, the divine inscription in the mind. Proceeding within the figura of economy through the dynamis of the living intelligence, Newman is safe inside the One Church.

Non in dialectica complacuit Deo salvum facere populum suum.[12]

4

Reasoning Machines Have Feelings, Too

The Transformation of John Stuart Mill (1806–73)

John Stuart Mill, the nineteenth-century political philosopher, was characterized by his contemporaries, and he characterizes himself, in the *Autobiography*, as a "mere reasoning machine." He reports that John Sterling, a disciple of Coleridge and the man who later became his friend, told how he and others "had looked upon me (from hearsay information) as a 'made' or manufactured man, having had a certain impress of opinion stamped on me which I could only reproduce."[1] Sterling was suggesting that Mill appeared to be a die-casting of Jeremy Bentham. Having no mind of his own, he replicated the Utilitarian. Mill's Utilitarian philosophy was often "denounced as cold calculation," his political economy as "hard-hearted," and his antipopulation doctrine as "repulsive to the natural feelings of mankind" (*MA* 67). His sectarianism caused him to define problems narrowly and to limit the possible solutions. He used the term *theoretically indifferent* to describe his attitude toward poetry, but it would do just as well to describe his attitude toward any political philosophy not based on utility, any theory of knowledge not based on sense perception, or any methodological approach not based on logical analysis.

By age twenty Mill was so thoroughly engrossed in Utilitarian philosophy and so vigorously motivated toward political reform through utility that, by his own admission, he was unable to recognize the limitations of the system or the severe consequences of his dedication. When his involvement in social reform ceased to hold any pleasure for him and his scant store of internal resources dried up, he suffered a severe emotional breakdown. He viewed himself as a political philosopher, but, when he had to apply his philosophy to personal concerns and political reform, Utilitarianism failed him. It would not suffice in the public arena nor in the private. The *Autobiography* is the narrative of John Stuart Mill's transformation. The inscribed persona of the narrative changes from "school-boy logician" to "philosopher of feeling." The *was* persona is characterized as Utilitarian, the *is* as social Romantic. Mill's political philosophy is first hard-hearted then philosophico-poetical. The *before* persona has the qualities of a reasoning machine, the *after* has traits of the true teacher.

The School-boy Logician

Of children's books, any more than of playthings, I had scarcely any, except an occasional gift from a relation or acquaintance: among those I had, Robinson Crusoe was pre-eminent, and continued to delight me through all my boyhood. It was no part however of my father's system to exclude books of amusement, though he allowed them very sparingly. (*MA* 7)

There is very little in the *Autobiography* of John Stuart Mill to suggest that the me of the text was ever allowed to be a child. Mill's child persona manifests few childlike characteristics or behaviors. As a boy with few children's books or toys, *Robinson Crusoe* is one of his rare delights. Urged to begin a study of classical languages at the age of three, he is early committing Greek vocables to memory. A major portion of the child's day is spent at his father's desk preparing Greek lessons while his father writes. Another significant segment of the young child's time is taken up in the lessons he prepares for the early morning walks with his father, during which he discusses works like Xenophon's *Anabasis* and the histories of Philip the Second, Philip the Third, and Frederick of Prussia. Mathematics, history, government, logic, religion, and ethics are included in the regular instruction as the two walk together. Beginning Latin at age eight, Mill soon gains an overview of the history of civilization, along with an understanding of major political, economic, and philosophical ideas. In addition to these rigorous studies, the young boy is assigned the responsibility of teaching Latin to his siblings.

And from this time, other sisters and brothers being successively added as pupils, a considerable part of my day's work consisted of this preparatory teaching. It was a part which I greatly disliked; the more so, as I was held responsible for the lessons of my pupils. (*MA* 8)

Young Mill, a grouchy tutor at ten, by the age of twelve, has studied geometry, algebra, and differential calculus and has read the major Latin and Greek texts.

And lastly, Aristotle's *Rhetoric,* which, as the first expressly scientific treatise on any moral or psychological subject which I had read, and containing many of the best observations of the ancients on human nature and life, my father made me study with peculiar care, and throw the matter of it into synoptic tables. (*MA* 9)

The persona of the *Autobiography* hardly sounds like the typical twelve-year-old. The astonishing case continues to build:

> I entered into another and more advanced stage in my course of instruction; in which the main object was no longer the aids and appliances of thought, but the thoughts themselves. This commenced with Logic, in which I began at once with the *Organon,* and read it to the Analytics inclusive. . . . Contemporaneously with the *Organon,* my father made me read the whole or parts of several of the Latin treatises on the scholastic logic. . . . After this, I went, in a similar manner, through the "Computatio sive Logica" of Hobbes. (*MA* 12)

In spite of the fact that many authorities had impugned syllogistic logic, Mill's father spends great effort impressing upon the son its particular utility. Walking along Bagshot Heath, the father demands that the son "frame some conception of what constituted syllogistic logic." When Mill fails to do so, his father makes explanation. Mill fails again; he cannot grasp his father's meaning. He contends, however, that he grew to believe that nothing was of more value in his education than this early practice of school logic:

> I am persuaded that nothing, in modern education, tends so much, when properly used, to form exact thinkers. . . . They may become capable of disentangling the intricacies of confused and self-contradictory thought, before their own thinking faculties are much advanced. (*MA* 13)

School-boy logician, then, stands as image for the before persona of the *Autobiography* of John Stuart Mill. Mill describes himself in a letter to Carlyle as "a school-boy fresh from the logic-school, [who] had never conversed with a reality; never seen one; knew not what manner of thing it was."[2] The school-boy logician image joins a youthful frame to an adult mind and conjures up the picture of a wizened, old head resting on an infant body. As the rationalistic training continues and his dedication to liberal philosophy increases, the school-boy's head outgrows his body.

> I could do no feats of skill or physical strength, and knew none of the ordinary bodily exercises. . . . I constantly remained long, and in a less degree have always remained, inexpert in anything requiring manual dexterity; my mind, as well as my hands, did its work very lamely when it was applied, or ought to have been applied, to the practical details which, as

they are the chief interest of life to the majority of men. . . . The education which my father gave me, was in itself much more fitted for training me to *know* than to *do*. (*MA* 22–23)

From the earliest pages of the *Autobiography* we are confronted with a persona who is logical, analytical, serious, dedicated, a persona with head knowledge. The head is growing larger and rapidly; human knowledge, heart knowledge, will take much longer. The school-boy logician is all scholar. There are no boyish pranks, no skinned knees, no frightening dreams. There are only reading, thinking, walking, talking, writing. At this point Mill gives total intellectual deference to his father and justifies the name he assigns himself—school-boy logician—in light of his father's educational ambitions for him, "a very unusual advantage which had fallen to my lot, of having a father who was able to teach me, and willing to give the necessary trouble and time" (*MA* 22). This passage is one of many in which we hear the voice of the elder Mill proceeding out of the mouth of the younger. It is a rational voice and causes the persona to parrot ideas not as yet his own and to respond to intellectual discussions in a pedantic and mechanized fashion. Mill is encouraged by his father to exhaust "my efforts to find it out for myself," but his father never seems to be satisfied with his answers:

> I recollect also his indignation at my using the common expression that something was true in theory but required correction in practice; and how, after making me vainly strive to define the word theory, he explained its meaning, and shewed the fallacy of the vulgar form of speech which I had used; leaving me fully persuaded that in being unable to give a correct definition of Theory, and in speaking of it as something which might be at variance with practice, I had shewn unparalleled ignorance. (*MA* 20)

Despite his hard work and dedication to intellectual pursuits, the school-boy logician is routinely made to feel foolish by his teacher father. Mill sees his father as having all the answers and blames himself for his father's indignation. Not only does the school-boy try (and fail) to speak with his father's voice; he sees himself through his father's eyes; he is "unparalleled in ignorance."

Utilitarian

If the young Mill is dedicated to the intellectual pursuits assigned him by his father, and speaks in his father's voice and sees through his father's eyes, the dedication aroused in him by the Utilitarian philosopher, Jeremy Bentham, is no less intense. When he begins to study Bentham's political theory in *Traite de legislation,* he takes on a new loyalty and a new voice: "When I laid down the last volume of the *Traite* I had become a different being" (*MA* 42). Mill comes to believe that Bentham is responsible for bringing about a revolution in the "general modes of thought and investigation in the nineteenth century." Bentham is the first to apply inductive method to the disciplines of politics and morals. He places existing political institutions alongside these standards and shows how they fail to measure up.[3] From the time that Mill reads Bentham's *Traite de legislation,* in 1821, he has one main object in life, the improvement of mankind. The document insists that mankind's improvement is possible through the application of a Utilitarian system in which the ethically good is determined by the motivation of human nature to obtain happiness or pleasure and avoid pain. What the individual should do and how social organizations should function can be determined by the principle of the greatest happiness for the greatest number. The clash between individual and social interest will disappear with conduct based on utility. Mill recalls the power of the *Traite* in his life:

> It gave unity to my conceptions of things. I now had opinions; a creed, a doctrine, a philosophy; in one among the best senses of the word, a religion; the inculcation and diffusion of which could be made the principal outward purpose of a life. And I had a grand conception laid before me of changes to be effected in the condition of mankind through that doctrine. (*MA* 42–43)

The baby *Homo rationalis* has changed to budding Utilitarian.

In 1823 Mill forms the Utilitarian Society and names himself Utilitarian. The Utilitarian persona is the carbon copy of Jeremy Bentham, who exercises a pervasive influence on all the young Mill's thinking. Like his father, who carries forward the philosophy of Utilitarianism with firmer conviction, if with less notoriety, than Bentham himself, Mill replicates the great Utilitarian in thought and action. It would seem the highest of compliments when Bentham asks Mill, only two years later, at the age of nineteen, to edit *Traite de legislation.*

Charles Austin, William Eyton Tooke, William Ellis, George Graham, and John Arthur Roebuck appear to be an extension and reinforcement of the Jeremy Bentham political circle in which the youthful Utilitarian is caught up. In several debating societies Mill is able to test his understanding of Utilitarianism on his friends, who, in turn, reinforce these ideas. Like a group of windup tin soldiers, this narrow political band marches to the tunes of others, holding "as doctrine" Bentham's philosophy of utility, Adam Smith's political economy, Hartley's associationalism, and Malthus's population principle (*MA 64*). As Utilitarian, Mill relies on external authority for definition and on economic utility for a comprehensive political philosophy. *Associationalist* and *political economist* are complementary names for the Utilitarian persona.

As Utilitarian, at age seventeen the Mill persona takes on the role of "correspondent" with the East India Company. Starting as junior clerk in the office of Examiner of India Correspondence, Mill progresses quickly to chief conductor of correspondence between India and the Native States and, ultimately, to examiner. He sees the correspondent position as advantageous to the pursuit of his real interests and relates that this work, though not "distasteful drudgery," frees him to devote the major portion of the "mental powers of a person used to abstract thought" to Utilitarian reform. For the next thirty-five years Mill makes his living as East India correspondent and makes his name as political philosopher and writer. He is credited with over fifteen major works and numerous articles and essays.

> The writings by which one can live, are not the writings which themselves live, and are never those in which the writer does his best. Books destined to form future thinkers take too much time to write, and when written come in general too slowly into notice and repute, to be relied on for subsistence. Those who have to support themselves by their pen must depend on literary drudgery, or at best on writings addressed to the multitude; and can employ in the pursuits of their own choice only such time as they can spare from those of necessity. (*MA 51*)

In addition to conserving mental energy and providing time for political writing, Mill sees his position with the East India Company as having practical value. As correspondent, the qualities and characteristics of the practical diplomat—understanding the necessities of compromise, learning the art of sacrificing the nonessential to preserve the essential, developing the skill to anticipate and forestall difficulties—complement the Utilitarian persona. As correspondent, Mill is well aware that the "practical conduct of public affairs has been of considerable value to me as a theoretical reformer" (*MA 52*).

At twenty years of age, an age when most young men are just beginning to give serious attention to their careers, John Stuart Mill has already served as a correspondent, written for the *Globe,* the *Morning Chronicle,* the *Par-*

liamentary History and Review, and edited both Bentham's famous *Traite de legislation* and his father James's *Elements of Political Economy.* He is regarded as a leader by his contemporaries who join with him to form the Utilitarian Society and is respected as a perceptive and analytic young thinker by the illustrious men who are his father's friends and correspondents: Bentham, David Ricardo, Thomas Robert Malthus, Joseph Hume, John Austin, George Grote, and Jean Baptiste Say. Mill is totally and blissfully immersed in the pursuit of knowledge and the Utilitarian movement. His personal satisfaction is bound up in this singular goal, "to be a reformer of the world."

> I was accustomed to felicitate myself on the certainty of a happy life which I enjoyed, through placing my happiness in something durable and distant, in which some progress might be always making, while it could never be exhausted by complete attainment. This did very well for several years, during which the general improvement going on in the world and the idea of myself as engaged with others in struggling to promote it, seemed enough to fill up an interesting and animated existence. (*MA* 80)

The young reformer is happy to be attached to a significant movement. He is satisfied that, though full attainment of Utilitarian goals is improbable, sufficient progress is being made to warrant his commitment. Hints in the text suggest that the Utilitarian's sense of well-being will not last: "This did very well for several years"; "it seemed enough"; "but the time came when I awakened from this as from a dream" (*MA* 80). These statements, as they interrupt his "interesting and animated existence," suggest that the Utilitarian persona is existing in a dreamworld and is missing out on real living. It is at this juncture that the Utilitarian begins to examine Utilitarian philosophy and himself as Utilitarian philosopher.

> In this frame of mind it occurred to me to put the question directly to myself, "Suppose that all your objects in life were realized; that all the changes in institutions and opinions which you are looking forward to, could be completely effected at this very instant: would this be a great joy and happiness to you?" And an irrepressible self-consciousness distinctly answered, "No!" (*MA* 81)

Since Mill's personal happiness is so inextricably bound up in liberal reform, it is difficult to separate the two. The first examination does seem to focus, however, on Mill's personal involvement in reform and his disappointment with its failure to bring him happiness. The examination of the Utilitarian self, absent of joy and happiness, is then extended to an examination of the Utilitarian system. Mill examines the doctrine of plea-sure and pain as motivation for social reform and challenges it from several standpoints: (1) the intensity of pain required to produce aversion seems too severe; (2) there are no "natural tie[s]" between the pleasure/pain asso-ciations and the things to be desired or avoided; and (3) the "habit of analy-sis" dilutes the strength of the associations. The careful examination of self and philosophy results in a critical breakdown of the logic-machine, the "Motive-Millwright." Carlyle understands the problem:

> Fantastic tricks enough man has played, in his time; has fancied himself to be most things, down even to an animated heap of Glass: but to fancy himself a dead Iron-Balance for weighing Pains and Pleasures on, was reserved for this his latter era. . . . And now the Genius of Mechanism smothers him worse than any Nightmare did; till the Soul is nigh choked out of him, and only a kind of Digestive, Mechanic life remains. In Earth and in Heaven he can see nothing but Mechanism; has fear for nothing else, hope in nothing else: the world would indeed grind him to pieces.[4]

Carlyle's indictment of Utilitarianism is too late to be of help to Mill. Since *Sartor Resartus* was published in 1833, seven years after he suffers his breakdown, Mill is forced to discover the limitations and consequences of a liberal political philosophy and a rational education on his own. It is small wonder, then, that at age twenty his disillusion is overwhelming.

> I was thus, as I said to myself, left stranded at the commencement of my voyage, with a well equipped ship and a rudder, but no sail; without any real desire for the ends which I had been so carefully fitted out to work for: no delight in virtue or the general good, but also just as little in any-thing else. The fountains of vanity and ambition seemed to have dried up within me, as completely as those of benevolence. (*MA* 84)

Wholly without motive or goal, without "benevolence" or "delight in virtue," John Stuart Mill is at his "crisis point." The school-boy logician, like any young scholar, is at the stage when traditional supports fall away and usual joys fail. The logic-machine can no longer identify himself solely with Utilitarian social reform. The student must find his own way; he must secure his own rite of passage.

Examining his personal limitations and the limitations of his rational education and liberal political philosophy, Mill becomes dejected, full of doubt, lonely, miserable, with "nothing left to live for" (*MA* 81). He recog-nizes that the habit of analysis has worn away all feeling. The loss of sensi-tivity for the improvement of mankind is paralleled by his inability to generate feelings to deal with his own improvement. He realizes that what is needed is some internal resource to counteract the pervasive sense of stultification. None has been cultivated; he has nothing to draw on. Mill concludes that the contemporary description of "a Benthamite, as a mere reasoning machine," is true of him. He confesses that his zeal for the improvement of mankind "had not its root in genuine benevolence" (*MA* 66) and, in the *Early Draft*, adds "and therefore we had at this time no idea of real culture. In our schemes for improving human affairs we overlooked human beings" (*MA* fn. 67). Mill admits that no political system can be successful that is founded solely on the material needs of society.[5] He acknowledges that Bentham is incapable of designing a comprehensive political system that takes human beings into account when he has so little experience of human beings himself.

> We did not expect from Bentham correct systematic views of ethics, or a sound treatment of any question the moralities of which require a profound knowledge of the human heart; but we did anticipate that the greater moral questions would have been boldly plunged into.[6]

Mill, seeing himself in the mirror of his examination of Bentham's limitations, can, at this point, do no more than Bentham. He is not ready to develop a system for social improvement when he himself has so little experience with human feeling or with persons outside his narrow political circle. The Utilitarian must await some experience of genuine human feeling before becoming involved again in social improvement. Mill is in the crisis of inward examination; he is in need of transformation, something to relieve the "feeling dead within me." Like his feelings, the Motive-Millwright's faith in Utilitarian reform is dead; all deference to authority figures, in particular to Bentham and his father, is gone. Tyrannized by the "Genius of Mechanism," the reasoning machine is himself ground to pieces.

Philosopher of Feeling

> I frequently asked myself, if I could, or if I was bound to go on living, when life must be passed in this manner. I generally answered to myself, that I did not think I could possibly bear it beyond a year. (*MA* 85)

The anguish continues. It is Marmontel's *Memoirs* that move the young, yet already dead, radical from absence of feeling to the experience of feeling. Reading the *Memoirs*, Mill discovers that the inward self is worthy of consideration. While Jean François Marmontel was not a writer of great repute, he was an autobiographer who was not afraid to write about the experience of feelings. The *Memoirs* bring the scholar to tears—some of his first, no doubt.

> A vivid conception of the scene and its feelings came over me, and I was moved to tears. From this moment my burthen grew lighter. The oppression of the thought that all feeling was dead within me, was gone. I was no longer hopeless: I was not a stock or a stone. (*MA* 85)

Mill weeps as he reads how the young Marmontel has overcome his personal sorrow at the death of his father and how he vows to be the strength his family needs. Mill relates no instance of identification with Marmontel's actual circumstances. He merely relates "a vivid conception of the scene," "feelings," and "tears." Readers may suspect, however, that, in giving up deference to authority, Mill, like Marmontel, suffers the loss of his two "fathers"—Mill and Bentham. There is also some hint that material needs are not the only ones that Marmontel and Mill wish to provide those to whom they pledge their help. Marmontel, then a mere boy, promises his family more than material needs; he "would supply the place of all that was lost." The absent father leaves the family destitute—of income and of a father's love and support—all of which the young boy pledges to provide. Similarly, Mill sees himself and his country in need. Utilitarian philosophy is no substitute for human feeling, nor will a strictly economic philosophy suffice to bring about political reform. From absence of feeling to experience of feeling—at the convergence of two autobiographies—we see the Utilitarian transformed to philosopher of feeling.

The philosopher of feeling regains his strength as he discovers the value of genuine human emotion. Marmontel, cure for absence of feeling, prepares Mill to read Wordsworth. Wordsworth is antidote for Bentham, and his poetry a corrective for logical analysis.

> What made Wordsworth's poems a medicine for my state of mind, was that they expressed, not mere outward beauty, but states of feeling, and of thought coloured by feeling, under the excitement of beauty. They seemed to be the very culture of the feelings, which I was in quest of. In them I seemed to draw from a source of inward joy, of sympathetic and imaginative pleasure, which could be shared in by all human beings; which had no connexion with struggle or imperfection. . . . From them I seemed to learn what would be the perennial sources of happiness, when all the greater evils of life shall have been removed. (*MA* 89)

This most famous excerpt from the *Autobiography* shows the Utilitarian transformed to an initiate of the Romantic School; he is under the influence of "thought coloured by feeling, under the excitement of beauty." For the Utilitarian existence was a struggle for material and intellectual improvement. For the philosopher of feeling cultivation of the inward self opens up a whole new world for exploration and examination. The pursuit of a rational education and a liberal politics left the Utilitarian in a state of distress. The pursuit of internal culture provides the medicine the philosopher of feeling needs. He reports:

> There have certainly been, even in our own age, greater poets than Wordsworth; but poetry of deeper and loftier feeling could not have done for me at that time what his did. I needed to be made to feel that there was real, permanent happiness in tranquil contemplation. Wordsworth taught me this, not only without turning away from, but with a greatly increased interest in, the common feelings and common destiny of human beings. (*MA* 89)

In contrasting Bentham's materialistic system with that of the Romantic poet, the school-boy logician, now philosopher of feeling, begins a pursuit of internal culture. By reading poetry about "incidents and situations from common life" and in the language of men closest to nature, Mill's already highly developed interest in the improvement of mankind is enhanced; he begins to develop a political philosophy designed for human beings rather than for utility.

Reasoning machine turned Romantic,[7] John Stuart Mill begins to give the imagination free rein and the pursuit of internal culture serious attention. Mill attests that "the maintenance of a due balance among the faculties, now seemed to me of primary importance. The cultivation of the feelings became one of the cardinal points in my ethical and philosophical creed" (*MA* 86). Here we see the new Mill. He *was* absent of feelings; he *is* cultivating them. In this new persona the philosopher of feeling wonders if he can design a political system that moves outward—past Bentham *and* Wordsworth—that takes into account both logic and poetry, analysis and imagination, the material and the human. If Bentham has failed to design an adequate system for political reform, can Mill do better?

> It [Utilitarianism] will enable a society which has attained a certain state of spiritual development, and the maintenance of which in that state is otherwise provided for, to prescribe the rules by which it may protect its material interests. It will do nothing (except sometimes as an instrument

in the hands of a higher doctrine) for the spiritual interests of society; nor does it suffice of itself even for the material interests. That which alone causes any material interest to exist, which alone enables any body of human beings to exist as a society, is national character.[8]

The school-boy logician could never have critiqued Bentham's system so severely, but as philosopher of feeling Mill begins to investigate the strengths and limitations of existing systems both at home and on the Continent. He finally comes to see the importance of understanding "national character." The Utilitarian turned social Romantic believes that

> the true teacher of the fitting social arrangements for England, France, or America, is the one who can point out how the English, French, or American character can be improved, and how it has been made what it is. A philosophy of laws and institutions, not founded on a philosophy of national character, is an absurdity.[9]

Some of the "absurdities" of the Utilitarian system are overcome by getting at or understanding the national character. This requires what Bentham was incapable of: an understanding of human beings and the collective mind. Thus, Mill begins construction of a political system that takes human beings into account and attempts to maintain a balance between the intellectual and emotional faculties and material interests.

Mill is aware that knowledge of the "general opinions of mankind," his definition of the collective mind, is requisite to the development of a viable political system. He also believes that it is the power of the imagination that makes the collective mind accessible to the philosopher and the philosopher to the society.

> The general opinion of mankind is the average of the conclusions of all minds, stripped indeed of their choicest and most recondite thoughts, but freed from their twists and particularities: a net result, in which everybody's particular point of view is represented, nobody's predominant. The collective mind does not penetrate below the surface, but it sees all the surface; which profound thinkers, even by reason of their profundity, often fail to do: their intenser view of a thing in some of its aspects diverting their attention from others.[10]

It is in this interplay of imaginations—Mill's and the "collective mind"—that the Mill persona takes on the attributes of "true teacher of the fitting social arrangements for England." In formulating his own system for the improvement of society, he teaches human beings how to work together to achieve their common goals: liberty, education, *and* material needs. As true teacher, the school-boy is ever a school-boy. In addition to acquiring the attributes of the true teacher from the study of "the general opinions of mankind," the Mill persona acquires new attributes from new teachers. The "lessons learned" from Coleridge, Carlyle, the Saint-Simonians, and the Continental philosophers are detailed in the "Figura" section. Encounters with the "collective mind" and with these new teachers provide the philosopher persona with new resonances and new attributes.

Political Philosopher / Teacher

At the conclusion of the *Autobiography* we find the philosopher/teacher with a well-rounded set of attributes. He is no longer a monolith; he is neither a single-issue political philosopher, nor does he manifest the one-dimensional personality of the hard-hearted Utilitarian. The before persona was logical, then he was poetic, and, finally, in Carlyle's terms, he is philosophico-poetical. Mill comes to believe that both logical and imaginative attributes are necessary aspects of the political philosopher persona.

> I found the fabric of my old and taught opinions giving way in many fresh places, and I never allowed it to fall to pieces, but was incessantly occupied in weaving it anew. . . . When I had taken in any new idea, I could not rest till I had adjusted its relation to my old opinions, and ascertained exactly how far its effect ought to extend in modifying or superseding them. (*MA* 94)

Like Carlyle's tailor, the political philosopher is weaver, synthesizer. He adjusts and modifies; he retains and discards. He retailors political systems. John Stuart Mill is transformed from one who propounds the political ideas of others to one who constructs (reconstructs) and disseminates a coherent and comprehensive political system of his own. He puts every faculty he possesses (logical and imaginative) to

> supply, not a set of model institutions, but principles from which the institutions suitable to any given circumstances might be deduced . . . the human mind has a certain order of possible progress, in which some things must precede others, an order which governments and public instructors can modify to some, but not to an unlimited extent: That all questions of political institutions are relative, not absolute, and that different stages of human progress not only *will* have, but *ought* to have, different institutions. (*MA* 97)

A mere logician would reject such an open-ended set of principles. He would want a system with clearly defined limits and parameters. The poet, in contrast, might avoid active involvement in the political process altogether. Combining the strengths of both, the philosopher/teacher persona, through the power of the analytic *and* the imaginative, devises a progressive set of principles for social improvement and gets down to the business of implementing them in the society. The "reasoning machine" is now both reasonable and imaginative. The logician/poet has reached the status of true reformer—a fully integrated and productive political philosopher.

In reading the *Autobiography* from the perspective of the persona, we have discovered, in addition to the obvious transformation of the Mill persona from school-boy logician to philosopher of feeling, that the Mill persona, like the Newman persona, is complex. The rhetorically constituted Mill is political philosopher looking back on school-boy logician, reasoning machine, and Utilitarian so as to show, not traces of the social Romantic and the philosophico-poetical, as Newman did when he infused the Anglican persona with Catholic traces, but, rather, to show *absence* of feelings. Mill and his readers know that he will (does) overcome his crisis of inward examination, but a narrative of transformation, as it is rhetorically constituted, requires that Mill construct a persona that conveys a self absent of feeling so as to convince his readers of a conversion to a self of feeling. He constructs himself first as a school-boy who has no childish feelings, who is mainly concerned that he memorize his Greek verbs and get his calculus correct. He constructs his adolescent self as a Utilitarian who has no pubescent drives or desires; his concerns are tied to the "greatest good for the greatest number." He writes his before persona as absent of feeling so that he can narrate a transformation to a self of feeling. This narrative also explains how a self transformed can construct a transformed political philosophy. The before and after personae—school-boy logician, reasoning-machine, Utilitarian, and social Romantic, philosopher of feeling, true teacher—attest that John Stuart Mill has changed.

Reeducation: The Figura of Mill's Philosophical Transformation

In addition to our appreciation for his contributions to political theory, we most often remember John Stuart Mill for his unusual education. Quite different from that of his contemporaries, Mill's education was extremely rigorous in both content and pedagogy. As mentioned earlier, it began with the study of Greek at the age of three and, by the time he was fourteen, had encompassed Aristotle and Hobbes and was soon to be launched on a study of liberal political theory.

In the "Persona" section we looked at how the before and after characteristics of school-boy logician and philosopher of feeling assume that a change has occurred in the life of John Stuart Mill. The nature of the change is implied by these two names for the persona; it is specified in the figura of "reeducation." *Reeducation* serves to explain the nature of Mill's transformation in the *Autobiography*. Repeated references to "schools," "pupil," "schoolboys," "teachers," "teachers of teachers," "learning, unlearning," "lessons," "education," "elocution," "examine," "analyze," "studies in law," and "studies in logic" fill the text. From beginning to end the significance of learning and knowledge are emphasized.

The *Autobiography* begins with the acknowledgment of Mill's indebtedness to his education for moral and intellectual development.

> But I have thought that in an age in which education, and its improvement, are the subject of more, if not of profounder study than at any former period of English history, it may be useful that there should be some record of an education which was unusual and remarkable. . . . It has also seemed to me that in an age of transition in opinions, there may be somewhat both of interest and of benefit in noting the successive phases of any mind which was always pressing forward, equally ready to learn and to unlearn either from its own thoughts or from those of others. (*MA* 3)

As *Sartor Resartus* is about transformation by retailoring, Mill's *Autobiography* is about transformation by reeducation. All tailoring is retailoring; all education is reeducation. It is learning and unlearning, an unending process. We find this same emphasis near the end of the memoir. While the discussion centers around Mill's political activities, the final paragraph illustrates the importance of doing the work of the scholar.

> Since that time little has occurred which there is need to commemorate in this place. I returned to my old pursuits. . . . I have written various articles in periodicals . . . have made a small number of speeches on public occasions, especially at the meetings of the Women's Suffrage Society, have published the "Subjection of Women," written some years before . . . and have commenced the preparation of matter for future books, of which it will be time to speak more particularly if I live to finish them. Here, therefore, for the present, this Memoir may close. (*MA* 185)

Mill closes his book as he began it, with education. He is doing the work of one who values learning and, at this point, learning for men and women. Studying, writing articles, giving public lectures, and making plans for future books, at the age of sixty-four no philosopher/teacher could hope to do more. Mill finished the final revision of the *Autobiography* in 1870. It, along with *Utility of Religion and Theism* and volume 4 of *Dissertations and Discussions,* were published posthumously.

Combined with these illustrations, the language, images, and metaphors of the entire text suggest reeducation as a figura for John Stuart Mill's transformation. *Reeducation* implies all the traditional senses of education: academic (disciplinary) knowledge, professional preparation, matriculation, coming of age, self-reliance, separation. *Reeducation* also implies that there is something missing in the initial education. For Mill it is the education of the "whole" person. With his first education his intellect receives careful attention; his emotions are totally disregarded. The first education is overtly self-conscious; the reeducation is a startling discovery of the internal self and the resources of the emotions.

Mill's reeducation, as he describes it, also implies a conversion experience. In earlier conversion narratives, like those of Augustine and Bunyan, there is something given up (sin) and something received (Spirit). In Mill's conversion (transformation, reeducation) he speaks of being ready to "learn and unlearn" (*MA* 3). An authentic education and conversion to "true teacher" require that Mill unlearn deference to logic and learn appreciation for poetry, that he unlearn total dependence on the intellect and learn reliance on the imagination.

The operative metaphors of the *Autobiography,* then, cluster around the idea of reeducation. They communicate the sense that the old education will not suffice, that there are new lessons to be learned. The missing elements in the initial education are so significant that a crisis is precipitated and a conversion ensues before the reeducation is complete. Allowing the figura of reeducation to guide this exploration of the *Autobiography,* we might investigate a series of "lessons" in the authentic education of the philosopher. Lesson 1 might be seen as initiatory, the exposition and justification of a rational education and a liberal political philosophy; lesson 2 as the crisis, the examination of the consequences of creating a reasoning machine; and lesson 3 as the reeducation, the exploration of the authentic matriculation of the philosopher of feeling. At each lesson there is a different teacher, and at each lesson the examination is focused on different texts. The three lessons of Mill's reeducation transform him from school-boy logician to philosopher of feeling. This implicit schematic sets the "educational objective" of the text of the *Autobiography.*

Lesson 1: Boys Will Be Logicians and Utilitarians

Rationalistic education and training in liberal political philosophy shape the persona of lesson 1. These lessons give the appearance of a genuine matriculation. Lesson 1, the stage of deference to intellectual authority figures and the accumulation of received notions, is a necessary stage in a traditional education, but it is a far distance from graduation. Operating under lesson 1, the school-boy logician perceives this stage in his education as the actual matriculation stage. He is convinced that he has things all worked out, he has the analytical skills to think through any difficulty, and he subscribes to a political philosophy that will rid England of its problems. At this point he is not arrogant, but he is dead sure. He does not at all perceive this stage in his life as "pre"-matriculation. In his mind he has graduated with honors, well ahead of his class.

> If I have accomplished anything, I owe it, among other fortunate circumstances, to the fact that through the early training bestowed on me by my father, I started, I may fairly say, with an advantage of a quarter of a century over my contemporaries. (*MA* 20)

This twenty-five-year educational advantage gives its student an unshakable confidence in the future and in his ability to bring about political reform. This early and disciplined education, "bestowed on him by his father," serves the student well.

Utilitarian Teachers. If the student of lesson 1 is unusual, he is no more so than his teachers. Mill's first teacher was neither a hired tutor nor a local schoolmaster; he was the most demanding and rigorous of instructors, his father. The elder Mill, as schoolmaster, allows none of the son's years to be wasted (nor his hours nor his minutes). His father designs a rigorous education for the son, who not only accedes to it; he approves it.

> In the course of instruction which I have partially retraced, the point most superficially apparent is the great effort to give, during the years of childhood, an amount of knowledge in what are considered the higher branches of education, which is seldom acquired (if acquired at all) until

the age of manhood. The result of the experiment shews the ease with which this may be done, and places in a strong light the wretched waste of so many precious years. (*MA* 19)

With such an advantage, his readers might wonder, why does Mill need reeducating?

Himself a scholar, the elder Mill carries out an amazing educational experiment. The entirety of the *Autobiography*'s chapter 2, "My Father's Character and Opinions," is devoted to a discussion of James Mill's role in his son's education, as are major portions of the first and sixth chapters. The son describes the teacher/father as a Stoic, an Epicurean, a Cynic.

> In his personal qualities the Stoic predominated. His standard of morals was Epicurean, inasmuch as it was utilitarian, taking as the exclusive test of right and wrong, the tendency of actions to produce pleasure or pain. But he had (and this was the Cynic element) scarcely any belief in plea-sure. . . . He never varied in rating intellectual enjoyments above all oth-ers. (*MA* 30–31)

This man, who rated intellectual pursuits above all others, accepted no lapses in thinking in his son and allowed him little time for the exploration of personal interests or the practice of private recreations. The son recalls, "The element which was chiefly deficient in his moral relation to his children, was that of tenderness" (*MA* 32), and in the *Early Draft* he admits that "mine was not an education of love, but of fear" (*ED* 66). The teacher of lesson 1 got results but at what price? Mill tells us, somewhat cautiously, "I hesitate to pronounce whether I was a loser or gainer by his severity" (*MA* 32).

The elder Mill introduces his son to a second teacher, the political philosopher Jeremy Bentham, whose tutelage, while less direct, made new demands on the young scholar. Bentham and the elder Mill ("the earliest Englishman of any great mark, who thoroughly understood, and in the main adopted, Bentham's general views of ethics, government, and law: and this was a natural foundation for sympathy between them") were familiar companions, studying, writing, and traveling together. For the period from 1814 to 1817 Mill spent much time at Bentham's residence at Ford Abbey and tells us that "this sojourn was, I think, an important circumstance in my education" (*MA* 35). Mill also attributes Bentham's brother Sir Samuel and his family another kind of education, a more Continental one. During his residence with them at Montpellier he attended "excellent winter courses" in bodily exercises ("in none of which however I made any proficiency"), chemistry, metaphysics, logic, and higher mathematics. Breathing "for a whole year the free and genial atmosphere of Continental life," Mill has a short respite from the English mentality and his Utilitarian teachers (*MA* 37).

Utilitarian Texts. The student of lesson 1 counts too much on external authority for definition and on a system of economic utility for a comprehensive political philosophy. This authority, exercised by his teachers, also resides in the texts they have written or that they give him to read and revise. Having completed a course of study that would confound most college graduates, the adolescent is given Bentham's *Traite de legislation* to read and, at nineteen, his *Rationale of Judicial Evidence* to edit.

"Utilitarian texts" stand here as an image for the received knowledge that Mill is acquiring from the elder Mill and Jeremy Bentham. The focus at this stage is on the written theories and experiences of others. Mill reads and/or edits all of Bentham's major works on morals and politics and adopts them as his own. The youthful vigor for learning is matched by youthful commitment to the philosophies of others and, in particular, Utilitarianism. Mill is impressed by Bentham's application of the inductive method to areas heretofore unexamined inductively, reasoning from particular facts or individual cases to a general conclusion, treating wholes by separating them into parts, resolving abstractions into things. Mill might learn to value other views, find new teachers, and examine new kinds of texts, but he never gives up the practice of analysis gained in these early lessons. He never ceases to consider "the power and practice of analysis as an essential condition both of individual and of social improvement" (*MA* 86).

In lesson 1 received ideas, not human beings, are examined; intellectual growth, not inward development, is the focus. Mill recalls the improbability of internal examination at this stage of his matriculation: "I never thought of saying to myself, I am, or I can do, so and so. I neither estimated myself highly nor lowly; I did not estimate myself at all" (*MA* 21).

The explanation for the limited education of lesson 1 is to be found in the restrictive nature of its pedagogy and in the limited view of its pedagogues and their texts. Young Mill's "first" education, though narrow and in many ways mechanical, prepared him to understand and critique the economic or material aspects of social reform. It prepared him to discuss with his father, Bentham, and their friends and associates the moral, ethical, legal, and political implications of current government practices. It taught him to parrot Bentham's solutions to the economic and social problems plaguing England. But, as he recounts in the *Autobiography*, it did not prepare him for living and, consequently, for genuine social reform.

What Mill needs, and what the autobiography describes, is to matriculate in a less restrictive institution than the Utilitarian School. He needs to study with less "peculiar" teachers than his father and Jeremy Bentham. So, in lesson 2 we see Mill begin a new study, one that investigates the consequences of a rational education and a liberal politics. We see him take an active role in his own education, put himself under the tutelage of Wordsworth, and place Wordsworth's Preface to the second edition of *Lyrical Ballads* and "Ode: Intimations of Immortality" alongside Bentham's *Introduction to the Principles of Morals and Legislation*. The student of lesson 1 transfers from the Utilitarian School to the school of individual experience—the Romantic School. Lesson 1, then, is the first stage in Mill's rigorous yet inadequate education. It forces him into a personal crisis.

Lesson 2: Crisis—The Consequences of Creating a Reasoning Machine

Victim to an "undernourished Inward Spirit," John Stuart Mill comes to the crisis point in his education. During what he calls the "melancholy winter" of 1826–27 he finds himself incapable of his usual occupations but goes on with them mechanically, "by mere force of habit." Having been so drilled "in a certain sort of mental exercise, that I could still carry it on when all the spirit had gone out of it" (*MA* 85).

As with most young, maturing students, this is the time for Mill when traditional supports fall away and usual joys fail. The student is forced to find his own way. He can no longer identify himself solely with Utilitarian social reform. He has no love to confide in; he has not as yet met Harriet Taylor. He is not to discover the unselfishness that was not that of "a taught system of duties, but of a heart which thoroughly identified itself with the feelings of others, and often went to excess in consideration for them" for another four years, and they do not marry for another twenty-one years (*A* 112). No doctrine, no one he loves, no one but himself—Mill's examination must turn inward. It must be focused on the reasoning machine himself. Mill's reeducation is at its most critical stage. The crisis of the scholar, an examination of received notions, and the attendant challenge to authority figures, must be followed by an examination of the limitations and potentials of the school-boy logician. The rite of passage from external to internal determination is impossible without this critical assessment.

Romantic Teachers. In the crisis stage of lesson 2 Mill's Utilitarian teachers are displaced by the school-boy himself. The school-boy has come of age; he is no longer bound to his old teachers, nor is he intimidated by their authority. Mill must be his own teacher and at the same time become a student to the Romantic poets. The assignment is almost too much for him. As Mill recalls:

> it was time to learn and unlearn. It has also seemed to me that in an age of transition in opinions, there may be somewhat both of interest and of benefit in noting the successive phases of any mind which was always pressing forward, equally ready to learn and to unlearn either from its own thoughts or from those of others. (*MA* 3)

Before he can unlearn deference to old teachers, Mill gets help from Marmontel and Wordsworth. Marmontel teaches him what neither his father nor Bentham cared to teach him—how to cry. The flood of tears waters Mill's "dry, heavy dejection" and initiates Mill's transformation from absence of feeling to experience of feeling. In precipitating experience of feeling, Marmonel prepares Mill to study with Wordsworth, and Wordsworth teaches Mill that through the experience of poetry "the feeling therein developed gives importance to the action and situation, and not the action and situation to the feeling."

Romantic Texts. In lesson 2, the texts of Utilitarian political theory are displaced by autobiography and poetry. On reading Marmontel's *Memoirs,* Mill discovers his own buried feelings and begins to experience, for the first time perhaps, his neglected, inward spirit. The focus shifts from the texts of others to the text of the self. The *Memoirs* precipitates the experience of feeling necessary to move Mill beyond the crisis of lesson 2; an autobiography within an autobiography configures the transformation from no feeling to feeling. If Marmontel's autobiography stands as bridge between absence of feeling and experience of feeling, it also stands as bridge between the examination of logical texts and the examination of Romantic texts. It is at this point that the logical texts (ideas, influence, writings, of Bentham and the elder Mill), if not replaced, are, for the time, supplanted by the imaginative verbal artworks of the Romantic poets.

Education in Bentham's school had purposely excluded the study of poetry from the curriculum. Mill footnotes Bentham's attitude toward poetry from *The Rationale of Reward:*

> Indeed, between poetry and truth there is a natural opposition: false morals, fictitious nature. The poet always stands in need of something false. When he pretends to lay his foundations in truth, the ornaments of his superstructure are fictions; his business consists in stimulating our passions, and exciting our prejudices. Truth, exactitude of every kind, is fatal to poetry. The poet must see everything through coloured media, and strive to make everyone else do the same. (*MA 68*)

In addition to Bentham's injunctions against poetry, Mill was also warned against the poetic tendency in existing political philosophy. Bentham exposed the imprecise language used in previous modes of political reasoning as "allusions to reason," "phrases," "sacramental expressions." He felt that phrases like *moral sense, common sense, rule of right,* and *laws of nature* were fictions. They contained no argument: they were but vague generalizations and had no place in political philosophy.[11]

In lesson 1 the school-boy logician studied the texts of the Utilitarians. In lesson 2 he studies his inward self, which includes an examination of the consequences of liberal political philosophy and a rational education on the development of that self. He also begins a study of the Romantic poets in an effort to round out the narrowness of his earlier studies and experiences. In lesson 1 the school-boy published works that parroted the voices of the Benthamites. In lesson 2 little written work was completed at all; the crisis period in the matriculation of the student was a time for feeling and reflection, a taking of accounts, an inward look. External supports and authority figures are set aside, and the "candidate for graduation" begins to develop his own internal resources. The (pre)matriculation stage of lesson 1, with its preference for the intellect, logical texts, and Utilitarian teachers is displaced by the crisis stage of lesson 2 and the discovery of emotions, poetic texts, and Romantic teachers. Lesson 2 becomes, in part, a do-it-yourself education. Mill has become both his own teacher and a student to the Romantic poets.

> Sweet is the lore which Nature brings;
> Our meddling intellect
> Mis-shapes the beauteous forms of things:—
> We murder to dissect.

Enough of Science and of Art;
Close up those barren leaves;
Come forth, and bring with you a heart
That watches and receives.[12]

Lesson 3: The Authentic Matriculation of the Philosopher of Feeling

Lesson 3 is final examination time for John Stuart Mill. The question for this lesson is: "Can the philosopher of feeling design a system that goes beyond Bentham and Wordsworth—that takes into account both logic and poetry, analysis and imagination?" This stage in his reeducation causes Mill to turn to new teachers and new texts for assistance. On his way to designing the political system of *On Liberty*, Mill studies "the general opinions of mankind" and investigates the political philosophies of Coleridge, Carlyle, the Saint-Simonians, and other Continental philosophers. Through personal contact and/or encounter with their writings these new teachers help Mill prepare to write a new political philosophy. They lead him to enlarge on, rather than reject out of hand, his earlier positions. Mill tells us:

> I did not, for an instant, lose sight of, or undervalue, that part of the truth which I had seen before; I never turned recreant to intellectual culture, or ceased to consider the power and practice of analysis as an essential condition both of individual and of social improvement. But I thought that it had consequences which required to be corrected, by joining other kinds of cultivation with it. The maintenance of a due balance among the faculties, now seemed to me of primary importance. (*MA* 86)

Mill discovers the "consequences" of an analytic approach to both public and individual concerns during the crisis of lesson 2. During lesson 3 he "corrects" these consequences by acquiring new teachers and new textbooks.

New Teachers. One of Mill's most influential new teachers is Coleridge, whom Mill characterizes as the "completing counterpart" to Jeremy Bentham and whose influence Mill describes "as the great awakener in this country of the spirit of philosophy, within the bounds of traditional opinions."[13] Through *Church and State* and *Biographia Literaria* Coleridge teaches Mill the ideas of permanence and progressiveness. Coleridge teaches Mill to value the purposes and truths of traditional institutions and doctrines as a way to ensure some permanence in societies. Coleridge believed that "the very fact that any doctrine had been believed by thoughtful men, and received by whole nations or generations of mankind, was part of the problem to be solved, was one of the phenomena to be accounted for."[14] Coleridge also teaches Mill to investigate philosophical or political positions that differ from his own as a way to guard against close-mindedness and to foster progressive thinking. Mill contends that "both the theory and practice of enlightened tolerance in matters of opinion, might be exhibited in extracts from his [Coleridge's] writings more copiously than in those of almost any other writer we know."[15]

Coleridge's positions on permanence and progressiveness serve to remind Mill of the value of past traditions and the necessity of enlightened tolerance in designing political systems. These divisions of the interests of society into "two antagonist interests," as Coleridge characterizes them, show up in Mill's mature writing and in his dealings with others. He repeatedly calls on "Conservative thinkers and Liberals, transcendentalists and admirers of Hobbes and Locke," to remember

> the importance, in the present imperfect state of mental and social science, of antagonist modes of thought: which it will one day be felt, are as necessary to one another in speculation, as mutually checking powers are in a political constitution. A clear insight, indeed, into this necessity is the only rational or enduring basis of philosophical tolerance; the only condition under which liberality in matters of opinion can be anything better than a polite synonym for indifference between one opinion and another.[16]

From Thomas Carlyle, another of Mill's new teachers, he learns that he must replace a political philosophy based solely on the appetites with an enlarged system that accounts for other aspects of human well-being. Carlyle's *Sartor Resartus* teaches Mill that material well-being is insufficient in the making of good citizens and good government.

> I asked myself: What is this that, ever since earliest years, thou hast been fretting and fuming, and lamenting and self-tormenting, on account of? Say it in a word: is it not because thou art not HAPPY? Because the THOU (sweet gentleman) is not sufficiently honored, nourished, soft-bedded, and lovingly cared-for? Foolish soul! What Act of Legislature was there that *thou* shouldst be Happy? A little while ago thou hadst no right to *be* at all. What if thou wert born and predestined not to be Happy, but to be Unhappy! Art thou nothing other than a Vulture, then, that fliest through the Universe seeking after somewhat to *eat;* and shrieking dolefully

because carrion enough is not given thee? Close thy Byron; open thy
Goethe.[17]

Carlyle's injunction suggests that Utilitarian political philosophy can be
reduced to the simple proposition of filling the stomach. As Mill encounters
Carlyle's thinking, which is not only outside the Utilitarian School but
holds it up to ridicule, he comes to understand the narrowness of Utilitarian reform. Integration of Carlyle's ideology into his thinking is quite different, however, from his usual method. He acknowledges that Carlyle's
writings "seem a haze of poetry and German metaphysics" and that "what
truths they contained" he is "already receiving from other quarters."

> Instead of my having been taught anything, in the first instance, by Car-
> lyle, it was only in proportion as I came to see the same truths, through
> media more suited to my mental constitution, that I recognized them in his
> writings. (*MA* 105)

Mill admits that, when Carlyle shows him the manuscript of *Sartor Resartus,* he "makes little of it," and, while Carlyle's writings may have taught
Mill little political philosophy directly, they did come to have "wonderful
power" for him as poetry—a new form of instruction he has just recently
discovered.

> But the good his writings did me, was not as philosophy to instruct, but as
> poetry to animate. . . . I felt that he was a poet, and that I was not; that he
> was a man of intuition, which I was not; and that as such, he not only saw
> many things long before me, which I could only, when they were pointed
> out to me, hobble after and prove, but that it was highly probable he
> could see many things which were not visible to me even after they were
> pointed out. (*MA* 105–6)

Mill is suggesting that the poets may often see things before the philosophers and that their visions, when shared, provide a new kind of instruction
for him. Poetry, or basic imaginative activity, as he defines it, teaches us
how our political systems actually work or fail to work. From the poetry of
Carlyle (and, through Carlyle, Goethe) Mill learns that the imaginative
individual has a responsibility for the improvement of society.[18] He comes
to understand the relationship of poetry to political reform: "It enables us,
by a voluntary effort, to conceive the absent as if it were present, the imaginary as if it were real, and to clothe it in the feelings which, if it were real,
it would bring along with it. This is the power by which one human being
enters into the mind and circumstances of another."[19] Mill learns from the

Romantic poets that, if reformers can enter the minds and circumstances of others, they may be more fully prepared to develop political systems that are coherent and comprehensive—that make sense for all citizens.

The Continental philosophers also serve as Mill's new teachers in the final stages of his authentic education. The Saint-Simonians, a group of French thinkers often referred to as the social Romantics, help Mill develop a view of the natural order of human progress that is dependent on shifts between organic and critical periods. Organic periods are defined as those times when society functions under a positive creed that guides actions and defines needs. The creed is outgrown when all possible progress is made and the society enters a period of questioning, criticism, and negativism. This shift, designated as a critical period, is a critical change, but it is not a complete overthrow. The critical period is followed by a synthetic period in which ideas from the old period, having passed through the critical period, are expanded and adapted. While the Saint-Simonians espoused human progress, they were opposed to private property and founded a society based on mutual ownership and technology. They urged exploitation of the achievements of the industrial revolution for the good of the society and proposed innovative systems for social interaction. Seeing his own era as a critical one, Mill learns from the Saint-Simonians to distinguish between a critical period in a society's history and its normal functioning. He also learns to be skeptical of a political economy based solely on private property.

In lesson 3 the philosopher comes of age. He completes his schooling for the design of a political philosophy that will take into account both the human and the material. The lessons learned from his study of Wordsworth, Coleridge, Carlyle, and the Saint-Simonians provide a corrective to Bentham's radical political philosophy, "by joining other kinds of cultivation with it." The school-boy is ready to teach others; the education is complete—Commencement Day is here!

Mill begins to produce works that have his own stamp on them. They challenge, expand, and enlarge the texts of lesson 1. The writings he produced in lesson 1 were the words of others, issuing from his own pen. The pen stopped writing during the crisis of lesson 2. It is in lesson 3, "The Remainder of My Life," that Mill completes his most important work on political theory. He founds and edits the *London Review* (1835), writes *Principles of Political Economy* (1848), *On Liberty* and *Thoughts on Parliamentary Reform* (1859), and *The Subjection of Women,* with Harriet

Taylor Mill (1869). This mature writing reflects a continuing commitment to logical analysis and the lessons he learned from Bentham and his father. It also suggests a fresh view of the human condition, with its reliance on the imagination, that he has learned in his lessons with the poets and the Continental philosophers.

John Stuart Mill's *Autobiography* is a narrative of transformation as reeducation. This rigorous and often painful project involves learning and unlearning, analysis and imaginative reflection. The focus of Mill's studies shifts from an examination of the material to the examination of the human. Whereas the student of lesson 1 is concerned with external reform, the student of lessons 2 and 3 is concerned with internal culture and human well-being. Whereas the curriculum of lesson 1 mainly focuses on logic, later lessons take up poetry and Continental philosophy. Whereas the student of lesson 1 relies on head knowledge and is considered a reasoning machine, the candidate for graduation has "got a heart." And, if the location of Mill's institution of higher learning does not move away completely from the school of Utilitarianism, it does house a few classrooms dedicated to the values of the social Romantics. Like Mill's plan for educational reform that will "prevent the infirmities of democracy by training the intelligence of the people," Mill's authentic education prepares him to become "a true teacher for the fitting social arrangements of England."

The Dynamis of "Thought Coloured by Feeling"

Transformation configured as reeducation characterizes John Stuart Mill's changes. But how does he change from logic-machine to one who cultivates the inward self? Since, in Mill's own words, "there seemed no power in nature sufficient to begin the formation of my character anew" (*MA* 84), what is the force, or power, to which his transformation is attributed? What are the means capable of being "instrumental to that object"? What sort of transforming power is operative in Mill's reeducation that causes him to reevaluate the bases of his thought and action?

Examining the *Autobiography* from the perspective of the dynamis will serve to illuminate the motive force of his transformation.

What made Wordworth's poems a medicine for my state of mind, was that they expressed, not mere outward beauty, but states of feeling, and of thought coloured by feeling, under the excitement of beauty. . . . From them I seemed to learn what would be the perennial sources of happiness, when all the greater evils of life shall have been removed. (*MA* 89)

The "medicine" of Wordsworth's poetry arouses feelings that lead to Mill's transformation. The phrase that Mill uses to describe his experience of Wordworth's poetry, "thought coloured by feeling," serves to characterize the dynamis of Mill's transformation. It aptly describes the motive force of a transformation that is configured as reeducation. *Thought* means an operation of the mind upon an object, idea, event. It is reflection, meditation, cogitation, intellect, imagination; it is attention, consideration, heed. Mill is first and foremost a thinker; in other words, thought is his business or stock-in-trade. It is thought, study, and analysis that have allowed him to acquire a remarkable education and to achieve early public success in those places where knowledge and education count for so much, with political philosophers and, in particular, with the Utilitarians. It is also "the habit of analysis," Mill tells us, that "has a tendency to wear away feelings." Feelings in sufficient strength might "resist the dissolving influence of analysis," but for the Englishman, in contrast to the Frenchman, "feelings stand very much in his way. . . . And in truth the English character, and English social circumstances, make it so seldom possible to derive happiness from the exercise of the sympathies, that is it not wonderful if they count for little in an Englishman's scheme of life" (*MA* 83, 84, 91).

When Mill turns his thought to examining Utilitarian political philosophy itself, he realizes that his "schemes for improving human affairs" had "overlooked human beings." When he turns his thought to examining the scope of his own personal world, he finds it lacking as well. He is devoid of all human feeling; he has lost interest in the improvement of mankind, and he is totally incapable of dealing with his personal crisis. While the power of thought has made Mill the man he is, it has also brought him to his crisis point. He discovers that the power of thought alone, either logical or reflective, is insufficient for his present needs.

It is when thought meets with or is colored by feeling through the experience of poetry and autobiography that Mill begins to see life anew and to revise his plan for the improvement of mankind. Marmontel's *Memoirs* and Wordsworth's poetry elicit a wash of feelings not experienced heretofore. They cause "a small ray of light" to break in upon his "gloom" (*MA* 85). Unlike the blinding light that struck Saint Paul at his conversion, it is only a "small ray," but it is the beginning of Mill's conversion. He is no longer "stock" nor "stone"; his "burthen" is lighter; he is relieved of his "irreme-

diable wretchedness." It is through the power of the emotions or feelings
that Mill comes to understand "what would be the perennial sources of
happiness, when all the greater evils of life shall have been removed."

On discovering that existence is more than a matter of struggle for material and intellectual improvement, a whole new world opens up for Mill. It
is the world of the imagination, the cultivation of the inward self. Mill recognizes that it is not the "beautiful pictures of natural scenery" that elicit
feelings of "inward joy." It is the imagination that is significant. It gives
voice to the poet and majesty to the mountain. The imagination

> enables us, by a voluntary effort, to conceive the absent as if it were pres-
> ent, the imaginary as if it were real, and to clothe it in the feelings which,
> if it were indeed real, it would bring along with it.[20]

The dynamis of thought colored by feeling is the imagination. If the imagination is allowed to function freely, the absent can be made present; the
imaginary may be imbued with a passion that challenges real-life experience.

The imagination also serves another important function for Mill as
political philosopher: it keeps him in touch with the everyday living. In the
Preface to the second edition of the *Lyrical Ballads* Wordsworth speaks of
the principal object "proposed in these poems":

> to choose incidents and situations from common life, and to relate or
> describe them, throughout, as far as was possible in a selection of lan-
> guage really used by men, and, at the same time, to throw over them a cer-
> tain colouring of imagination, whereby ordinary things should be pre-
> sented to the mind in an unusual aspect; and, further, and above all, to
> make these incidents and situations interesting by tracing in them . . . the
> primary laws of our nature: chiefly, as far as regards the manner in which
> we associate ideas in a state of excitement.[21]

When Mill was struggling so desperately during the crisis, he believed that
the flaw was in his own life; he came to understand that there was also a
flaw in Bentham's system, a deficiency of the imagination. Wordsworth
leads him to see this deficiency and to desire its remedy in the cultivation of
inward feeling.

The dynamis of thought colored by feeling is the power that resolves the
crisis in Mill's personal life, and it is also the motive force of his revised
political philosophy.

> This is the power by which one human being enters into the mind and
> circumstances of another. . . .Without it nobody knows even of his
> own nature . . . nor the nature of his fellow-creatures, beyond such

generalizations as he may have been enabled to make from his observation of their outward conduct.[22]

Bentham had attempted to create a practical political philosophy with little or no understanding of human nature. Mill contends that Bentham had experienced few human feelings himself and that, because he had little contact with any persons outside Utilitarianism, he had no idea what sort of system was actually needed for social improvement.

> Bentham's knowledge of human nature is bounded. It is wholly empirical; and the empiricism of one who has had little experience. He had neither internal experience nor external; the quiet, even tenor of his life, and his healthiness of mind, conspired to exclude him from both. He never knew prosperity and adversity, passion nor satiety. . . . He knew no dejection, no heaviness of heart. He never felt life a sore and a weary burthen. . . . His own lot was cast in a generation of the leanest and barrenest men whom England had yet produced. . . . Knowing so little of human feelings, he knew still less of the influences by which those feelings are formed. . . and no one, probably, who, in a highly instructed age, ever attempted to give a rule to all human conduct, set out with a more limited conception either of the agencies by which human conduct *is* or of those by which it *should* be, influenced.[23]

John Stuart Mill might well have continued in Bentham's steps had it not been for the transforming power of the imagination. *On Liberty,* published five years after the first draft of the *Autobiography* and more than thirty years after his mental crisis, demonstrates the force of the dynamis of imagination as it empowers Mill's writing. Considered his most important work, with the exception of the *Autobiography,* it greatly expands the Utilitarian view of the greatest happiness of the greatest number. Mill shows that regard for others comes from a genuine inward concern for both the self and society, not from the association of pleasure with material welfare. He also comes to agree with European thinkers that political institutions should be seen as relative to time and place and that social reformers, through education and legislation, can bring about only limited external modification. He insists that society should interfere with individual action only to prevent harm to others.

> Whatever crushes individualism is despotism, by whatever name it may be called, and whether it professes to be enforcing the will of God or the injunctions of men.[24]

Although Mill ceased to consider representative government as an absolute, he never wavers from his allegiance to liberal democracy and his commitment to political reform. In the previous excerpt he insists that both domination by the aristocracy and the despotism of public opinion lead to the corruption of justice, the promotion of private interest over public, and the association of material goods and property with happiness. He is convinced that a society that has as its main goal the accumulation of wealth can have no thought of improving conditions for the masses.

> I regard utility as the ultimate appeal on all ethical questions; but it must be utility in the largest sense, grounded on the permanent interests of man as a progressive being. Those interests, I contend, authorise the subjection of individual spontaneity to external control, only in respect to those actions of each, which concern the interests of other people.[25]

For Mill a liberal society places positive value on individuality. It not only tolerates but encourages free public discussion; it is a humane society and one that produces reasonable citizens. *On Liberty* focuses on promoting a more tolerant public. Freedom from oppression is not so much the issue; legislation, representation, and suffrage do not make for real liberty. What is needed, under Mill's system, is a liberal, tolerant populace standing behind a liberal government. Persons who, rather than being preoccupied solely with pleasure, are sensitive to the needs and feelings of their neighbors, will be able to create and maintain institutions that promote the welfare of all. Individuals take precedence over institutions or the systems for improving them.

> If there are any persons who contest a received opinion, or who will do so if law or opinion will let them, let us thank them for it, open our minds to listen to them, and rejoice that there is someone to do for us what we otherwise ought, if we have any regard for either the certainty or the vitality of our convictions, to do with much greater labour for ourselves.[26]

Through the power of the imagination, thought colored by feeling, John Stuart Mill put forward a theory of civil and social liberty that has not lost its force with time. His political thought may not have caught on in England in his day, but his ideas on personal and social liberty shape much of democratic thinking in the present culture.[27] Mill has shown us what makes for good individuals and good government.

The dynamis of the imagination is Mill's source for internal joy and heightened experience. It is the reservoir of inward culture and its wellspring; it is motive power for the transformation of the reasoning machine. As the power of thought is colored by feeling, a man and his political philosophy are transformed. A reasoning machine would never have written a text about a personal crisis and a transformation empowered by the imagination, but this is exactly what John Stuart Mill did. His *Autobiography* both attests to transformation through the power of the imagination and stands as evidence of this power. Dynamis twice testifies as it is the power for the specification *and* the elaboration of Mill's transformation from school-boy logician to philosopher of feeling.

5

From Beetle Collector
to Acclaimed Naturalist

The Transformation of Charles Darwin (1809–82)

In 1755 the Lisbon earthquake shattered the best of all possible worlds and exposed a basic flaw in the clockwork universe. The static, ordered world was flying apart, and a dynamic universe full of tension, forces, and fields awaited investigation. Less than eighty years later the volcanic rocks of the mountains of Ascension were resounding under Charles Darwin's geological hammer.[1] Soon to become one of the world's most highly acclaimed scientists, his explorations shattered old views of how life forms developed and resulted in the single most significant scientific theory since Copernicus.

The Autobiography of Charles Darwin[2] is the story of the *man* behind the theory of evolution, the maturing of his mind and his development as a scientist. What kind of man was he? What was his world like? How did he make sense of things? How did he characterize the maturation of his thinking and to what did he attribute his development as a scientist? Written in 1876 ostensibly for his own amusement, the enjoyment of his children and grandchildren, and at the urging of an unidentified German editor, the *Autobiography* is an abstract of Darwin's life. Darwin was born in 1809 into a wealthy, upper-class home in Shrewsbury, England, the son and grandson of distinguished physicians. Stories of his unsuitability for the profession of medicine, his leaving Edinburgh, his taking a B.A. degree at Cambridge with little distinction, his engagement as naturalist on the HMS *Beagle* voyage, his marriage to his cousin, Emma Wedgewood, and their subsequent move to a permanent home in Down, where Darwin engaged in his work on evolution for the next forty years, are familiar. The *Autobiography* presents a life of stability, hard work, and tranquillity.

Yet, in contrast to this picture of personal stability and quietude, the idea of transformation is central to everything we know about Charles Darwin. His name is synonymous with change: transmutation, adaptation, variation, evolution. To determine the force or mechanism for variation in animals and plants occupies Darwin for the better portion of his professional life. In the midst of his investigations Darwin is forced to discard the view of a onetime creation and, with it, a fixed and hierarchical universe. He comes to believe that the universe is ancient and dynamic, much older than Bishop Ussher's 4004 B.C. The environment is alive, and it acts and interacts with the plants and animals in its surroundings. In rejecting a onetime creation and the *Scalae Naturae,* Darwin discovers a process that is noncyclical and ongoing. He learns that what brings about development, what pushes the world on, is struggle, force, tension, and adaptation. The idea of a onetime creation of all life forms in straight-line succession, proceeding from simplest to most complex, is discarded in favor of the evolutionary idea of the ongoing struggle of survival.

Beetle Collector

It is much the same with the text of the *Autobiography.* The narrative relates Darwin's evolution as a scientist. It characterizes his life-changing experiences as the gradual realization of an innate scientific potential. The agent of change is not the external God of conversion; he has undergone no salvation experience. The report of his life could hardly read like that of John Bunyan, who, upon receiving the words "My grace is sufficient for thee," relates:

> At which time, my Understanding was so enlightened, that I was as though I had seen the Lord Jesus look down from Heaven through the Tiles upon me, and direct these words into me; this sent me mourning home, it broke my heart, and filled me full of joy, and laid me as low as the dust.[3]

Bunyan believes the "condition of the Dogge and Toad" to be better than his own. He counts himself as nothing without God's sufficient grace to order his life. In contrast, Darwin's gradual transformation is actualized through his own innate attributes operating within a dynamic world environment.

With his lively curiosity, be it for dog, toad, earthworm, or beetle, Darwin constructs the narrative of himself around his innate capacities and zeal for scientific knowledge.

> But no pursuit at Cambridge was followed with nearly so much eagerness or gave me so much pleasure as collecting beetles. It was the mere passion for collecting, for I did not dissect them and rarely compared their exter-

nal characters with published descriptions, but got them named anyhow. I will give a proof of my zeal: one day, on tearing off some old bark, I saw two rare beetles and seized one in each hand; then I saw a third and new kind, which I could not bear to lose, so that I popped the one which I held in my right hand into my mouth. Alas it ejected some intensely acrid fluid, which burnt my tongue so that I was forced to spit the beetle out, which was lost, as well as the third one. (*DA* 62)

This anecdotal sketch gives some indication of Charles Darwin's youthful characteristics. Darwin, as avid beetle collector, is so zealous that he pops one into his mouth to seize another and so careless that his tongue is burned when the beetle ejects its acrid fluid.

"Boyish beetle collector" stands as image for the *before* persona of the *Autobiography.* In contrast to these naive qualities, a picture of a mature "acclaimed naturalist" appears at the end of the text of Darwin's life:

My books have sold largely in England, have been translated into many languages, and passed through several editions in foreign countries. I have heard it said that the success of a work abroad is the best test of its enduring value. I doubt whether this is at all trustworthy; but judged by this standard my name ought to last for a few years. . . . My industry has been nearly as great as it could have been in the observation and collection of facts. What is far more important, my love of natural science has been steady and ardent. This pure love has, however, been much aided by the ambition to be esteemed by my fellow naturalists. (*DA* 139, 141)

Darwin develops from a youthful and zealous beetle collector to a mature and respected scientist. What is unique about this development is that both its before and after aspects contain within their terms the notion of scientist. Even as ardent collector, Darwin manifests the qualities and habits of mind that identify a young man in pursuit of a lifelong career in natural science. Darwin is not "converted" to science, as Bunyan was to saintliness or as was Mill to a Social Romanticism; he presents himself as scientist— untrained and immature, to be sure, but nonetheless scientist—at the outset. Collector and naturalist, before and after, these are the attributes of the persona that constitute the scientist, boy and man.

The early sections of the *Autobiography* indicate that Darwin had a happy, rather carefree childhood, and, though his mother died when he was eight years old, he remembers little about her and appears quite content to have been cared for by his sisters. While these sections describe no youthful anguish, and in their rambling quality portray Darwin as nonchalant and unaffected, they are balanced by Darwin's doubts about his scientific prospects. Struggling with what he believes are limiting character traits, Darwin portrays himself as somewhat careless in his studies: "I was considered by all my masters and by my Father as a very ordinary boy, rather below the common standard in intellect" (*DA* 28). He sees himself as unmotivated: "I became convinced from various small circumstances that my father would leave me property enough to subsist on with some comfort" (*DA* 46). He lives for collecting and shooting: "My zeal was so great that I used to place my shooting boots open by my bed-side when I went to bed, so as not to lose half-a-minute in putting them on in the morning" (*DA* 54).

Against these instances of irresponsibility, Darwin recalls that during the summer of 1825, before coming to Edinburgh, at the age of sixteen, he serves as attending physican to some poor women and children in Shrewsbury, at one time having about a dozen patients. His father declares that he "should make a successful physician" (Darwin's father felt that the chief element of a physican's success was to excite confidence), but, according to Darwin, "what he saw in me which convinced him that I should create confidence I know not" (*DA* 48). Darwin also notes that he prepared and read two short papers on marine zoology (at the time he is only seventeen) for the Plinian Society (*DA* 50). Yet his interests quickly move to other things: stuffing birds and meeting with the Wernerian and Royal Medical Societies. Showing no clear direction to his lively interest in the sciences, Darwin provides other instances of the embryonic scientist: he reads "with care several books on chemistry" (*DA* 46); botany, "I was interested at this early age in the variability of plants!" (*DA* 23); and geology, "I felt the keenest delight when I first read of the action of icebergs in transporting boulders, and I gloried in the progress of geology" (*DA* 53). Charles Darwin tries on the names of beetle collector, physician, marine zoologist, chemist, botanist, and geologist as he explores the natural world around him.

> With respect to science, I continued collecting minerals with much zeal, but quite unscientifically—all that I cared for was a new *named* mineral, and I hardly attempted to classify them. . . . I almost made up my mind to begin collecting all the insects which I could find dead, for on consulting my sister, I concluded that it was not right to kill insects for the sake of making a collection. From reading White's *Selborne* I took much pleasure in watching the habits of birds, and even made notes on the subject. In my simplicity I remember wondering why every gentleman did not become an ornithologist. (*DA* 45)

Naming himself rock hound, entomologist, and ornithologist, the evolving scientist is developing wider interests. These various scientific roles illustrate the potential, or "possibility," of the mature scientist and, as varied and unfocused as they are, prepare the reader to believe the "proof"4 of the scientist that Darwin provides in the *Autobiography*.

While Darwin often fails to take these superior scientific interests and abilities seriously (and realizes them only in retrospect), others recognize his potential early on. In addition to being invited regularly to Cambridge botany professor Henslow's home, he is afforded numerous other opportunities to converse with the great scientists of the day.

> Looking back, I infer that there must have been something in me a little superior to the common run of youths, otherwise the above-mentioned men, so much older than me and higher in academical position, would never have allowed me to associate with them. Certainly I was not aware of any such superiority, and I remember one of my sporting friends, Turner, who saw me at work on my beetles, saying that I should some day be a Fellow of the Royal Society, and the notion seemed to me preposterous. (*DA* 67)

Thus, in the seeming confusion of a multitude of random scientific interests, the scientist is developing, meeting other scientific minds through both reading and personal contact, and strengthening his interests in the pursuit of science. All these transformations occur before the famous voyage of the *Beagle* in 1831. On the *Beagle* voyage Darwin experiences other such evolvings: he changes from the random pursuit of a multitude of scientific interests to dedicated commitment to the natural sciences, from casual storyteller to scientific journalist, from "Barbarian" to a "gentleman of science," and, most significantly, from an "evolutionary suspicion" to belief in evolutionary theory.

Novice Naturalist

On getting the "travel bug" from reading Humboldt's *Personal Narrative*, with its glorious descriptions of Teneriffe, Darwin makes plans for passage there. His travel plans are quickly altered when he receives word from John Henslow that "Captain Fitz-Roy was willing to give up part of his own cabin to any young man who would volunteer to go with him without pay as naturalist to the Voyage of the *Beagle*" (*DA* 71). The ship was making a three-year voyage around the world (which turned out to be five) to produce map surveys of crops in the new world, chart the coast line, and collect indigenous flora and fauna. It appears that Robert Fitz-Roy, the twenty-six-year-old captain of the *Beagle*, being the son of Lord Charles Fitz-Roy and grandson of the duke of Grafton, did not care to mix with the lowly crew. Robert, fearful that this self-induced isolation might lead to suicide, invites Darwin on the voyage. Since Darwin is from a "good" family, Fitz-Roy hopes he will make an acceptable dinner companion. Yet Darwin almost "misses the boat." First, his father opposes the voyage, and his Uncle Josiah (the "requisite man of common sense, who advises you to go" [*DA* 71]) must convince the senior Darwin to consent to the trip. It is Darwin's nose, however, that turns out to be the greatest obstacle to his making the voyage. In another anecdotal passage he describes the incident:

> Afterwards on becoming very intimate with Fitz-Roy, I heard that I had run a very narrow risk of being rejected, on account of the shape of my nose! He was an ardent disciple of Lavater, and was convinced that he could judge a man's character by the outline of his features; and he doubted whether anyone with my nose could possess sufficient energy and determination for the voyage. But I think he was afterwards well-satisfied that my nose had spoken falsely. (*DA* 72)

Humorous accounts of this sort fill the *Autobiography;* Darwin, like his father, loved to tell stories, and these anecdotes convey the qualities of humor and general goodwill in the Darwin persona. The "nose" anecdote, in particular, provides a contrast between the Fitz-Roy and Darwin personae. Darwin sees Fitz-Roy's impressionistic correlation of physical features with personal attributes as standing in opposition to his own more scientific explanations for things.

On 27 December 1831, after repeated delay, the *Beagle* sails away from Plymouth. For five years Charles Darwin explores the "wonders of the world," making reference to a childhood book that inspired his first "wish to travel to foreign countries": St. Jago with its white and hard-baked rock of lava and sea shells, the Tropics with their glorious vegetation, the great deserts of Patagonia, the forest-clad mountains of Tierra del Fuego, naked "savages," coral reefs and islands, St. Helena, the Galapagos archipelago, and South America (*DA* 80–81). Darwin wastes not a minute; he immediately immerses himself in serious investigation. He attributes various accomplishments on the voyage to

> the habit of energetic industry and of concentrated attention to whatever I was engaged in, which I then acquired. Everything about which I

thought or read was made to bear directly on what I had seen and was likely to see; and this habit of mind was continued during the five years of the voyage. I feel sure that it was this training which has enabled me to do whatever I have done in science. (*DA* 78)

The voyage provides the training the young scientist needs in order to pursue the study of the transmutation of species for the next twenty years. It is on the voyage that naive delight in anything near at hand is replaced by a mature and purposeful investigation of the natural phenomena that Darwin encounters. Darwin changes from a boy in random pursuit of a multitude of scientific interests to a young man dedicated to the study of natural science.

As far as I can judge of myself I worked to the utmost during the voyage from the mere pleasure of investigation, and from my strong desire to add a few facts to the great mass of facts in natural science. But I was also ambitious to take a fair place among scientific men. (*DA* 80–81)

In addition to the focusing of his scientific interests on the *Beagle* voyage, Darwin describes a second evolving; he begins to take greater care in documenting his observations.

During some part of the day I wrote my Journal, and took much pains in describing carefully and vividly all that I had seen; and this was good practice. My Journal served, also, in part as letters to my home. (*DA* 78)

In fact, some of these very journal letters were passed on by his father to John Henslow, who read them at the Philosophic Society of Cambridge in 1835 and made quite a reputation for Darwin even before he returned from the voyage. It is no wonder that Darwin later relates that he owes to the *Beagle* voyage "the first real training or education of my mind" (*DA* 77). This training in scientific practice is one more transformation in Darwin's evolution as a scientist. He is changed from observer to investigator, from casual storyteller to scientific journalist.

As further proof of his evolving professionalism, Darwin relates a third instance of change in his scientific character during the voyage.

During the first two years [of the *Beagle* voyage] my old passion for shooting survived in nearly full force, and I shot myself all the birds and animals for my collection; but gradually I gave up my gun more and more, and finally altogether to my servant, as shooting interfered with my work, more especially with making out the geological structure of a country. I discovered, though unconsciously and insensibly, that the pleasure of observing and reasoning was a much higher one than that of skill and sport. The primeval instincts of the barbarian slowly yielded to the acquired tastes of the civilized man. (*DA* 78–79)

Darwin gives up his dearest pastime for his profession. His commitment to the practice of science displaces his love of hunting. The "idle sportsman" becomes a dedicated researcher; the "barbarian" becomes a gentleman of science. Darwin's father is to be particularly impressed with this change, since he had once told the young boy, "You care for nothing but shooting, dogs, and rat-catching, and you will be a disgrace to yourself and all your family" (*DA* 28).

The final evolving of the scientist during the *Beagle* voyage, from sus-picion to belief, is discussed at length in the next section, here only in so much detail as to indicate the change in Darwin's quality of mind, from that of suspicion to belief. Darwin takes with him on the voyage an "evo-lutionary suspicion." Like many men of science at this time, he "suspects" that species have a capacity for change. He returns from the *Beagle* voy-age with a belief in an evolutionary theory. This belief is confirmed by his reading of Lyell's *Principles* and his careful investigation of the plant and animal life and the geological formations along the voyage. It will take Darwin another twenty years to work out the theory and prepare it for publication.

From observer to investigator, from storyteller to journalist, from bar-barian to gentleman of science, from suspicion to belief, Charles Darwin undergoes a multiplicity of changes aboard the *Beagle,* concluding with one he hardly expects; on disembarking from the *Beagle* in 1836, he recalls:

> That my mind became developed through my pursuits during the voyage, is rendered probable by a remark made by my father, who was the most acute observer whom I ever saw, of a skeptical disposition, and far from being a believer in phrenology; for on first seeing me after the voyage, he turned round to my sisters and exclaimed, "Why, the shape of his head is quite altered." (*DA* 79)

This anecdote, like the others, conveys the characteristic humor in the Dar-win persona. It also shows the qualities of a dutiful and respectful son who refuses to take himself or his father too seriously. It is necessary that the father validate Darwin's transformation, for, if the father blesses, a significant transit has been accomplished: the child has become a man, a man of science, and, to go with the other alterations, an altered head!

Mature Scientist

After the *Beagle* voyage and a short stay in London the newly acclaimed naturalist marries and takes a quiet residence in Down, avoids unnecessary company, and settles into the life of a researcher. As indicative of the gradual transformation that has taken place in Darwin's life, compare the scientist quietly at work in Down with the earlier rowdy college student of Cambridge. First at Cambridge:

> Although as we shall presently see there were some redeeming features in my life at Cambridge, my time was sadly wasted there and worse than wasted. . . . I got into a sporting set, including some dissipated low-minded young men. . . . we sometimes drank too much, with jolly singing and playing at cards afterwards. . . . I also got into a musical set. . . . From associating with these men and hearing them play, I acquired a strong taste for music, and used very often to time my walks so as to hear on week days the anthem in King's College Chapel. This gave me intense pleasure, so that my backbone would sometimes shiver . . . and I sometimes hired the chorister boys to sing in my rooms. (*DA* 60–61)

Then at Down:

> Few persons can have lived a more retired life than we have done. Besides short visits to the houses of relations, and occasionally to the seaside or elsewhere, we have gone nowhere. . . . My chief enjoyment and sole employment throughout life has been scientific work; and the excitement from such work makes me for the time forget, or drives quite away, my daily discomfort. (*DA* 115)

Here, again, more evidence for the evolution of the scientist: the young, rowdy student, through a series of evolvings, has become a quiet, committed, and mature scientist. Dinner parties and social gatherings are replaced by attention to research and writing. This work provides such fulfillment that Darwin is distracted from the pain of his long-running struggle with ill health.

One other set of illustrations provides proof of the changes that have occurred in Darwin's practice of science.

> One little event this year has fixed itself very firmly in my mind, and I hope that it has done so from my conscience having been afterwards sorely troubled by it; it is curious as showing that apparently I was interested at this early age in the variability of plants! I told another little boy (I believe

it was Leighton, who afterwards became a well-known Lichenologist and botanist) that I could produce variously coloured Polyanthuses and Primroses by watering them with certain coloured fluids, which was of course a monstrous fable, and had never been tried by me. (*DA* 23)

Contrast this anecdote from Darwin's youth to the following passage from his later years:

I may mention that I keep from thirty to forty large portfolios, in cabinets with labelled shelves, into which I can at once put a detached reference or memorandum. I have bought many books and at their ends I make an index of all the facts that concern my work; or, if the book is not my own, write out a separate abstract, and of such abstracts I have a large drawer full. Before beginning on any subject I look to all the short indexes and make a general and classified index, and by taking the one or more proper portfolios I have all the information collected during my life ready for use. (*DA* 137–38)

The serious and determined tone in this last passage is in definite contrast to the "monstrous fable" about the primroses. And yet the language of the primrose passage suggests that Darwin was (at an early age) interested in the "variability of plants" and was embarrassed that he had not applied rigorous scientific method to his primrose experiment. In his youth he had created a fable in place of an experiment, but this lively interest in variation evolves into serious professional concern. The evolution of the scientist continues throughout his lifetime; Darwin never ceases his scientific efforts. Up to the very end he is rethinking, revising his ideas and his writings. In a letter to J. S. Hooker (1869), which has been copied on the flyleaf of the *Autobiography,* Darwin confides:

If I lived twenty more years and was able to work, how I should have to modify the Origin, and how much the views on all points will have to be modified! Well it is a beginning, and that is something.

As final proof of the scientist, Darwin lists, in the style of a cataloger, all the works he has produced, accompanying each listing with a brief description of the work, indicating the length of time he took to complete each one, and relating the number of copies sold. From the first published work in 1844, *Journal of Researches* (the observations from the *Beagle* voyage), to the final contribution in 1881, *The Formation of Vegetable Mould through the Action of Worms,* Darwin shows himself to be a thorough researcher and scientist who continues productive writing, despite ill health, into the very last years of his life (*DA* 116–39). Darwin closes the *Autobiography:*

> Therefore, my success as a man of science, whatever this may have amounted to, has been determined, as far as I can judge, by complex and diversified mental qualities and conditions. Of these the most important have been—the love of science—unbounded patience in long reflecting over any subject—industry in observing and collecting facts—and a fair share of invention as well as of common-sense. With such moderate abilities as I possess, it is truly surprising that thus I should have influenced to a considerable extent the beliefs of scientific men on some important points. (*DA* 144–45)

The "man of science" is both complex and industrious. Childlike in his love of science and invention, mature in his patience, common sense, and industry, Darwin brings the zeal of the boyish beetle collector into the work of his mature years.

Darwin characterizes himself, in these mature years as he writes his autobiography, as "attempt[ing] to write as if I were a dead man in another world looking back at my own life" (*DA* 21). While we as readers may be somewhat surprised by Darwin's phrase "in another world," since his evolutionary claims appear to have no truck with "other worlds" for the dead, we recognize that the reflexive persona of the *Autobiography,* the "dead man," is a rhetorically constituted observer who, looking at the "evidence," develops the "proof" of the scientist—before and after, zealous youth and acclaimed naturalist. *Dead man* and *another world* may then be seen not as backsliding on Darwin's part but, rather, as Darwin's attempt to construct an unbiased, distanced "myself" to present the narrative of his scientific transformation.

How Things Develop: Evolution as Figura for Scientific Transformation

In contrast to narratives, like Mill's, that are shaped by a singular, onetime conversion experience, Charles Darwin characterizes his narrative of transformation from beetle collector to mature scientist as a number of spontaneous discoveries and insights. He sees his development, while incremental, as having a random quality. Nor does he inscribe his narrative in catastrophic terms; the metaphors and figures Darwin uses to record the maturing of his mind and his development as a scientist suggest that a gradual, yet spontaneous, transformation is occurring. Time and again we read:

"It at once struck me." (*DA* 120)
"It then first dawned on me." (*DA* 81)
"Nevertheless I made one interesting little discovery." (*DA* 50)
"I . . . instantly rushed off to communicate my surprising discovery to him." (*DA* 66)
"But I was then utterly astonished." (*DA* 60)
"I can remember the very spot in the road whilst in my carriage, when to my joy the solution occurred to me." (*DA* 120–21)
"I have become a little more skillful in guessing right explanations and in devising experimental tests." (*DA* 136)
"One little event this year has fixed itself very firmly in my mind." (*DA* 23)
"My love for science gradually preponderated over every other taste." (*DA* 78)

The acclaimed naturalist looking back over his life sees himself as having evolved as a scientist, growing a little more skillful in "guessing right explanations" and his "love of science gradually preponderating" over all his other interests and involvements. "Evolution" serves well as figura for specifying the unique features of Darwin's transformation from beetle collector to acclaimed naturalist. For Darwin to come to the place where he could perceive his own development as evolutionary and characterize his transformation in other than crisis/conversion terms, however, was not easy. He would begin with an evolutionary suspicion of how plants and animals of the natural world achieve their present forms, confirm that suspicion, discover the mechanism for this transmutation, write the *Origin,* and, finally, inscribe his own life change experiences in evolutionary terms.

In 1831 when Darwin sailed off on the *Beagle,* he took with him only an evolutionary suspicion about the natural world but no sense of his own evolving as a scientist. His evolutionary suspicion was derived, in part, from his grandfather, Erasmus, who had presented a theory of generation or descent in the *Zoonomia* over sixty years earlier (1796). Although Darwin discounted his grandfather's work because of its highly speculative nature, it is likely that it served to introduce him to the notion of evolution at a very early age. Perhaps he thought of it as "wild theorizing,"[5] or perhaps he might have completed the *Origin* much sooner had he been able to discuss the project with his grandfather. Since the *Autobiography* provides no answer, we can only say that what Charles got from Erasmus was evolutionary suspicion, a serious predilection toward an evolutionary theory.

It is on the voyage that the evolutionary suspicion changes to confirmation. He attributes much of this confirmation to the reading of Lyell's *Principles of Geology.*

> The science of Geology is enormously indebted to Lyell—more so, as I believe, than to any other man who ever lived. When I was starting on the voyage of the *Beagle,* the sagacious Henslow . . . advised me to get and study the first volume of the *Principles,* which had then just been published, but on no account to accept the views therein advocated. . . . I am proud to remember that the first place, namely St. Jago, in the Cape Verde Archipelago, which I geologised, convinced me of the infinite superiority of Lyell's views over those advocated in any other work known to me. (*DA* 101)

Lyell's *Principles* and Darwin's application of them in the field convince him of the notion of evolution—that species do have the capacity for change—but that is not what concerns Darwin for the next twenty-three years (and throughout the rest of his life, in one way or another). He is convinced of evolution, but what he seeks to do is discover the mechanism of the evolutionary process: What causes variation? To what can evolution be attributed beyond the innate capacities of the species?

In 1838 Darwin discovers the possibility of a mechanism for his evolution, but it is over twenty years later, in 1859, that he finally publishes his theory of evolution in *The Origin of Species.*

> In October 1838, that is, fifteen months after I had begun my systematic enquiry, I happened to read for amusement Malthus on *Population.* . . . It at once struck me that under these circumstances favourable variations would tend to be preserved, and unfavourable ones to be destroyed. The result of this would be the formation of new species. Here, then, I had at last got a theory by which to work. (*DA* 120)

Reading Malthus gives Darwin the notion that food supply might well be one element of the mechanism of evolution. If the food supply expands arithmetically and population grows geometrically, then there must be some sort of selection process tied to the animal's ability to survive in the face of scarcity. Those species survive and reproduce that can access the limited food supply. Thus, unlike his contemporaries, who thought of evolution with little interest in the mechanism,[6] or today's readers, who think of evolution simply as slow, gradual change, when Darwin speaks of evolution in the *Origin,* or when he describes his own development as evolutionary, he is positing a process that includes both the notion of the transmutation of species and the mechanism for that transformation. In attempting to explain evolution and its mechanism, Darwin uses terms that are metaphorical: *natural selection, struggle, insular economy, survival of the fittest*. It is because he uses language that is familiar and accessible to his audience that he is often criticized for being less than scientifically rigorous. An excerpt from the first version of *The Origin*, the *Sketch of 1842*, is an early example of Darwin's anthropomorphic explanation of development.

> What a struggle between the several kinds of trees must here have gone on during long centuries, each annually scattering its seeds by the thousand; what war between insect and insect—between insects, snails, and other animals with birds and beasts of prey—all striving to increase, and all feeding on each other or on the trees or their seeds and seedlings, or on the other plants which first clothed the ground and thus checked the growth of the trees![7]

In the *Sketch* and the *Essay of 1844* Darwin refers to a *selecting being* "infinitely more sagacious than man," an obvious personification of natural selection. In the instances of the "struggle of the trees," "the War of the insects," and the "being infinitely more sagacious than man" Darwin is creating a vocabulary to explain a unique process; he is employing metaphor to present his case for evolution. The final version of the *Origin* is much less anthropomorphic and "poetic," but Darwin does not refrain entirely from the use of metaphor in proposing his evolutionary theory. Evolution is presented as a complex of metaphors that interact so as to provide the possibility for the proof of the theory.

Edward Manier, drawing on Mary Hesse's work on scientific inference and metaphor, argues that the metaphors of "a being more sagacious than man," the "insular economy," and the "struggle for existence" are necessary to the theory of evolution. He orders their functions into five categories: (1) critical-persuasive, (2) heuristic, (3) semantic, (4) explanatory, and (5) affective. Darwin's metaphors persuade readers away from opposing theories by carrying "suggestive echoes of those positions he seeks to supplant." The heuristic function of the metaphors joins "explanatory fictions with available information in order to organize and make plausible the search for additional 'laws' and conditions which might explain the transmutation of the species." The semantic function "contribute[s] to a new scientific vocabulary, and through it, to a new way of describing and perceiving nature." The explanatory function of the metaphors of selection, insular economy, and struggle set up the possibility for the testing and collecting of data, so that the randomness of the "sagacious selector" is checked by the insular economy and the struggle for existence. Finally, the affective function of the metaphors serves to resolve conflicts in the community of scientists and masks problematic implications of evolutionary theory for the public.[8]

In sum, evolution, for Darwin, is more than an innate capacity for change in the species; it includes the mechanism for the transformation within its theory. This mechanism is described by a set of metaphorical phrases that have cognitive *and* affective significance. The metaphors function so as to make the proof of the theory more probable and plausible. Darwin's theory of evolution is composed of and rests on a network of images or metaphors that encapsulate the transformation narrative—natural selection, a being more sagacious than man, insular economy, and struggle for existence. *Evolution,* or Darwin's term, *transmutation,* is itself a metaphor for transformation—of species and for Darwin's own development.

If evolution were a "revolutionary" term for nonrevolutionary change in Darwin's day, several other meanings have accrued to the term over time that may distort our understanding of the figura of evolution in the *Autobiography.* *Evolution* has come to stand as a general term for any kind of non-revolutionary transformation. We speak of a poem evolving for the writer. Linguists suggest that language evolves; at present it is becoming more simplified, with fewer verb endings (or is it becoming more complex with whole new vocabularies for fields of specialization?). Political scientists point to some countries in which revolution is occurring and to others in which new political systems are evolving. Psychologists work with clients whose personalities are evolving, and they maintain that all of us are changing, adapting to our circumstances every day, hour, minute. Sociologists point to evolving cultures; they may speak of a shift to a matrilinear society or the gradual breakup of community values. These few instances, among many others, suggest that we employ the metaphor of evolution in a variety of ways. We most often ignore the aspect of *mechanism* in these descriptions; we do not attempt to qualify *evolution* in the sense that Darwin did. We have used the term so freely that the verb *evolve* has come to have more power for us than the noun *evolution* had for Darwin. It has come to stand for any ongoing, continuous change.

All of this is to say that if we make the statement "Darwin evolved as a scientist" to describe his transformation, we are, as present-day readers, generally not getting at the full sense of *evolution* that Darwin uses to explain change in the natural world and in his own life narrative. The maturation of Darwin's thinking, and the possibility and proof of his development as a scientist from the perspective of the figura of evolution, requires Darwin's expanded sense of *evolution* as it implies innate capacity, mechanism, and ongoing transformation. Evolution is the *Autobiography*'s unity; it describes the type of transformation; it is its basis, or ground, and its limits, or range. In Manier's terms the figura of evolution allows for the possibility of the transformation of the young and nonchalant beetle collector to a serious scientist. The first instances of scientific potential in the young scientist are found in Darwin's tales of his naive scientific practice. They are so unobtrusive as to be discounted as boyish junk collecting. At the age of eight Charles Darwin was sent to day school in Shrewsbury.

> By the time I went to this day-school my taste for natural history, and more especially for collecting, was well developed. I tried to make out the names of plants, and collected all sorts of things, shells, seals, franks, coins, and minerals. The passion for collecting, which leads a man to be a systematic naturalist, a virtuoso or a miser, was very strong in me, and was very clearly innate, as none of my sisters or brother ever had this taste. (*DA* 22–23)

The potential is evident: the interest in scientific pursuits and the possibility of the future scientist are visible at the young age of eight. Add to this anecdote the numerous tales of youthful collecting, experiencing, and observing everything in the purview of youthful eyes, and we see Darwin piling up possibilities for the evolution of the scientist. The mature scientist is observing the youthful scientist evolve. Within the figura of evolution we are also provided the proof of the transformation, with Darwin's descriptions of the mature scientist at work. They show how his process of change is ongoing, continuing throughout the life. The narrative demonstrates how he never ceases in the development of his mind or in the pursuit of his profession in science. Near the end of the *Autobiography* he writes:

> On the favorable side of the balance, I think that I am superior to the common run of men in noticing things which easily escape attention, and in observing them carefully. . . . From my early youth I have had the strongest desire to understand or explain whatever I observed, —that is, to group all facts under some general laws. These causes combined have given me the patience to reflect or ponder for any number of years over any unexplained problem. . . . I have steadily endeavoured to keep my mind free, so as to give up any hypothesis, however much beloved . . . as

soon as facts are shown to be opposed to it. . . . I cannot remember a single first-formed hypothesis which had not after a time to be given up or greatly modified. (*DA* 140–41)

This extensive excerpt and many others provide proof of the scientist as they point to the gradual and continuous development of Darwin's scientific mind, his innate capacity for science, "superior to the common run of men in noticing things . . . and in observing them," and in his dedication to scientific practice.

We could say, then, that from the perspective of the figura of evolution (following Manier) Darwin's life narrative, like the *Origin*, is shaped by possibility and proof of the evolution of the scientist. The possibility section is more metaphorical and, I would add what Manier excludes, more anecdotal. These anecdotal passages function much like the metaphors, having critical-persuasive, heuristic, scientific, explanatory, and affective roles. We might surmise that Darwin felt both stories—his narrative of the origin of species and the narrative of his own transformation—were too "big," too overwhelming, for his readers. The anecdotal style sets up the possibility of the great scientist and of one of the greatest scientific discoveries, by breaking the "big possibility" into many "little possibilities," or anecdotes. If one narrative is too big, then perhaps many little narratives and networks of images and metaphors may prepare the reader to accept the proof that Darwin provides at the end of the *Autobiography,* for the full maturing of the scientist, and in the second section of the *Origin,* for proof of the evolution of species.

The proof sections of the two works are more objective in character. As with the *Origin,* the proof section of the *Autobiography* provides data, listing times when Darwin has given up old views, reporting events that have led to new hypotheses, enumerating his cataloging and collecting system, and documenting articles and books that he has published.

Spanning the anecdote of the eight-year-old Shrewsbury day school student and the "hard evidence" of the mature and reflective scientist, the *Autobiography* is filled with instances of Darwin's evolutionary development. Still and all, evolution—in its scientific sense, in which those species survive and reproduce that are best adapted to changes in the environment and that will reproduce or outbreed other less well-adapted species in the struggle for survival—is metaphorical in a different way than the figura for Darwin's transformation. Darwin is not a species; his is not a slow, gradual change over centuries or eons. Rather, his is a transformation configured as evolution in the sense that his innate capacities for science interact with the environment in a time and a place that are right for the appearance of an evolutionary scientist. The multiple, random instances of transformation provide the possibility and proof that the youthful persona was ever changing, adapting to the endlessly new, "deviating indefinitely," growing as a scientist. The mechanism, or power, for Darwin's transformation will be detailed in the "Dynamis" section.

The Dynamis of "Zeal and Environment"

The transformation that Charles Darwin narrates in his *Autobiography* is from beetle collector to acclaimed naturalist. The figura of evolution serves to illuminate the characteristics of the persona of the scientist (novice and professional) and provides the metaphor for this transformation in the text. Viewing Darwin's *Autobiography* from the perspective of the dynamis may help us see how we get from beetle collector to naturalist, how we come to understand the power to which transformation is attributed in the text. As Darwin himself puts it, "But passing over the endless beautiful adaptations which we everywhere meet with, it may be asked how can the generally beneficent arrangement of the world be accounted for?" (*DA* 88).

Darwin was posing his question with regard to the variation of the species. The question is posed here with respect to Darwin himself. In the "Figura" section care was taken to articulate what Darwin meant by evolution: a process of gradual, noncatastrophic transformation requiring species with innate capacities for transformation *and* an environmental selection mechanism. Darwin understood one dynamic aspect of change— the innate capacity for change or variation in species. Following the *Beagle* voyage, he spent another twenty years working to understand the other— the environmental mechanism. We are at a similar juncture. The innate scientific potential in the Darwin persona has been identified; what is needed is to discover the mechanism, or dynamis, of transformation within the figura of evolution.

To phrases like "my love for science gradually preponderated over every other taste" and "when to my joy the solution occurred to me," cited earlier, could be added: "the habit of energetic industry and of concentrated attention," "proof of my zeal," "pursuit . . . followed . . . with eagerness," "strong and diversified tastes," "much zeal for whatever interested me," "I gloried in the progress of Geology" (*DA* 78, 62, 43, 33). These are but a few of numerous textual references to Darwin's dynamic capacity for transformation in the *Autobiography*. If, however, we attend to Darwin's own meaning for evolution, what is still needed is an environmental mechanism to interact with this innate capacity, or "zeal." Darwin sees the environment as dynamic and attributes the dynamis of transformation in his own life to both internal and external forces—his zeal for science and a dynamic world circumstance. It is only through the interaction of the two that Darwin's evolution can be, to use Manier's phrase, "rendered probable."

The environment for Darwin's theory of evolution, as posited in the *Origin*, was one of "wonderfully complex and changing circumstances" (*DA* 90); the environment that surrounded Darwin's own life was much the same. Manier defines Darwin's notion of environment as not "a mere geographic site or station" but, rather, "a matrix of possibilities for life—a matrix which is itself a function of the vital activities of still other organisms . . . as opportunities which call for coadaptation."[9] What were the "matrix of possibilities for life" (we might substitute "for the scientist") in Darwin's environment? What constituted his "wonderfully complex and changing circumstances?" The text of the *Autobiography* points to numerous elements that make up the environment for the scientist. They are considered here under the general categories of the family, the scientific community, and the natural world.

The Dynamic Environment of Family Life

The first and most obvious environmental possibility for the development of the scientist is Darwin's own family and its scientific interests and pursuits. His father, Robert Darwin, is a commonsense man of science, a doctor.

> My father's mind was not scientific, and he did not try to generalise his knowledge under general laws; yet he formed a theory for almost everything which occurred. (*DA* 42)

Here Darwin is speaking not of "inherited traits" but, rather, of day-to-day family activities and behaviors. Darwin's father is a practical man who takes an anecdotal approach to the medical profession. He regularly relates humorous professional stories to his son, and Darwin includes a number of them in the *Autobiography*. It is this practical man who exemplifies the dedicated professional to his son.

Grandfather Erasmus, also a physician, is the speculative scientist who proposes a theory of generation or descent in 1796. Though he dies (1802) before Charles is born (1809), we can imagine that there was a clearly established tradition of scientific discussion in the family home. While Darwin was unable to engage in discussions with Erasmus directly, he did have his grandfather's writings: *Zoonomia, The Botanic Garden, Phytologia,* and his volumes of notes. Darwin discounts their effect on him but suggests that "it is probable that the hearing rather early in life such views maintained and praised may have favoured my upholding them under a different form in my *Origin of Species"* (*DA* 49).

Family wealth and status are also critical factors in Darwin's environment. They make possible his participation in the voyage of the *Beagle* as ship's naturalist and Darwin's association with men of science, both at family social events and in England's best schools. While his father considers him quite lazy and without clear professional goals, the family wealth and status ensure that Darwin can devote his life to scientific pursuits without the need to earn a living from his work.

The Dynamic Environment of the Scientific Community
Once out of the family home and upon entering the university, Darwin has an opportunity to encounter many extraordinary scientific minds, yet he insists that his college years were of no value to his development. He recalls that "during the three years which I spent at Cambridge my time was wasted, as far as the academical studies were concerned, as completely as at Edinburg and at school" (*DA* 58). Math was "repugnant"; in classics he attended only compulsory lectures. Public science lectures were voluntary, "but I was so sickened with lectures at Edinburgh that I did not even attend Sedgwick's eloquent and interesting lectures" (*DA* 59–60).

In spite of his condemnation of his academic endeavors, Darwin's college years were not wasted. The university was the place where his lifelong associations with men of science began. Among these scientists the most notable and significant, so far as the *Autobiography* indicates, are Henslow, Lyell, Sedgwick, Hooker, and Huxley.

John Stevens Henslow was a professor of botany at Cambridge and the man to whom Darwin attributes the greatest influence on his career. He cataloged British plants (1829) and wrote a dictionary of botanical terms (1857). He also had an extensive knowledge of entomology, chemistry, mineralogy, and geology. Henslow is responsible for arranging Darwin's first geological tour around Shrewsbury with Sedgwick, for getting Darwin the position on the *Beagle,* for sending him off with a copy of Lyell's *Principles of Geology* (1830) to read during the voyage, and for introducing Darwin's letters from the *Beagle* to the Philosophical Society of Cambridge.

Sir Charles Lyell, English geologist, was another contributor to Darwin's "wonderfully complex" environment. Lyell's *Principles* provided the form for Darwin's own writing and the methodological approach for his scientific investigations.

Adam Sedgwick, professor of geology at Cambridge, took Darwin on his first geological "field trip," giving him practice assignments that were of no use to his own research but were instruction in scientific practice for the young scientist. It was Sedgwick who first announced to Darwin's father, on the occasion of Charles's successful return from the *Beagle* voyage, that he could "take a place among the leading scientific men" (*DA* 81).

Joseph Hooker's place in Charles Darwin's environment was as "one of my best friends through life." Hooker was an English botanist who researched the geographical distribution of plants. He supported Darwin in the *Origin* controversy, and it was he who, along with Lyell, strongly urged Darwin to get the essay on transmutation of the species into print before Wallace. *The Origin of Species* was finally published in November 1859.

Novice scientists must be taught if they are to develop. They must also be sheltered and supported. This appears to be Thomas Huxley's role in Darwin's environment. The English biologist and educator was Darwin's mentor in science.

> He has been a most kind friend to me and would always take any trouble for me. He has been the mainstay in England of the principle of the gradual evolution of organic beings. Much splendid work as he has done in Zoology, he would have done far more, if his time had not been so largely consumed by official and literary work, and by his efforts to improve the education of the country. (*DA* 106)

It was Huxley who took it upon himself to make the Victorians aware of the need for science in the education of their young people. He defended scientific methodology even to the English courts.

Charles Darwin's *Autobiography* is filled with references to these and other men of science. They are spoken of with fondness and respect. They appear, like Darwin himself, to be men of integrity, committed to the practice of science. They function as "opportunity for coadaptation." As they influenced, challenged, and supported him, he did the same for them. They made for a dynamic intellectual community in Darwin's environment. As a member of this community of scientists, Darwin possessed a "burning zeal to add even the most humble contribution to the noble structure of Natural Science" (*DA* 68). He explains how he added his contribution.

> It has sometimes been said that the success of *The Origin* proved "that the subject was in the air," or "that men's minds were prepared for it." I do not think that this is strictly true, for I occasionally sounded not a few naturalists, and never happened to come across a single one who seemed to doubt about the permanence of the species. Even Lyell and Hooker, though they would listen with interest to me, never seemed to agree. I tried once or twice to explain to able men what I meant by natural selection, but signally failed. What I believe was strictly true is that innumerable well-observed facts were stored in the minds of naturalists, ready to take their proper places as soon as any theory which would receive them was sufficiently explained. (*DA* 123–24)

Darwin employs the evolutionary *figura* once again; here he uses it to explain how scientists take up "new" science. "Innumerable, well observed facts" stored in the minds of scientists might be seen as similar to an innate capacity; the arrival of a theory that would order and explain the facts of evolution might be seen as the trigger or mechanism.

If the times were right for Darwin's explanation of his evolutionary theory, they were also right for the transformation of a scientist characterized by an evolutionary metaphor. Grandfather Erasmus Darwin had postulated a theory of descent sixty years earlier; his speculative theory was rejected, and he was, by and large, ignored as a man of science. It was to wait for the discoveries of the grandson for the idea of evolution to take hold and for a member of the Darwin family to establish his theory and his place within the scientific community. As Robert K. Merton has indicated:

> It is the absolute number of such inventors, rather than their proportion to the entire population, which is of primary significance for the rate of innovation. But, on the other hand, the mere number of "potential" inventors (i.e., individuals who have the capacity for invention) will not notably affect the rate of invention unless there is free communication between the inventors, a system of cultural values which places a high estimation upon innovation and an accumulation of knowledge which is at the ready disposal of the would-be inventors.[10]

The scientists who peopled Darwin's environment meet Merton's criteria for effecting innovation. From Darwin's own account they are in "free [and supportive] communication," and they place high value on innovation and the accumulation of knowledge, which they readily put at Darwin's disposal.

The Dynamic Environment of the Natural World

The natural world is the scene of Darwin's scientific investigation and evolutionary theory. He discusses its interdependencies and struggles in the *Origin*.

> A plant on the edge of the desert is said to struggle for life against the drought, though more properly it should be said to be dependent on the moisture. A plant which annually produces a thousand seeds, of which only one of an average come to maturity, may be more truly said to struggle with the plants of the same and other kinds which already clothe the ground. The mistletoe is dependent on the apple and a few other trees, but can only in a far-fetched sense be said to struggle with these trees, for, if too many of these parasites grow on the same tree, it languishes and dies. But several seedling mistletoes, growing close together on the same branch, may more truly be said to struggle with each other. As the mistletoe is disseminated by the birds, its existence depends on them; and it may methodically be said to struggle with other fruit-bearing plants in tempting the birds to devour and thus disseminate its seeds.[11]

In the *Autobiography* the natural world is, quite obviously, the geographical location of Darwin's work, but it is far more than that. In the text the natural world functions as agency for the transformation of the scientist. For Darwin "the universe is alive." As opposed to the static, unchanging, hierarchical world of his predecessors, it is dynamic. If the study of rocks, birds, beetles, primroses, and gases had interested the young Darwin, geological formations, botanical distribution, and animal variation hold even greater interest for the mature scientist. Darwin's "struggle" with his lively environment is to make sense of it, to investigate it, to find adequate explanations for its changes, and to articulate those explanations effectively to his associates and the society at large. As new areas of scientific investigation open up to him and as he makes new discoveries, he, like the birds that are "tempted by the mistletoe," finds the natural world an irresistible temptation to his scientific mind and zeal.

> He came to the islands [Galapagos] already impressed by the similarity of the extinct armored glyptodonts to their living relative, the armadillo. . . . He had stared at a penguin's wing and had perceived that by certain

modifications a wing could be made to beat its way through either water or air. Was it logical to suppose that all these clever adaptations to circumstance had been plucked out of a vacuum? . . . Did life in some manner respond to the environment? . . . How could climate, about which people talked so glibly, adapt a woodpecker for climbing trees or a hummingbird to probe into a flower?[12]

As Darwin's environmental horizons widen, stretching from Shrewsbury to the Galapagos, and his investigations of the natural world range from the "ova of Flustra" to the *Descent of Man,* it is his zeal that marks his commitment to science. This commitment is even more exemplary when compared with one of Darwin's contemporaries, Philip Henry Gosse, who chose religious conservatism over scientific inquiry.

Sir Edmond Gosse, English literary critic and author of the autobiography *Father and Son,* is only ten years old when Darwin's *The Origin of Species* appears. He tells how Lyell proposed that, "before the doctrine of natural selection was given to a world which would be sure to lift up at it a howl of execration, a certain bodyguard of sound and experienced naturalists, expert in the description of species, should be privately made aware of its tenour."[13] Sir Edmund's father, the naturalist Philip Gosse, was approached by both Hooker and Darwin after meetings of the Royal Society. The senior Gosse, a fairly respected zoologist, was also an ardent adherent of a Protestant sect known as the Plymouth Brethren. Sir Edmund tells us how

> every instinct in his intelligence went out at first to greet the new light. It had hardly done so, when a recollection of the opening chapter of Genesis checked it at the outset. He consulted with Carpenter, a great investigator, but one who was fully as incapable as himself of remodeling his ideas with regard to the old accepted hypothesis. They both determined, on various grounds, to have nothing to do with the terrible theory, but to hold steadily to the law of the fixity of the species.[14]

Philip Gosse writes his own theory to challenge Lyell's geological history of man, "which, as he fondly hopes will take the wind out of Lyell's sails, and justify geology to godly readers of 'Genesis.'"[15] In *Omphalos* Gosse insists that

> there had been no gradual modification of the surface of the earth, or slow development of organic forms, but that when the catastrophic act of creation took place, the world presented, instantly, the structural appearance of a planet on which life had long existed.[16]

The resulting incident is well-known; the *Omphalos* is rejected by both the scientific and Christian communities. Gosse is derided by the press, who take his argument to its logical conclusion: "God hid the fossils in the rocks in order to tempt the geologists into infidelity."[17] Gosse turns his back on the spirit of scientific inquiry, insisting on a catastrophic creation in the face of monumental evidence.

Darwin, unlike the more conservative Gosse, is first and foremost a man of science. Once he surveys the natural world around him he is ready to speculate, to "guess," to imagine. He works diligently in his profession, *and* he ranges outside the norms of religious dogma and scientific treatise. His innate capacity for change (development, transformation) interacts with a dynamic environment in a "wonderfully complex" and marvelous fashion. The "war" between insects and snails astonishes him; he takes "delight" in discovering that mistletoe "tempted" the birds to disseminate its seeds. Neither bean pod nor earthworm escapes his "habit of energetic industry and of concentrated attention." Darwin's *Autobiography* provides us with a new kind of dynamis. It is a dynamis that sees the environment as an active agency in a transformation that is characterized by interdependency and struggle.

6

A Fuller Conception of Life

The Transformation of Margaret Oliphant (1828–97)

Margaret Oliphant Wilson Oliphant was born in Wallyford, Scotland in 1828. She was the youngest child and only daughter of Francis Wilson and Margaret Oliphant and grew up with two brothers, Frank and Willie. Around age sixteen she began a writing career that continued for over fifty years. In 1852, at age twenty-four, she married a cousin on her mother's side, Frank Oliphant, an artist and stained glass designer. Together they had six children, only three of whom survived past infancy. At thirty-one Oliphant was widowed and left with three small children. Her daughter, the eldest of the three, died only four years later. Her two sons, who lived to ages thirty-one and thirty-four, were her greatest joy and her deepest disappointment; bright and well-educated, they were never self-supporting. Oliphant provided the sole support for an extended family, which at times grew to as many as ten persons, by her writing. She survived all of her children, living to the age of sixty-nine. Oliphant is best known for her novel series, *Chronicles of Carlingford*, for the novels *Hester, Kirsteen,* and *Beleaguered City,* and for her criticism, biographies, histories, translations, and travel narratives.

This brief biographical summary of Margaret Oliphant is derived from the first edition of her *Autobiography and Letters.*[1] The edition, completed by her niece Denny Wilson and her cousin Annie Coghill, in 1899, reprinted in two other editions the same year and then again in 1974 and 1978, was a truncated version of her life narrative. Her first editors eliminated over one-fourth of the original manuscript. In these editions Oliphant is "idealized as a hard working mother" who dedicated her life and energies to the support of her extended family through her writing. This view of Oliphant has been furthered by critics (some from her own day and some more recent) who focus on her industry and productivity to the neglect of her professional qualities and characteristics. The Elisabeth Jay edition,[2] published in 1990 (without which we could not speak of Oliphant's different conception of the autobiography), reintroduces the material deleted from the original documents. The first edition (and its subsequent reprints) is a simple linear narrative; Jay's text preserves the chronological sequence of *composition,* rather than adopting the expedient of the 1899 editors, who rearranged the entries to provide a chronological and idealistic view of Oliphant's life. Jay's edition reveals a complex woman with depth of thought and feeling and a range of interests and knowledge who continued to develop her professional expertise throughout her long life. It is on this text that my discussion of Margaret Oliphant's *Autobiography* is based.

Less well known than the three other autobiographers in this study, I include Oliphant because her experiences are representative of a range of attitudes, values, conflicts, and tensions I see as operative in Victorian culture and, in particular, representative of the demands placed on women with professional careers and domestic responsibilities.[3]

Because Oliphant moved in so many different circles, the self of the autobiography is forced to confront aspects of the culture that were rarely faced by her contemporaries, John Henry Newman,[4] John Stuart Mill, or Charles Darwin. Their histories seem little touched by economic deprivation, death, social obligations, household or travel arrangements, or the education of children. Their autobiographies detail professional concerns: theology, politics, science. Similarly, Margaret Oliphant's *Autobiography* details professional concerns—she was a productive, successful writer—but it treats issues beyond those of the Victorian professional; it reports participation in a wider world. And that is why Margaret Oliphant's *Autobiography* serves well as concluding chapter to this text.

A Fuller Conception of Life

Oliphant's participation in a wider world is encapsulated in a statement found early in the *Autobiography:* "I don't suppose my powers are equal to hers [Charlotte Brontë's]—my work to myself looks perfectly pale and colourless beside hers—but yet I have had far more experience and, I think, a fuller conception of life" (*OA* 10). She uses the phrase "fuller conception of life" to explain the relationship between life and art. She sees both Charlotte Brontë, her literary idol, and George Eliot, her contemporary, as leading extremely narrow lives. Provoked into writing her autobiography by reading J. W. Cross's edition of *George Eliot's Life as Related in her Letters and Journals,* Oliphant notes, "I think she must have been a dull woman with a great genius distinct from herself" (*OA* 17). Seeing an even greater genius in Brontë, she is, nonetheless, aware that Brontë rarely journeyed far from her father's isolated parish in the Yorkshire Moors. Oliphant seems to be saying that she is more actively involved in the everyday world than were Brontë and Eliot and that this involvement gives her a fuller understanding of human beings and their actions.

Like Oliphant, I employ the phrase "fuller conception of life" as a means of comparison. I use it, however, in reference to the three other Victorians whose autobiographies are the focus of this study (I reserve the discussion of Oliphant's relationship with the Carlyles for the "Persona" section of the chapter). Newman, Mill, and Darwin each makes his profession central to his life narrative and, thus, limits its horizon to the worldview of the theologian, the political philosopher, and the scientist, respectively. In contrast, Margaret Oliphant's profession constituted only a part of her life and, hence, I contend, her autobiography encompasses a wider, fuller world.

Like Newman's *Apologia,* Oliphant's *Autobiography* is concerned with theological issues. In it she records close friendships with noted theologians of her day—John Tulloch, principal of St. Mary's College, University of St. Andrews, and the liberal Frederick Denison Maurice—and speaks of writing the biography of Edward Irving, the millenarian minister. The *Autobiography* is full of prayers and reflections that register intense doubt and measured faith. While Newman desired nothing more than to join "two luminous beings," his mind and God's, Oliphant speaks of "wild outcries of reluctance, with groans of pain, with remonstrances against God's will" (*OA* 12). Oliphant's anguish bears little resemblance to Newman's more reserved expression. Nevertheless, she felt sufficient spiritual and intellectual kinship to complete an article on Newman for *The Victorian Age of English Literature.*

Oliphant's fuller conception of life also included politics and social reform. Like John Stuart Mill's family, Oliphant's was "tremendously political and Radical, my mother especially and Frank" (*OA* 19–20). They were particularly active in the days of the Anti–Corn Law agitation. Oliphant, then only fourteen, amazed everyone by securing more signatures on the petitions than the "authorised agents." Of this bit of upstaging, she remarks, "I was a tremendous politician in those days" (*OA* 26). The family also became involved in welfare work and distributed relief to the families in the North End of Liverpool.

Another political concern that Oliphant shared with Mill had to do with the rights of women. Merryn Williams suggests that Oliphant has been misrepresented by some critics, who call attention to her statement about

"Stuart Mill and his mad notion of the franchise for women" (*A&L* 211), while disregarding the rest of the letter and much else that Oliphant wrote on the subject. Williams argues that Oliphant's views were complex. She was "not a reactionary; she had much to say about the condition of women in her time." She believed that "the Married Women's Property Act was necessary" and that women could do men's work but that "too much mental work" had caused the loss of two of her babies. Whereas in the 1880s Oliphant acknowledged men's superiority because of their physical strength, a decade later she wrote sympathetically of emancipated young women.[5] And, as Williams points out, Oliphant was "typecast as antifeminist, yet concerned throughout her life with the problems of women."[6] Even if Oliphant found herself at odds with Mill over methods and means, she shared his awareness of the political and social problems facing women.

Oliphant's literary life was a far remove from the scientific pursuits of Charles Darwin, yet in the *Autobiography* she speaks of science with good humor. She records that, while living in Scotland, she took long walks to visit Mrs. Wilson, who advised her to bring up her children on "museums and the broken bread of Science, which I [Margaret] loathed, pointing out to me with triumph how this system had succeeded with her own sons" (*OA* 93). Oliphant understood that science was the passion of her day, and she wrote a number of articles for *Blackwood's Edinburgh Magazine* on the subject.

Margaret Oliphant did not make a reputation for herself in theology, although religious figures were often central characters in her fiction, and she wrote respected works on a number of theologians. Nor did she invest her energies, in her later years, in active political reform, though she did write often on political issues. And she was clearly not involved in scientific pursuits of even an amateur nature, as was the case with many of her Victorian contemporaries, yet she was not unaware of the place of science in her culture and spoke favorably in *Blackwood's* of the biography of Mary Somerville, the Scottish naturalist. Instead, she was a writer whose many literary talents resulted in a large body of fictive and nonfictive writing. If we couple her interests in theology, politics, and science with her family involvement and the associations of a long and productive literary career, we begin to understand how "a fat, little, commonplace woman, rather tongue-tied," can speak of a fuller conception of life (*OA* 17).

If we consider, additionally, that each of Oliphant's professional, social, and family circles had their own sets of conventions and expectations, we can understand the conflicts, ambivalences, and ironies that run through her narrative. What Oliphant discovered was that the more worlds she inhabited the more conventions she must confront and that those conventions were often in conflict. In the section that follows I will show how these conflicting conventions shaped Oliphant's conception of the autobiography in general and the discourse and generic forms of her *Autobiography* in particular.

A Different Conception of Autobiography

Margaret Oliphant's fuller conception of life led her to a unique perspective on autobiography. Between 1881 and 1884 she wrote critical reviews of the autobiographies of Benvenuto Cellini, John Evelyn, Madame Roland, Lord Herbert of Cherbury, Samuel Pepys, Lucy Hutchinson, Alice Thornton, Edward Gibbon, Margaret, duchess of Newcastle, and Cardinal Goldoni. Oliphant introduces each review with a brief critical discussion around a particular theme in autobiographical studies (usually only a page or two): why individuals write autobiographies, what is the value of autobiography, what should autobiography do, and, for Oliphant especially, what is common to the autobiographies of the ordinary and the great. This is followed by Oliphant's lengthy summary of the autobiography itself, loosely constructed around the theme of the introduction.

This work made Oliphant aware of the limits of conventional autobiography and caused her to reject the "professional" model for a fuller account in constructing her own autobiography. She believed that focusing solely on her writing, her professional career, and the methods by which she constructed her characters, developed her plots, or collected her research, would create a distorted autobiography. In fact, she criticized those writers who constructed their autobiographies in this way.[7] In contrast to Newman, Mill, and Darwin, then, Oliphant's fuller conception of autobiography makes her text an appropriate final chapter for my work on Victorian autobiography.

Both Laurie Langbauer and Elisabeth Jay offer convincing analyses of Oliphant's conception of autobiography. Langbauer locates Oliphant's interest in autobiography in the series of articles she wrote on the genre for *Blackwood's*.[8] Langbauer argues that, "no matter their own status or part in the world's extraordinary affairs, what interests all these writers, she [Oliphant] finds, are the most absolute commonplaces."[9] Be they ladies or nursemaids, famous or obscure, Oliphant believed that autobiographers thrust their "own little worlds" into history by relating tales of common everyday events and that they find "their infant or their apple-tree of more importance than the convulsion of nations." Langbauer shows how Oliphant extended the idea of commonplaces to a larger worldview. Linking commonplace details and the realm of politics, the events of everyday life with those of nations, "Oliphant feels that . . . the 'narrowest domestic record' is as 'interesting and instructive as any other part of the perennial drama' of social relations that make up what we call history proper."[10] Langbauer, then, sees Oliphant's conception of the autobiography as centered in the prosaic, the ordinary, and finds this conception closely aligned with Thomas Carlyle's ideas on history and biography.[11]

Whereas Langbauer locates Oliphant's conception of autobiography in the commonplaces, Elisabeth Jay locates it in the "human story" and bases her argument on a passage near the end of the *Autobiography* in which Oliphant instructs:

> If Denny publishes this, or any part of it, she will, of course, or any one else who may have the charge of it, cut out any of these details she pleases. It is not likely that such family details would be of interest to the public. And yet, as a matter of fact, it is exactly those family details that are interesting,—the human story in all its chapters. (*OA* 130)

Jay notes that Oliphant was "appalled" and "astonished" that there were no human stories in the autobiographies of her novelist contemporaries, George Eliot and Anthony Trollope.[12] Jay then argues that "without the human story" Oliphant felt her life would be "incomprehensible." "For she could not, of course, appeal to the single-mindedness of commitment to the artistic life that might produce an autobiography shaped according to the myth of progress that Avrom Fleishman has demonstrated to be so beloved by nineteenth-century male writers."[13] Thus, Jay sees Oliphant's conception of the autobiography as tied to the human, rather than to art, and Oliphant as rejecting a myth of progress for the "bits" and "fragments" (echoes of Carlyle) of a life. Jay concludes her argument by showing how Oliphant's first editors violated her conception of autobiography.

> The editors of her *Autobiography* entirely missed the self-directed irony of her repeatedly expressed conviction in these last years that most people would rather read a cheerful tale of a "simple, busy, happy life" and set to work to delete as much as they could of the most agonizingly self-questioning material since they were unable to see that it was precisely in these passages that she had attempted something new. (*OA* 145)

Jay insists that Oliphant's editors forced her text into the shape of a conventional autobiography by eradicating many of its human elements; she calls the product of their efforts "a desolate Victorian folly."[14]

While wholeheartedly endorsing these factors as sources for Oliphant's conception of autobiography, I add a third: Oliphant's place in Victorian culture. I argue that her place was many places and that these places shaped her ideas of the complex nature of the autobiographical persona and the forms in which she presented the fuller narrative of her life. To say that, for Oliphant a fuller conception of life meant happier or richer, or simply more "involvement," is to miss the full sense of her thinking. The *Autobiography* reveals that her life was full of grievous loss, much anxiety over finances, and hard, taxing work. But her life was full; she lived in the thick of things. And this suggests another, stronger sense of *full* that also shows up in the *Autobiography*. When the life is full, it is also full of conflicting expectations, and those conflicting expectations are the essence of Oliphant's conception of life and life narrative. They are at the heart of the conflicts, ambivalences, and ironies that dominate her autobiographical discourse.

Oliphant's statement that she has had a "great deal of her own way," but at the cost of ceaseless labor and of "carrying a whole little world with me wherever I moved," is telling (*OA* 17). "Carrying a whole little world" encompasses both a fuller conception of life and the expectations that attend moving in many different circles. I see Oliphant's "carrying her whole little world" as more than a little culturally determined. Victorian culture dictated that Oliphant care for and educate her children, and the *Autobiography* records that through "ceaseless labour" she met these expectations. The culture also permitted Oliphant, if grudgingly, to write for profit, but it also required that she live constantly with the tyranny of the Victorian literary marketplace.

The care of her own three children, the adoption of three others, and the "taking in" of various relatives and friends, along with the creation of ninety-eight novels, around fifty short stories, over four hundred critical and review articles, and a number of biographies and travel books, made for a crowded cottage and a long list of expectations.[15] Packing her children, entourage, and writing accoutrements for a trip to Edinburgh or Paris was quite a little world to cart around. Integration of work and family— that elusive dream of today's woman—was not a possibility for Oliphant. Her writing and her family life bumped into each other, rubbed shoulders, and shoved each other for priority of place but were never clearly separated or fully integrated. Because she carried this little world around wherever she went, her writing suffered countless interruptions. Twenty-four different entries written across a thirty-five-year period suggest that she never had "two hours undisturbed" in her whole life (*OA* 30), but it is a remarkable feature of the *Autobiography* that the interruptions also initiate much of the autobiographical discourse. The tragic deaths of her children constitute a major portion of at least twenty of the twenty-four entries.

Contact with the human and the everyday is evident in the structure of Oliphant's life narrative, as well. As a woman's story, Oliphant's autobiography is not "a myth of progress," as Avrom Fleishman characterized the Victorian male autobiography.[16] Rather, it is a "refracted autobiography," composed of "anecdotes and portraits that present her own case obliquely."[17] As Oliphant herself terms it, it is "a prosaic little narrative," initiated, interrupted, generated, and *compromised* by the everyday. And, I argue, it was expressed in generic forms best suited to the ordinary: travel narratives, passages of mourning (eulogies, memorials, and internal dialogues), prayers (pleas and reproaches), and portraits of persons who intersect her many life paths (novelist, biographer, historian, translator, critic, daughter, sister, wife, mother, cousin, aunt).

In sum, the continual weight of her whole little world often wearied Oliphant, but, as is clear from her text, it resulted also in a fuller conception of autobiography and a different form of expression, one that encompassed a wider world—a world of family, travel, theology, politics, *and* literature and their attendant expectations. The *Autobiography* voices the conflicts of Oliphant's fuller life. It records how economic pressures put her in conflict with literary expectations and how these expectations, in turn, put her in conflict with family demands. It speaks of class pressures that put her aristocratic expectations in conflict with her democratic values, of conflicts between "vulgar trade" and art, and between the priorities of her children's privileged education and her own economic status.

Oliphant's conception of life and life narrative led her to replace the masculine Victorian persona of certitude with a feminine persona of amplitude. Her ambivalence toward her own development, personal and professional, caused her to replace the myth of progress evident in the autobiographies of Newman, Darwin, and Mill with a compendium of autobiographical figures and forms appropriate to the "ordinary" rather than the "extraordinary" life. Her refusal to accept easy explanations caused her to take an ironic stance toward the power to which she attributed the changes in her life. I am not yet ready to say that these are features unique to women's autobiographies, but they do set Margaret Oliphant's *Autobiography* apart from those of her Victorian male counterparts. As Langbauer reminds us, for Oliphant "not having everything worked out is generative";[18] and, as Oliphant herself would tell us, "There was no other way."

"Breadwinner" or "A Bigger Me"?
Conflicting Roles and the Oliphant Persona

Margaret Oliphant interrogates and problematizes the autobiographical persona as she presents her life narrative. The certitude about the persona that is manifest in the autobiographies of Newman, Darwin, and Mill is absent from the Oliphant persona. Oliphant's construction of herself shows a gender role confusion that is complicated by her role as professional writer. If the mother persona always asks, "Was I a good mother?" will not the professional writer (and literary critic) ask, "Was I a good writer?" And, when the culture's demands on the mother and writer are in conflict, will not the construction of the autobiographical persona involve the untangling of these questions?

Oliphant's rhetoric reflects her struggle. Self-descriptive phrases like "making pennyworths of myself" (*OA* 95), "laborious life" (*OA* 14), "not quite grown up" (*OA* 13), "how I have been handicapped in life!" (*OA* 15), "poor little unappreciated self" (*OA* 17), and "torn in two" (*OA* 37) are juxtaposed with phrases like "friendless, but totally undismayed" (*OA* 89), "my head was steady as a rock" (*OA* 29), "simple, yet self-possessed" (*OA* 36), "a spirit almost criminally elastic," "never worn out by work or crushed by care," "rash," " dare-devil," "dashing forward in the face of all obstacles" (*OA* 135). Further evidence of the struggle may be seen in the names by which Oliphant identifies herself: "mother," "mother childless," "breadwinner," and "production machine so little out of order" (*OA* 56) are contrasted to "a minor literary talent" (*OA* 39), "literary lady" (*OA* 88), "almost . . . one of the popularities of literature" (*OA* 91), and "a bigger me" (*OA* 57). The literary persona interrogates the mother persona, and the author role is problematized by the role of provider.

All through this text I have contended that autobiography can be read as a narrative of transformation and that, as a text of a life, it presents the persona in a before and after configuration. The autobiographer is saying, "I was not always as I now am." Margaret Oliphant frames the construction of her persona somewhat differently. She is skeptical that the narrative self can reach such certitude. To the end of her autobiography she interrogates her identity; in essence she is asking: "I was this, but I was also that, and now I am that, or am I this? Am I both? Does it matter?" The consequence of Oliphant's interrogation of herself as autobiographical subject is that she rejects certitude for amplitude, a single perspective for a plurality.

The persona transformation that is most apparent and to which Oliphant gives more voice (and space) is the transformation from mother to mother childless. She is, at the first of the narrative, mother, a widow left to support three small children, and, at the end, mother childless; all her children have predeceased her. The mother's misery is "dreadful care"; she is concerned that her children want for nothing, that they grow up amid "fine trees and wild nooks and corners" (*OA* 123). Of far greater concern, however, is that her sons have not become independent, self-reliant: "I think often if all had gone well . . . had Frank been a prosperous man in India . . . and Tiddy been a rising lawyer as was hoped, and Cecco, if delicate, still able with care to keep on,—it would all have been so natural, not anything wonderful, just the commonplace of life" (*OA* 147–48). She must admit, however, that their education "has not come to much"; Frank dies in India, and neither of her two boys "achieved those high hopes which I seemed so fully justified in forming." Like most doting mothers, Oliphant believes that they were "well-equipped and beyond the average in ability" but notes sadly that they "did nothing to verify this to the world" (*OA* 80). Both Tiddy and Cecco remained dependent on Oliphant until their deaths, Tiddy from alcoholism and Cecco from a lingering respiratory illness. Later she admits that she has been "faulty in their education [their expensive formal education and her general indulgence], but what was wrong was done in love and not wrongly meant" (*OA* 82).

The mother childless's misery is "awful blank" (*OA* 58). Better, she believes, to have failed sons than to have no sons at all, to live with dreadful care than with an awful blank. Remembering the family trip to Switzerland before the children all went their separate ways, she remarks that this was "the last time the three boys [Tiddy, Cecco, and nephew Frank] were to spend together, for many years, we thought,—for ever in this world, as it turned out" (*OA* 150).

While the transformation from mother to mother childless arouses our deepest sympathies, to encompass the full range of Oliphant's complexities I explore two images from the *Autobiography*—"breadwinner" and "a bigger me"—to show how Oliphant replaces what appears to be, in Victorian autobiography at least, a masculine persona of certitude with a feminine persona of amplitude. I contend that Oliphant's transformation from breadwinner to a bigger me is not "once for all" but, rather, is a change bounded by a set of terms that encompass her many and variable changes and that serve as reference points in Oliphant's ongoing discussion over the problematic nature of her autobiographical persona.

Getting to Know Margaret Oliphant: Names, Forms, and Identity

We can "get to know" Margaret Oliphant through the names she gives herself and the various identities implied by the breadwinner and bigger me personae. We can also "get to know" the Oliphant persona through the forms that constitute the *Autobiography:* chronological and travel narratives, eulogies, memorials, internal dialogues, prayers, and portraits. In both instances Oliphant problematizes the construction of the autobiographical persona, and concludes, finally, that neither she nor her readers can "know" her, that "we have no certainty of anything even in the most intimate circle of our individual being."[19]

The Names
Breadwinner and *a bigger me* are names by which Margaret Oliphant identifies herself in the autobiography. As they define the conflict between the mother and the artist persona, they serve as summary terms for the numerous roles Oliphant must assume and the various functions she must perform during her lifetime.

Victorian Breadwinner. Oliphant's role as breadwinner is implied throughout the *Autobiography.* She makes numerous references to providing "daily bread" (and sometimes butter) for her children, serving "mammon" rather than God in support of her family, fulfilling the female role without male financial support, and fulfilling the male role without male privilege.[20] Oliphant is not just a mother in the ordinary Victorian sense—the woman in charge of the household and the care of the children. She must earn the household income as well. The breadwinner identity assumes mother and provider, caregiver and food gatherer.[21]

Oliphant's own mother figures prominently in the development of her identity. This is hardly the case with the other Victorians in this study. Newman makes reference to a sister whose name he does not mention; neither his mother nor his father appears in the *Apologia*. Darwin's mother died when he was only eight years old; the *Autobiography* reveals that he seems never to have felt the loss. Mill's father looms so large that his mother is barely a shadow, kindly yet "drudging away" her life.

In sharp contrast to these "absent" mothers, Oliphant's mother was her "all in all."[22] Margaret Wilson was hardworking; "she kept everything going, and comfortably going on the small income she had to administer." She was poor but generous, once giving her own flannel petticoat to a poor, freezing woman. She entered into everything with "the warmest energy and animation," was "radical and democratic and the highest of aristocrats all in one." "There was absolutely nothing she would not have done or endured for her own" (*OA* 20–22). Her daughter was no different. The *Autobiography* records many instances in which her mother's traits of high energy and intelligence, her values of generosity and democracy, and her willingness to "endure all" are replicated in the daughter. It is important to remember, however, that Margaret's mother traced her lineage to aristocracy—the Oliphants of Kellie in Scotland—and, though poor, followed the conventions of her class ("so far as that went she might have been a queen") and taught them to her daughter. "I was brought up with the sense of belonging . . . to an old, chivalrous, impoverished race. I have never got rid of the prejudice" (*OA* 21–22). The clash between aristocratic expectations and democratic values caused yet another conflict for Oliphant.

Little Dragon. Margaret Oliphant took on the responsibilities of mother and provider at a relatively young age. At twenty-one she was sent to London to look after her brother Willie, who had serious drinking problems but had to finish his final term at school. Margaret was "a little dragon watching over him with remorseless anxiety." She not only kept him from drinking; she also insisted that they go without dinner to pay Willie's bills. Willie finished school and for a short time served as a minister in a small village in Northumberland but was soon brought home in shame. Margaret supported him in one way or another for the remainder of his life. She let him copy out her manuscripts for publication and allowed him to publish four of her novels under his name. She provided Willie's financial support for the last twenty-five years of his life—"my poor, good, tenderhearted, shipwrecked Willie" (*OA* 27). Margaret's mothering of Willie presages her future.

Breadwinner Wife. When Margaret married her cousin Frank in 1852 she was not relieved of her breadwinner responsibilities. Rather, she cared for the home and, later, her children, and she contributed to the family income, "writing all the while." She fully assumed the role of breadwinner when Frank became ill and they traveled to Italy for his health. She became his nurse as his condition worsened and his sole provider when he had neither the will nor the strength to paint. Maintaining her husband and family on advances for her articles in *Blackwood's,* the breadwinner wife, after less than eight years of marriage, becomes widowed breadwinner.

Widowed Breadwinner. Oliphant might have moved out of the breadwinner role had she married Rev. Robert Story after Frank died in Rome in 1859. She became acquainted with Robert the next summer while she was working on a biography of Edward Irving, who had been a friend of his father. The proposal of marriage is only hinted at in the *Autobiography*'s first entry, but much later she speaks of Story in endearing terms: "good fellow, good friend, though we have drifted so far apart since then" (*OA* 95).

Rejecting marriage for "the lonely life," Oliphant set out to support three small children, "without any props." The newly widowed breadwinner was determined to provide a home and sustenance for her children. Despite rather unpretentious dwellings—the homes ranged from a "quaint little house" in Elie, a "droll little house" in Edinburgh, to a "tiny," "humble" house in Ealing—it was a "good time" for Oliphant. Her career was taking off, and her earnings were substantial. Friends were amazed at her seeming cheerfulness; she, on the other hand, recalls, "I don't remember that I ever thought it anything the least out of the way, or was either discouraged or frightened, provided only that the children were all well" (*OA* 96). But, when her little family joined friends for a trip to Italy and Maggie, her daughter, and the eldest, died unexpectedly in Rome, Oliphant's heart was heavy and broken once again.

Adopted Mother. Oliphant's breadwinner role was expanded greatly when she assumed responsibility for her brother Frank's children. What began as a temporary situation turned into a permanent arrangement; Oliphant took care of her widowed brother until his death and three of his four children thereafter, one daughter living with another aunt. Frank Jr., her brother's oldest son, was received by Cecco and Tiddy as "a true brother" (*OA* 130). The two little girls, Denny and Madge, however, "had been very unresponsive children, not 'forthcoming' . . . shy mice, half-shy, half-defiant, as I think children often are whose childhood has been broken up by transplantation to another house." When they left home for school in Germany and were placed among strange-speaking people in a strange place, they wrote Oliphant begging to come home. Oliphant had "hard work refusing," and the girls soon got over their homesickness, but it was at this time that they became her "true children, the unquestioned daughters of the house, and with no further cloud upon the completeness of their adoption—they of me, as well as I of them. The first is often the more difficult of the two" (*OA* 151).

Breadwinner of the Empty Nest. With the year 1875, Oliphant writes, "began a new life." This was the year of "the empty nest": Frank Jr. was in India, Tiddy was at Oxford, Cecco was finishing up at Eton, and Denny and Madge were in Germany. The breadwinner was proud that she had placed her sons, nephew, and nieces in the best schools available and had prepared them for the assumption of their "rightful" places in society, but her pride was soon overcome by anxieties, "almost more than I can bear" (*OA* 151). Oliphant's anxieties arose from her sons' misbehavior. The "winsome and light-hearted" Cyril (Tiddy) began to lead a desultory life, and Cecco was soon following in his footsteps.

> My dearest, bright, delightful boy missed somehow his footing, how can I tell how? I often think that I had to do with it, as well as what people call inherited tendencies, and, alas! the perversity of youth, which he never outgrew. . . . Why should I try to explain? He went out of the world leaving a love-song or two behind him and the little volume of 'De Musset,' of which much was so well done, and yet some so badly done, and nothing more to show for his life. And I to watch it all going on day by day and year by year. (*OA* 152–53)

This passage—omitted by Oliphant's niece and cousin from their edition—expresses the anger and disillusionment of a mother who watched one of her children leave the nest only to discover that he was ill prepared to assume responsibility for himself. It is in passages such as these that Oliphant constructs herself as "failed mother" and agonizes over whether she had made things too easy for her children.

Breadwinner as Before. If Oliphant did not avoid her breadwinner role by marrying Rev. Story, she might have eventually relinquished it when her children were settled. But this was not to be. In a diary entry dated 1887[23] she relates that things were looking up: Cecco had passed his library exam with flying colors, and in an entry dated 1 October she writes that the queen herself had recommended Tids for a position in the education department. But then came the "downfall." Cecco was rejected for the library position because of poor health, and Tids was not awarded his position in education. No reason is given other than that he had not taken a first class, but Oliphant hints that the real reason for Tiddy's rejection was his drinking. "And so the hopes collapsed and we were as before" (*OA* 158). In her disappointment and shame Oliphant must continue on "as before." She has her "boys" to raise—and they are, by now, twenty-eight and thirty-three years old.

No More Mouths to Feed. This is the time of the "mother childless." Nephew Frank died in India in 1879, Tiddy in 1890, and Cecco in 1894. Referring to the death of her eldest son, Tiddy, in the entry marked "2nd October 1894," Oliphant mourns, "Four years have not quite passed since the terrible event which rent as I have said my life in two." Add to this event the death of Cecco, and all she can say is that her life is "gone altogether, like a bladder that has burst. I have no life any longer. . . . The younger after the elder and on this earth I have no son—I have no child. I am a mother childless" (*OA* 79). This gripping passage shows Oliphant with no purpose for living: she has no life, if she has no sons. But she lived on for another two years, and, though she had no sons to support, she finished out her days making careful provision for her niece Denny and her cousin Annie. We could say that she never gave up her breadwinner role, but to say that this role fully defines the Oliphant persona is to ignore her fuller conception of life and life narrative; she and her narrative are bigger than this.

A Bigger Me: The Artist Persona

> It would be vain to try to explain him to such a mind, which is of a different species and knows not even the language which Scott speaks. It is the nationality perhaps, the national brotherhood that makes me feel as if it were a bigger me that was speaking sometimes, as if I could enter into anything. . . . I feel I know him almost as I know myself. (*OA* 57)

Margaret Oliphant makes this statement in reference to her feelings about Sir Walter Scott, who had been attacked by "some fool in the newspaper" who charged that Scott "cared nothing for his books, except as a way of making money." In opposition to the fool, Oliphant understood and appreciated Sir Walter's work because they shared professions and nationality. As part of a "brotherhood" of Scottish writers, Oliphant sees herself as "a bigger me." I use the phrase as an image for those aspects of Oliphant's persona that have to do with her artistry. A *bigger me* encompasses such roles as "storyteller," "literary lady," "a minor literary talent," and "almost . . . one of the popularities of literature" and adds to Oliphant's sense of a fuller conception of life.

Storyteller. Like her breadwinner persona, Margaret Oliphant's authorial persona, her bigger me, owes much to her own mother. Besides being "companion, friend, and counsellor," her mother was also "minstrel" and "storyteller" (*OA* 38). Oliphant admitted to Jane Carlyle that she often had difficulty distinguishing between her mother's stories and her own: "I could never tell whether it was I myself who remembered things or she" (*OA* 97). Of the first story she published in *Blackwood's*, "Katie Stewart," she recalls that her mother told her, on her wedding day, the "love-tale" of her mother's great aunt who had lived in Kellie Castle. The aunt "told all her experiences to my mother, who told them to me, so that I never was quite sure whether I had not been Katie Stewart's contemporary" (*OA* 36). In keeping with the tradition established by her foremothers, Oliphant sees herself as storyteller by heritage.

Literary Lady. While Oliphant had no difficulty identifying herself as storyteller, she was more skeptical about her role as "literary lady." One of her old friends, the clergyman David Laing, always referred to her as a literary lady (he didn't like literary ladies, but he liked her)—"a joke all my friends were fond of making with me—I never was much of a literary lady and certainly my pretensions were very small then" (*OA* 88). Here Oliphant is not referring to herself as a failed writer but as a failure in a *public* writer's role. Readers generally see this stance as indicative of Oliphant's irony, her way of understating her case. She develops this ironic stance further by critiquing her role as a "minor literary talent."

A Minor Literary Talent. In her novel, *The Athelings, or the Three Gifts* Oliphant describes the literary scene and the attendant, disconcerting (to her) social practices of the day. So-called minor literary talents were invited to the homes of their "lionizers" to entertain or amuse their guests. Oliphant disappointed her hostesses in this enterprise and frustrated her husband, who "tried in vain (as I now see) to form me and make me attend to my social duties" (*OA* 39). Part of the explanation for Oliphant's lifelong reticence to trumpet herself can be attributed simply to good manners; women of her social class did not brag. But she was, at first, shy and uncomfortable in these literary settings.

Almost . . . One of the Popularities of Literature. This same sort of ironic understatement is evident in Oliphant's characterization of herself as "almost . . . one of the popularities of literature." In her day she was clearly one of the important and popular novelists, her audiences surpassing many who earned more for their publications than she did. Since she was not certain that she belonged in the same league with writers of the highest caliber, however, she prefaced her description with a qualifying *almost.* Was she a member of the brotherhood of writers? Was she a bigger me? The Oliphant persona, constructed as such, enlarges the breadwinner persona. It implies that *breadwinner* is insufficient to define Oliphant's character and that she was a member of a larger community of writers. But the bigger me also allows Oliphant to interrogate the writer persona. Was she simply a "minor literary talent, or was she one of the popularities of literature?

The Forms

If we read beyond the names that Oliphant gives herself to the way in which she constructs herself in the various forms of discourse that shape the autobiography, the tensions, conflicts, and complexities of her autobiographical persona are more evident still. In the chronological narrative, the travel narratives, the grief passages, the dialogues with God, and the verbal portraits she paints of the persons in her surroundings, we discover an autobiographical persona in its very construction. What I mean by this is that Oliphant, as she experiments with autobiographical forms, explores the nature of the autobiographical persona. Her questions: Who am I—breadwinner or a bigger me, doting mother or minor literary talent?—are tied in provocative ways to the forms she chooses to continue her life narrative.

The Chronological Narrative. With the chronological narrative we discover "what happens" to Margaret Oliphant: when and where she was born, how she grew up, when she began writing, and how she faced her personal and professional trials. Yet it is worth remembering that the narration of the events of her life is not of a piece; rather, the events are scattered throughout the text and appear in the nonchronological sections as well the chronological ones. Most of the historical material, however, is prefaced with phrases like "Here, then for a little try at the autobiography" (*OA* 18) or "I forget where I left off in this pitiful little record of my life" (*OA* 60) or "I will try after this not to dwell so much on this subject . . . but resume the thread of my poor life—in this book I mean" (*OA* 55). These words, in addition to implying that Oliphant had only a "poor life" without her children, also suggest that the chronological narrative, the "thread" of her "book-life," was inadequate to the task of presenting the autobiographical persona. Oliphant, for the most part, rejected chronology as *the* form of autobiography. She saw it as one of many forms for constructing the life narrative. The reader must assist in the construction of the thread of her poor life.

The chronological narrative provides general information about Oliphant's qualities and characteristics: that her home life as a child was quiet, her father disliking all guests and his family being all "vitreol and vinegar"; that the family's major entertainment was reading; that she was disappointed in her initial experiences with the fine arts; that she was "tremendously political" in her younger years; that she hated social calls, preferring quiet suppers and the "true society" of close friends (*OA* 44); that she had a sense of humor; that she disliked intellectuals, preferring persons with a "benignant gentle dulness [sic] which always soothes me" (*OA* 124); that she loved her children; that writing gave her pleasure.

In the chronological narratives the reader also finds indications of the tension between the breadwinner and the bigger me aspects of her persona. For example, when Oliphant tells of her first love and subsequent engagement, the human dimension of the experience is displaced by artistic expertise: she turns the incident into a story, replete with soft light and glowing eyes.

> But the little incident remains to me, as so many scenes in my early life do, like a picture suffused with a soft delightful light: the glow in the young man's eyes; the lowered tone and little speech aside; the soft thrill of meaning, which was nothing, yet much. Perhaps if I were not a novelist addicted to describing such scenes, I might not remember it after—how long? Forty-one years. (*OA* 24)

While Oliphant refused to construct her life narrative along the lines of a novel, her personal memories are selected, colored, and heightened by her artistic sensibilities. The chronological narrative also reveals, conversely, that her artistic persona may have been thwarted by the breadwinner. In resolving to keep her household and "make a number of people comfortable at the cost of incessant work," Oliphant admits: "I know I am giving myself the air of being *au fond* a finer sort of character than the others. I may as well take the little satisfaction to myself, for nobody will give it to me. No one even will mention me in the same breath with George Eliot" (*OA* 16–17). This bit of self-defensiveness is typical of places in the chronological narrative in which Oliphant wrestles with the question of her artistic worth. That she recognizes her position as self-defensive is yet another instance in which Oliphant interrogates the aspects of her constructed persona.

The chronological narrative also provides instances in which the artist persona comes to the fore. When Oliphant recalls the writing of the *Carlingford* series, the artist persona takes precedence. She boasts, somewhat hesitatingly, that the series "*almost* made me one of the popularities of literature. *Almost,* never quite, though 'Salem Chapel' really went very near it" (*OA* 91). Many such instances from the chronological narrative show Oliphant avoiding the tendency to construct the autobiographical persona in the shape of a novelistic character, opting rather to present the "life-book" persona in the interrogative mode, without certitude, and to leave the artist persona in a "commonplace set of circumstances" (*OA* 110).

The Travel Narratives. Although she was famous for her novels, Margaret Oliphant was also known for her travel narratives. She routinely took her entire entourage (children, relatives, friends, secretaries, housekeepers, nannies, and tutors) on extended holidays, and, because travel of this sort was expensive, Oliphant often requested advances on her books to support these trips and other luxuries. These travels often provided material for articles.

In addition to these pieces Oliphant employs the travel narrative as a major discourse form in the *Autobiography* and embeds extended travel narratives into the chronological account. Oliphant selected those travels that were most significant to the changes in her life. The selected travel narratives, like the chronological narrative, provide readers with general information regarding the Oliphant persona while highlighting the tensions between its nurturer and artistic aspects.

Two travel narratives stand out in the text, both journeys that ended in disaster. The first was occasioned by her husband Frank's illness. The couple were told that time in Italy—in the "sunny South"—would improve Frank's health. The family left England for Florence in January 1859, but Italy had no sun; it was bitterly cold and dreary. "I remember thinking that it might have been Manchester for anything one saw or felt that was like the

South," and Frank was suffering, unable to exert himself, "sitting silent without even books" (*OA* 69). While this embedded travel narrative forwards the chronological thread of the life narrative, we also learn more about the Oliphant persona, the strength of her character, some of her likes and dislikes, her habits and values. From the stay in Paris, we learn that Oliphant was a capable travel organizer, "having to take the management of things myself" (*OA* 66). From their stop in Lyon we learn that she was not extravagant but did believe that traveling second-class was a "stupid economy." The visit to Notre Dame de Fourvieres shows that Oliphant managed very well, even when they failed to bring enough money to pay their hotel bill. She claimed that "this sort of thing has never been a bugbear to me as to many people" (*OA* 67). The travel narratives also reveal Oliphant's love of the natural world as she describes "the delightful sweeps and folds of the Maritime Alps" and the "paradise gardens of oranges and hedges of aloes in Cannes." What she remembers of Florence is not the "art" but nature, "the view from Bellosguardo above all the treasures of the galleries."

Even though she preferred nature to art, Oliphant was touched by one painting in the Pitti. She was aware that "another baby was coming," and, when she saw Albertinelli's *Visitation,* the painting of "old Elizabeth, and Mary with all the awe of her coming motherhood upon her," she recalls: "I had little thought of all that was to happen to me before my child came, but I had no woman to go to, to be comforted—except these two" (*OA* 73). The feelings of mother and artist came together before the Albertinelli painting. This experience was one of Oliphant's few comforts when the trip to "sunny" Italy ended in the disaster of Frank's death in Rome and she was left pregnant, with two small children to support.

The second major travel narrative also ended in disaster, but it was occasioned by better times. She and her family were living happily in Ealing, she "being more gay than she had been in her life before," writing all the time, though she doesn't know how, what with all her "merry neighbours" and their "boating, games, laughter, and good talk" (*OA* 105). Geraldine Macpherson, the friend who had been with her when her husband died in Rome, persuaded Margaret and another friend, Mrs. Tulloch, to go to Rome with her. "I have no doubt if I heard of such a proceeding now I should think it the wildest plan," but with "delightful indifference to ways and means" they set out—"the little party of women, all of us about the same age, all with the sense of holiday, a little outburst of freedom, no man interfering, keeping us to rule or formality." This merry party ended abruptly when Oliphant's daughter Maggie suddenly died of gastric fever on 27 January 1864, and Oliphant was "plunged again under the salt and bitter waves" (*OA* 107–8).

Since Oliphant loved to travel, she claimed that she had to work harder and write more so that her family could enjoy the pleasures and benefits of many places. The travel narratives that Oliphant included in the *Autobiography*, however, have little to do with the "joys" of travel. Rather, in their disastrous consequences they exemplify the breadwinner and bigger me aspects of the persona. The mother/provider mourns for her husband and child; the writer constructs travel narratives on the theme of loss.

Grief and the Literature of Bereavement

With the exception of Annie, Denny, and Madge, Margaret Oliphant was predeceased by all her relatives.[24] Passages on the deaths of her family members constitute one of the larger segments of the autobiography.[25] It is in the grieving passages that Oliphant joins the voices of the mother and the poet in "continual strains" of sorrow: "Ah me, alas! pain ever, for ever. This has been the ower-word of my life. And now it burst into the murmur of pain again" (*OA* 108). The "grief passages," when examined chronologically, rather than in the narrative order in which they are presented, trace Oliphant's gradual transformation from mother to mother childless. Oliphant then joins her grief and her artistry in the construction of eulogies, memorials, and internal dialogues.

1854. Reading the grief passages in chronological order, we learn that Oliphant's first experience with death came when her mother died in 1854, "suffering no attendance but mine." Oliphant laments: "I never had come within sight of death before. And, oh me! when all was over, mingled with my grief there was . . . something like a dreadful relief." The grief was due to the loss of her "all in all." The relief was attributable to the fact that Oliphant's husband and mother did not get along, and now "there were no longer two people to please, but only one" (*OA* 37–38).

1855, February. Oliphant was to "come within sight of death" again in a very short time. Just five months later, in February 1855, her second daughter, Marjorie Isabella, only eight months old, died. Oliphant recalls that the great sorrow at the loss of her mother "did not give me, when she died, a pang so deep as the loss of the little helpless baby."

1855, November. Oliphant records the loss of still another infant son, a day old.

> My spirit sank completely under it. . . . Neither of these little ones could speak to me or exchange an idea or show love, and yet their withdrawal was like the sun going out from the sky—life remained, the daylight continued, but all was different. It seems strange to me now at this long distance—but so it was. (*OA* 38)

1858. Three years later another child, Stephen Thomas, a boy nine weeks old, died.

1859. Death came for the fifth time in five years when Margaret's husband, Frank, died of tuberculosis in 1859. The grief passages that accompany Frank's death seem to have less to do with sorrow than with Oliphant's anxiety for her children. She determined to leave Birkenhead, where they had been staying with her brother's family, because "I think it was rather more than I could bear to see his children rushing to the door to meet him when he came home, and my fatherless little ones ready to rush too, though it was so short a time since their father had been taken from them" (*OA* 88). While Oliphant makes brief references to her grief over the death of her husband, the absence of any extended expression of mourning for him is in marked contrast to the expressions of grief for other family members she includes later. Readers are left to puzzle over this omission. Was her grief not as great because the loss was not as significant? Or was Oliphant reluctant to speak of emotions related to marital love, while the public expression of concern for one's children was considered more acceptable? In any case, it is not long before Oliphant's grief "begins to lighten" (*OA* 95), and her heart comes up "with a great bound from all the strain of previous trouble and hard labour and the valley of the shadow of death" (*OA* 105).

1864. The next loss Oliphant experienced came four years later— a "graver era."

> A graver era, God help me, but I did not know when I wrote the words that I was coming to lay my sweetest hope, my brightest anticipations for the future, with my darling, in her father's grave. Oh this terrible, fatal, miserable Rome! I came here rich and happy, with my blooming daughter, my dear bright child, whose smiles and brightness everybody noticed,

and who was sweet as a little mother to her brothers. . . . Four short days made all the difference, and now here I am with my boys thrown back again out of the light into the darkness, into the valley of the shadow of death. (*OA* 4)

With the loss of her ten-year-old daughter, Maggie, her "brightness," Oliphant was thrust back into darkness and mourning. "Instead of my sweet, living loving child I have but a curl of the dear hair and another name upon the marble out at Testaccio," the Protestant cemetery in Rome (*OA* 5). Oliphant concludes her eulogy for Maggie with the deepest expression of grief: "Here is the worst of all. I am alone. I am a woman. I have nobody to stand between me and the roughest edge of grief. . . . I have to bear the loss, the pang unshared. My boys are too little to feel it, and there is nobody else in the world to divide it with me" (*OA* 9).

1890. Twenty-six years later Oliphant records the death of her son Tiddy. "This day last week we laid him in the grave, crowned with sunshine and with flowers. . . . What tragedy of all is so bitter and terrible as to have to say of a human creature, nobly endowed, beautifully formed, made for everything that was good, that before he had reached the crown of human strength it had come to be that there was no way but this—" (*OA* 48–49). There is a bitter edge to Oliphant's grief in this passage. Angered over her son's wasted life, she "patterns her memorial" to him on Christ's life; Tiddy was "just our Lord's age when He began his ministry." Yet there is a hollowness in the comparison: Tiddy had no ministry; his was a squandered life.

1894. At the death of her last son, Cecco, the mother childless takes account of her losses: "The little ones I have no occasion to think of, they are so far away, babies and no more. My Maggie was a deep rent in my life, but that too has gone into the distance." Now her two boys (she always called them boys even when they were men) are gone, the last being Cecco, who has "been his mother's boy all his dear life. He was born after his father died. He has known nobody but me, no protector, no provider, but his mother" (*OA* 79). Oliphant writes that she "will never again be able to quote him, or say 'Cecco says.' And she *will* speak his name; she will resist the impulse to bury his name in her heart" (*OA* 83; my emphasis). In an 1896 entry,[26] two years after his death, Oliphant talks with Cecco. She had been chiding herself for reading an old book of Sir Walter Scott's instead of praying.

When I was thus blaming myself I felt almost as if I was suddenly surrounded by a soft atmosphere of tender love and almost laughter, such as
sometimes was when I would blame myself for some of my familiar little
faults, which they rather liked in me than blamed. It was only a moment,
a kind of delightful humourous derision of boys, and I could almost think
I felt Cecco touch my forehead as he used to do and say "Poor Mamma".
. . . "Poor Mamma" as if she might not know her little folly and be indul-
gent in it. It gave me a great feeling of comfort. (*OA* 160)

Read chronologically, the grief passages reveal a long and sorrowful
transformation, the transit from a full to an empty house, from life to
death. But it is important to keep in mind that Oliphant's grieving reaches
greater intensity than is evident in my chronological survey. She does not
build a plot that gradually moves from a young, happy bride and mother—
her husband at his work, her children at her knee—toward the widowed
mother alone at the end of the narrative. Rather, the mother childless persona interrupts the discourse of the mother throughout the autobiography—in the chronological and travel narratives as well as the eulogistic passages—doubling, turning the grief back on itself, building to painful
intensity.

This morning I said I was dead and felt nothing, now I am all wildly alive,
suffering and aching and hardened in my sins, but of my mind not my
body, my body is well, well, the horrible thing. I could turn to and work
or write a love story or draw or skate or walk a mile—anything, anything—but my burden is more than I can bear. (*OA* 86)

With each loss Oliphant did indeed "turn to and work." If we read the
grief passages as literature, we discover an artist constructing eulogies,
memorials, and internal dialogues that alleviate her grief. In putting "the
long musings of my agony into words," she follows the example of Tennyson's *In Memoriam* (*OA* 11). She writes a eulogy for Maggie, creates a
memorial for Tiddy, and transcribes an internal dialogue with Cecco.
These expressions are never maudlin; they are some of her finest writing.
Like the chronological thread that can be traced through the autobiography, the "continual strain" of her thoughts is a deep scar that runs through
the text. The mother, moving relentlessly toward mother childless, mourns
the loss of her children. The artist constructs renderings of personal and
universal pain.

At several points Oliphant inserts phrases such as "the tenor of one's
entire life might have been changed," "the children, all so small, so happy,

so bright, my three little things—Maggie approaching eleven," "after the great calamity came," "I have often travelled that road since, but never so free or light of heart!" (*OA* 107). These phrases suggest that the writer cannot write about the past without present knowledge, without inserting her awareness of the sorrow that is to come.

Another instance is a chronological passage in which Oliphant writes about the birth of her youngest son, Cecco. As she writes of this "bonnie rosy baby" thirty-five years later, she mourns that it is this same child, Cecco, who is "lying in his coffin in the room next to me. . . looking more beautiful than ever he did in his life, in a sort of noble manhood, like, so very like, my infant of nearly thirty-five years ago. . . . All gone, all gone, and no light to come to this sorrow any more!" (*OA* 78). Each section of her narrative, no matter how gay and bright, is overshadowed by a death pall.

Oliphant's artistry—ordering the narrative of past events to coincide with present grief, initiating autobiographical accounts with present suffering—was recognized by readers such as Virginia Woolf, who had little positive to say about Oliphant's fiction but who saw the expressions of grief in the *Autobiography* as "a most genuine and moving piece of work."[27] They are Oliphant's contribution to the literature of bereavement, a literature in which *pain* becomes the "ower-word" of the mother *and* the poet.[28]

The Prayer Passages: Approaching and Reproaching God
Grief over the bitter losses of her husband and beloved children caused Oliphant to examine her faith and her attitudes toward God. When her pleas for release from sorrow fail and trite or conventional explanations for suffering are found wanting, she rails at God. "I keep on always upbraiding and reproaching God," she writes of her exchanges with God in Albano in 1864, and during that same year in Capri she makes "wild outcries of reluctance, with groans of pain, with remonstrances against God's will" (*OA* 9, 12). These "prayer passages," like the grief passages, provide additional insight into the Oliphant persona. Whereas the grief passages draw the voices of mother and poet together, the prayer passages mark the tensions and conflicts between the voices. The mother is angry; the artist is fatalistic.

Oliphant's dialogues with God attend each of the expressions of grief and follow a distinct pattern. The mother asks for comfort and receives none. She then upbraids God and asks him to let her die. When this second plea goes unanswered, the artist constructs her own explanations and comforts. Oliphant's dialogues with God over Maggie's death are illustrative of the prayer passage pattern. First, the mother mourns Maggie's loss and prays for comfort.

> I am alone always, alone in the world for ever. Help me, Oh help me Lord. I am a poor helpless woman without any strength and thou hast snatched away the props on which I leant. Stand by me and grant me a little patience till I die. (*OA* 13)

The despairing mother receives no comfort from a God who refuses to hear her cry:

> I have not been resigned. I cannot feel resigned, my heart is sore as if it was an injury. . . . God has taken her away out of my arms and refuses to hear my cry and prayer. My heart feels dead. . . . my heart cries out against God's will. Now I have to go limping and anxious through the world all the days of my life. (*OA* 4–5)

The mother then rails at God and begs for death.

> Stand by the forlorn creature who fainteth under Thy hand, but whom Thou sufferest not to die. (*OA* 9)

When God refuses to let her die, Oliphant sees him as cruel and wonders if He can be "trusted with Maggie." She realizes that the agonizing faith required of her is "to believe in the face of all appearances to the contrary, in opposition to my knowledge of myself, against the aching and yearning of my heart, that in this and all He does He has done well" (*OA* 7).

Failing in this kind of mother's faith, the artist begins to construct her own answers or comforts; she tries "to get a new aspect of this never-ceasing, ever-present loss which will make it less horrible, less blank and bitter." She comforts herself by remembering that Maggie did have "a happy life and never lacked any pleasure I could give her" (*OA* 6). She reminds herself that Maggie would eventually have married and left her anyway.

> My Maggie, if you had lived to be some man's love and wife and had gone away with him to the end of the world would I your mother have stood in the way of your happiness? God forbid—And how can I tell what bright life, what sweet existence is opening upon you now. (*OA* 12)

With each loss Margaret Oliphant is more alone, and her sorrow and anger build accordingly. By the time she loses her last child, Cecco, she is wailing to God to either "kill or calm" her, since she cannot kill herself (*OA* 86). The familiar, desolate passage at the end of the *Autobiography* is haunting in its poignancy. Written sometime after April 1895, it concludes the work. But Oliphant wrote again on the death of Cecco in a diary entry discovered by Jay and marked 1896. She has found comfort; Cecco seems to touch her shoulder and say "Poor Mamma." Her railings and reproaches against God are changed to a murmured prayer of thanks: "O my God—and oh my children" (*OA* 160).

Portraits: Knowing So Few Notables

From the "portraits," the verbal pictures Oliphant paints of unusual persons who stand out in her memory, we discover yet further illustrations of her artistry. And when she draws portraits of other writers and compares herself to them, we discover what she thinks about herself as artist.

Oliphant repeatedly reminds us that she disliked paying visits, that she felt "like a fish out of water." She also insists that she did not do well in literary society. She hated the pretensions of the famous, and she had difficulty listening to other writers pontificate on the philosophy of their creative processes or on the construction of their fictive characters. Nor could she play the expected role of minor literary talent. Often taken as "the poor little shy wife of some artist" (*OA* 41), she admits that she was a disappointment to her friends because she had "no gift of talk" and did nothing to make herself "agreeable or remarkable" in literary society (*OA* 138).

If one considers reports to the contrary,[29] as well as the portraits she constructed of her friends and acquaintances, the reader might wonder if Oliphant is being somewhat disingenuous when she apologizes: "It is rather a fictitious sort of thing recalling those semi-professional recollections. It is by way of a kind of apology for knowing so few notable people" (*OA* 144). She attaches this apology to portraits of persons whom she remembers because of some unique feature or other: Lance, the painter of fruits and flowers and still life, who asked her to put him in a book (*OA* 39); Mr. Fullom, who read for Colburn Oliphant's first book, a small personage, one whom "it was marvellous to think of as connected with anything that pretended to be intellectual" (*OA* 40); Mrs. Hall, only a fair writer and author of only a few novels but a kind woman who sent flowers for Maggie's christening (*OA* 40); Mary Howitt, the writer whose spiritualist daughter produced "wonderful scribble-scrabbles, over which she was very enthusiastic" (*OA* 41); Rosa Bonheur, the French painter, a "round-faced, good humoured woman, with hair cut short" like a man's, and "not very distinct in matter of sex so far as dress and appearance went" (*OA* 42); Miss

Mulock, tall and slim, with "a way of fixing the eyes of her interlocutor in a manner which did not please my shy fastidiousness"; Mr. Smedley, "an extraordinary being in a wheeled chair," a rich man's son, totally self-supporting as a writer of "sporting novels" (*OA* 43).

Oliphant draws a more extended portrait of another couple who interested her greatly, an old "unfrocked priest," Father Prout, and "the old lady about whom he circled." "It amused me to think," Oliphant tells us, "that these old people had perhaps indulged in a grande passion and defied the world for each other. I thought no worse of them somehow! which I am aware is a most immoral sentiment" (a touch of her irony here). Oliphant reflects that these elderly romances of "old fidelity and friendship" under her eyes were "made innocent, almost infantile . . . as of old babies, independent of sex and superior to it, amid all the obliterations of old age. I had several curious visitors of this kind" (*OA* 115–16).

This set of portraits, selected from the many that constitute her recollections, shows Oliphant as an artist, highlighting the unique features of individuals and placing them in her life narrative as she might arrange paintings on the walls of her house or, better still, like a set of mirrors that reflect Oliphant's values and preferences. They also call into question the critical allegations that Oliphant was a "prude" who only wrote "wholesome" stories.[30]

These portraits are but the sketches of Oliphant's acquaintances, "little glimpses of society." She draws more detailed portraits of close friends and literary acquaintances. The Macphersons were the couple who attended her when her husband was dying and in whose care she placed her alcoholic brother, Willie, for over twenty-five years. Robert is portrayed as "hot headed, humourous, noisy" yet "Nero to the heart," Geddie as "untidy, disorderly, fond of gaiety of every kind" (*OA* 74–75). The Blacketts, one of Oliphant's publishers, were also her friends; Mrs. Blackett was "a fine creature, very much more clever than he," but most "childlike"; he "was a little apt to blow himself out and assume importance" (*OA* 101). John Blackwood, the most important of Oliphant's publishers, "was already a friend," even in the earliest days of their professional relationship, "with that curious kind of intimacy which is created by a publisher's knowledge of all one's affairs, especially when these affairs mean struggles to keep afloat and a constant need of money." When the "balance changed a little" and Oliphant was no longer indebted to him, she continued to promote the belief that she was in his debt, because he still conceived of himself as her "genial benefactor." Oliphant also includes extended portraits of Isabella Blackwood, the Montalemberts, Annie Thackeray, Leslie Stephen, and Lord Tennyson. They offer subtle (and not so subtle) hints of Oliphant's preferences and relationships.

In the *Autobiography* Margaret Oliphant speaks at no greater length, nor more fondly, of any other persons (except for her mother and her children) than she does of Jane and Thomas Carlyle. One portrait of the two shows her respect for them and provides insight into the types of friendships that Oliphant established. When Cecco had a convulsion, Oliphant recalls that this was one of the few times "I quite lost my head." When Mrs. Carlyle arrived for a visit she found Oliphant sitting in front of the fireplace, holding Cecco in a blanket, and humming softly to him. Cecco startled her out of her shock by saying: "Why you singing hum-hum? Sing 'Froggy he would a-wooing go.'" Jane sat by her and encouraged and comforted her but did not stay long. That same evening she received a letter from Mrs. Carlyle telling her that Mr. Carlyle had made her sit down and write that "a sister of his had once had just such an attack, which never was repeated. God bless them, [the Carlyles] that much maligned, much misunderstood pair! That was not much like the old ogre his false friends have made him out to be" (*OA* 103). Oliphant's friendship with Mrs. Carlyle "was never broken from this time" (*OA* 98).

"Knowing so few notables," then, is a rhetorical space out of which Margaret Oliphant can draw portraits of persons from her everyday encounters. She searches out unique features in ordinary individuals and exaggerates these features by calling them to her readers' attention, to see if "the commonplace outside might not cover a painter or a poet or something equally fine" (*OA* 43). For example, she describes the children's nursemaid, "the noble Marie" of St. Adresse, as wearing a beautiful cap that made her look like one of the "medieval princesses wandering after the procession of the *Fete Dieu*" (*OA* 120). Just as she brings to light the extraordinary in the ordinary, Oliphant also unmasks the "great" by disclosing their ordinariness. Lord Tennyson is exposed as rude, Leslie Stephen as angry with God. Sir Charles Dilke, editor of the *Athenaeum,* is shown to have an inflated view of his own importance. Grace Greenwood (pen name of poet and journalist Sara Jane Lippincott) is portrayed as patronizing.[31] Like Thomas Carlyle, Oliphant saw the extraordinary in the ordinary and the ordinary in the great—the philosopher "disguised" in a tailor's apron and the fool wrapped in a king's royal raiment.

Portraits: What My Own Mind Is Worth

If, as mother, Margaret Oliphant was not afraid to examine the quality of her mothering, she was no less ready to examine her abilities as writer and her status in the literary community. She did not use a public forum to do so; she had no "theory on the subject." "I always avoid considering formally what my own mind is worth" (*OA* 14). In her private reflections, however, she faces these issues squarely. When Oliphant draws portraits of other writers and compares herself to them, we discover what she thinks of herself as an artist.

When Oliphant compares herself with Miss Mulock (Dinah Maria Craik), who was first a children's story writer and later authored such didactic novels as *The Ogilvies* and *John Halifax, Gentleman,* she sees herself as the superior storyteller. It was Oliphant herself who introduced Mulock to her publisher Blackett, and it was Blackett who secured Mulock's popularity with the public.

> She made a spring thus quite over my head with the helping hand of my particular friend, leaving me a little rueful,—I did not at all understand the means nor think very highly of the work, which is a thing that has happened several times, I fear, in my experience. Success as measured by money never came to my share. Miss Mulock in the way attained more with a few books, and that of very thin quality, than I with my many. I don't know why. I don't pretend to think that it was because of their superior quality. (*OA* 102)

Oliphant complains that, by all outward appearances, Mulock rates higher than she does. When she judges Mulock by the "very thin quality" of her work, however, Oliphant is implying that her own mind is worth more.

Oliphant compares herself to John Addington Symonds in terms of their mutual sufferings and the tenor of their memoirs. Symonds, historian, poet, critic, and translator, was "a pleasant, frank, hearty man, as one saw him from outside." Symonds's *Life,* in contrast, portrays him as having suffered severely from ill health. Oliphant, in comparing her life and work with Symonds's, concludes that she is not a complex person, nor does she have an elaborate tale to tell of herself. She perceives hers as "a life so simple" and her autobiography as a "prosaic little narrative," while Symonds's text is filled with morbid introspection and "elaborate self-discussion" (*OA* 99–100).[32]

In thinking of herself in comparison to Sir Walter Scott (one of her favorite Scottish writers), Oliphant clearly feels a part of a bigger me. She can match him page for page when she compares their work habits.

I have carried it on all this time steadily, a chapter a day, I suppose about twenty pages of an octavo book. Sir Walter when he was labouring to pay off his debts, speaks of writing a volume in twelve days I think. I have done it steadily in sixteen. He says no man can keep it up for long—but I have kept it up in spite of everything now for months and months.

Oliphant can work as hard and as long as Scott, perhaps longer, but the results are not the same. When she measures her artistry against Scott's, "the product is very different indeed—and the object so small beside his grand big magnificent struggle" (*OA* 55).

Referring to her work habits from an earlier time, Oliphant compares herself with Jane Austen. Recalling that she had to work at one corner of the family table "with everything going on as if she were making a shirt," she notes that Austen had to write in the same way. But, whereas Austin's family "were half ashamed to have it known that she was not just a young lady like the others, doing her embroidery," Oliphant's family were

quite pleased to magnify me, and to be proud of my work, but always with a hidden sense that it was an admirable joke, and no idea that any special facilities or retirement was necessary. My mother, I believe, would have felt her pride and rapture much checked, almost humiliated, if she had conceived that I stood in need of any artificial aids [a writing table or a room of her own] of that or any other description. (*OA* 30–31)

Oliphant goes no further with her portrait of Austen, and readers are left to wonder, does she avoid asking what her "mind is worth" with regard to Austen because she fears the answer, or is she, by comparing the similarities of their work habits, implying that they also share literary reputations of equal stature?

When Oliphant compares herself with her respected literary colleague, Anthony Trollope, she acknowledges that, though their methods are different, they are of equal literary status. She is quick to mention, however, that he always made more money. The bitterness she expresses in comparing herself with George Eliot and George Sand shows up in statements such as "George Eliot and George Sand make me half inclined to cry over my poor little unappreciated self," "No one even will mention me in the same breath with George Eliot" (*OA* 16–17), "Should I have done better if I had been kept, like her, in a mental greenhouse and taken care of?" (*OA* 15). Such remarks show a side of Oliphant "at odds with the qualities of charm and grace" her relatives wished to convey in their edition of the manuscript.[33] A mass of feelings lie buried under these statements; Oliphant is angered that her dedication to motherhood has resulted in failure and that her dedication to her art has yielded so little fame. For all her protests Oliphant wants to be considered as equal to Sand and Eliot. She concludes: "These two bigger women did things which I have never felt the least temptation to do—but how very much enjoyment they seem to have got out of their life, how much more praise and homage and honour. I would not buy their fame with their disadvantages, but I do feel very small, very obscure beside them, rather a failure all round" (*OA* 17). Although Oliphant insists that she would not trade places with either of the two, she faces with excruciating honesty the question of what her mind is worth. Desiring neither their privileges nor their fame, she intimates that, in terms of their literary powers, she does not quite measure up.

Of all the literary personages with whom Oliphant compares herself, it seems that she considered Charlotte Brontë the artist of the highest caliber. Brontë was, for Oliphant, her superior in literary power and stature, "my work to myself looks perfectly pale and colourless beside hers." Oliphant does not try to explain away this superiority by comparing personal advantages, work habits, popularity, or income, as she does with some of the other writers. Brontë's superiority is beyond question. Oliphant comes out ahead only in her fuller conception of life.

Superior to Mulock, prosaic in comparison to Symonds, following working habits similar to those of Scott and Austen, of equal literary status with Trollope, daunted by Sand and Eliot, perhaps reverential toward Brontë, Margaret Oliphant constructs a composite portrait of her own artistry. The multifaceted portrait is telling but no more so than Oliphant's fearlessness in determining to construct it.

Portraits of the Misunderstood

A final set of verbal portraits must not be overlooked. These are portraits of older women whom Oliphant encounters in her later years: 'Little Nelly," an unnamed widow—"clever, witty, pretty"—and Mrs. Duncan Stewart. Each of the three had been "misinterpreted by the public." Peterson sees these portraits as providing insight into the Oliphant persona, as they add the dimension of fear of public misunderstanding to Oliphant's other characteristics.[34] I submit that the portraits of these "misunderstood" women also add an empathetic, caring aspect to the Oliphant portrait, as she moves beyond her mother role to that of friend.

In the *Autobiography* the names Margaret Oliphant gives herself and the forms she uses to construct her narrative introduce a self in conflict over her identity. These sorts of conflict did not trouble Newman, Mill, or Darwin. They might find themselves at odds with their culture and construct narratives that defend their positions, but their autobiographies reveal little internal conflict over selfhood. Newman may have difficulty defending his transformation from Anglican to Catholic to his Anglican associates, but he never doubts that he will resolve the theological issues that concern him. When Utilitarianism fails Mill and he suffers a crisis of feeling (a serious but temporary conflict), he constructs a new plan for living and a new political philosophy. He *was* dead sure about Utilitarianism; he *is* dead sure about his new system. Neither is there any sense of conflict in the Darwin persona. Writing as one "back from the dead," Darwin charts the route of his professionalism. Looking back, he notes that he was always doing science and that he will continue to do so to the end of his life. In contrast to the certitude manifest in the Newman, Darwin, and Mill personae, Oliphant leaves the question of her identity unresolved to the end of the *Autobiography*.

It is fair to say that Oliphant was in conflict over her role identification because she was a first-generation working mother, but this single explanation is too simplistic. She was a mother who remembered her "halcyon days," with everything going well with her little ones, but who was not afraid to face up to her "miserable failure" as a mother of two desultory sons. She was a productive, successful writer who was not afraid to ask what her mind was worth. Had she not found it necessary to become a breadwinner, might she have been a better writer? Might she have stood alongside George Eliot, George Sand, or Charlotte Brontë? She admits that, breadwinner or not, she fails to measure up to their literary stature. But she can also acknowledge that she is a better writer than some who gained more popularity and earned more income from their work. On reflection she concedes that she doesn't think so little of herself. She belongs to a community of writers. She is a bigger me.

Interrogating each of her roles, Margaret Oliphant constructs a different sort of autobiographical persona from those of Newman, Mill, and Darwin. More like Carlyle's tailor, the self that Oliphant constructs in the *Autobiography* has many talents, functions in a number of roles, is full of assurance *and* doubt. Hers is a persona of amplitude, but it is an uneasy fullness. She can operate as daughter, sister, wife, mother, aunt, novelist, critic, editor, translator, historian, and biographer— but never with certitude.

Production or Overproduction?
The *Figura* of Oliphant's Literary Transformation

If Margaret Oliphant confronts the question of her identity in the *Autobiography* and does not resolve it, it is because she held a view of life and life-narrative that rejected simple answers. Thus, we can hardly expect that she would epitomize her life in terms of a single metaphor of transformation. Her ambivalence over the nature of her transformation was tied up in the tension between *production* and *overproduction*. If her work were only that of breadwinner, then the more she produced (overproduced), the more she earned; if, however, she saw her work as that of the artist, then productivity is an appropriate image for her transformation type.

Oliphant's ambivalence about her work was shared by some contemporary and subsequent critics who perpetuated the "myth of overproduction" that has dogged Oliphant's literary reputation. Her own ambivalence, I argue, had more to do with her practices as a literary critic and her methods as a writer than with doubts about her self-worth. Hers was the self-consciousness of the professional writer and critic.[35]

Critical Ambivalence

Production, the act or process of producing something either by nature or human industry or art, is, in economic terms, the creation of economic value through goods or services. Hence, productivity, in economic or artistic endeavors, is generally viewed positively, overproduction, negatively. With the economy problems arise if more goods and/or services are produced than can be absorbed. In the arts overproduction is often seen as indication of "hack work"; industry does not imply real talent when the artist grinds out work that is unpolished, work that caters to the public's taste at a "penny-a-line."[36]

Oliphant was clearly productive, but was she overproductive? As noted earlier, she wrote ninety-eight novels, around fifty short stories, over four hundred articles, travel pieces, a number of biographies and histories, and edited and translated many other works—a large oeuvre, by any measure. For the most part modern Victorian scholarship has characterized Oliphant as overproductive, charging that "she wrote too much too quickly and with too little intellectual equipment to do her work justice."[37] That is not to say that Oliphant was without critics in her own day. Henry James saw her as having her "say" more "publicly and irresponsibly" for half a century than any other woman; Thomas Hardy called her criticism "the screaming of a poor lady."[38] Leslie Stephen, George Saintsbury, and Hugh Walker used a version of the term *overproduction* to explain their hesitancy in placing her work in the same category with major literary figures.[39]

The "distinctly misogynistic tone" of a few male Victorian novelists, the reservations of some Victorian critics and Edwardian historians, and the "hack status" accorded Oliphant by many of today's scholars[40] contrast sharply with the high regard in which her work was held by many of her contemporaries; Francis, Lord Jeffrey, J. M. Barrie, Robert Louis Stevenson, Thomas and Jane Carlyle, Henry James, Anne Thackeray Ritchie, and Montalembert all gave high praise to one or another of her publications. Some contemporaries, Clarke notes, "ventured to compare her with Jane Austen, Scott, and George Eliot."[41]

In a return to the positive view held by many of Oliphant's contemporaries, a reappraisal of Oliphant's work is in progress.[42] Margaret Rubik contends that "much more uncompromisingly than many famous authors of the time [Oliphant] disappoints stereotyped expectations, ridicules maudlin Victorian values and denounces the false pathos and sentimentality of her contemporaries."[43] Rubik shows that Oliphant achieved these ends by a number of subversions: (1) when Oliphant draws positive heroines who are "much more intelligent than their male partners and who, instead of looking up to their lovers as mentors, actually manipulate and instruct them," she is subverting women's roles in Victorian society; (2) Oliphant's view of marriage in her fiction is "down to earth and unsentimental" and, on occasion, "savagely disillusioning"; when she concentrates on "average marriages with their daily frictions and trivial irritations," she is subverting the notion of the ideal marriage; (3) Oliphant often caters to the taste of her readers "by ending her novels with the customary wedding bells," but she overturns readers' expectations with narrators who question happy endings and speak skeptically of poetic justice; (4) and, finally, unlike other Victorian novelists who "turn deathbed scenes into lachrymose farewells," Rubik argues that Oliphant refuses to idealize death or demystify it with "maudlin assurances of eternal reward" and that she "refrain[s] from moralizing." In her tales that deal with religious characters Oliphant does not try to "teach a moral lesson"; she shows, rather, that the "Bible can be as much an excuse as a guide."[44] Rubik is making the case that Oliphant was anything but a hack writer, and she does so by pointing to the character of Oliphant's literary style and content.

John Stock Clarke takes on the question of Oliphant's overproduction directly. He argues that of all the myths or paradoxes "the most obsessive, inevitable, and damaging to Oliphant's credit as a distinguished novelist is the conviction that she crippled her talent by overproduction." He attributes this to the fact that critics have

> tended to take their opinions from other critics; for most of the twentieth century it has been generally felt acceptable to dismiss Oliphant as a writer with a vulnerable talent that was effectively killed off by the writing of two, three, or more books a year. Influenced by these preconceived ideas, commentators were ready enough to see in her work what they expected to see, rather than what a sympathetic reading would reveal.[45]

Clarke attributes to the Saintsbury and Walker literary histories[46] the dismissive views of Oliphant that were taken up later by critics. He is disconcerted to find such views appearing in *Blackwood's* as late as 1968.

Clarke, like Rubik, corrects the misinterpretations of Oliphant's work that have promoted the overproduction myth and concludes that, because Oliphant "was so voluminous a writer," only scholars who are willing to make a serious reassessment of her work, rather than take the word of other critics, can resolve the paradoxes of Oliphant's reputation.[47] And Linda Peterson, who has undertaken just such a reassessment, concludes: "If her [Oliphant's] *bildungsromane* were not canonized . . . it may not be just that Oliphant wrote too many, too quickly. It may also be that she refused to do the cultural work of Victorian patriarchy by keeping love and marriage at the center of fictions of female development."[48]

Oliphant's Ambivalence: "Did I Write Too Much?"

In the *Autobiography* entry marked only as "1894," in which she discusses her "industry," Oliphant makes it clear that she resented those who complimented her on the quantity of her work, rather than on its quality: "as to my 'industry.' Now that I am old the world is a little more respectful, and I have not heard so much about my industry for some time" (*OA* 137).

She believed that "the instinct of nature is against the prolific worker. In this way a short life, a limited period of activity, are much the best for art; and a long period of labour, occupied by an active mind and fertile faculties, tell against, and not for, the writer."[49] Like Trollope, toward whose memory these words are directed, Oliphant retained her "fertile faculties" throughout her long life. Her *Autobiography* can be read as the history of her literary productivity: early production, low tide, turning point, and high tide, drying up of the imaginative strain, return to productive work. These stages reveal the nature of Oliphant's transformation, with all its ups and downs, its interruptions and compromises.

Early Production as Evening Entertainment

"Did I write too much?" is not a question Oliphant raised in the youthful stages of her career; the question was, rather, how to find more time to write. Oliphant's earliest efforts were for her own and her family's amusement—evening entertainment for a quiet household. The *Autobiography* records that she wrote her first book, *Christian Melville,* in 1845. She was around sixteen years old at the time. Her second book, about church business and a "half-witted, undeveloped heroine," was never published. She was twenty-one when she published her first book, *The History of Mrs. Margaret Maitland* (1849), over which her mother "laughed and cried with pride" and for which she earned 150 pounds (*OA* 26, 29). In 1852 Oliphant met Major Blackwood and sent him her manuscript of "Katie Stewart," which he published in *Blackwood's* from July through November (*OA* 35).

When Oliphant married Frank later that same year and they moved to London, her writing continued. In the midst of caring for Frank, their two children, Maggie and Tiddy, and her household chores, "I was, of course, writing steadily all the time." These days were some of the happiest that Oliphant recalls, a "halcyon time." Even so, at this early date the issue that was to plague her throughout her lifetime had already emerged. She continues "getting about £400 for a novel, and already, of course, being told that I was working too fast, and producing too much" (*OA* 63). This comment suggests that her editors also held the popular view that industry and real talent are at odds.

Low Tide

By 1859 Margaret Oliphant had written "a half-dozen books or more, and had a little bit of reputation" (*OA* 72). But this early success and the halcyon time were interrupted when Frank became ill and Margaret took him to Italy for his health. It was during this period that Oliphant records one of the few times when overproduction was not at issue.

> I have the clearest vision of him [Frank] sitting close by the little stove in the corner of the room, wrapped up, with a rug upon his knees, and saying nothing, while I sat near the window, trying with less success than ever

before to write, and longing for a word, a cheerful look, to disperse a little the heavy atmosphere of trouble. (*OA* 70)

As Frank's health deteriorated, so did Oliphant's work for the Blackwoods. She has difficulty remembering just what she wrote at the time. She does recall that she completed a story set in Florence called *Felicita* and one of her worst novels, *The House on the Moor* (1861), to which she prefaces the apology: "This book was overshadowed and interrupted by the heaviest grief. The author says so, not to deprecate criticism, but to crave the tender forbearance of her unknown friends."[50] Oliphant's suffering is evidenced in her literary production, which had reached its lowest ebb at Frank's death. Her grief began to lift when in the following summer she moved her family from Birkenhead to Elie in Fife, Scotland. Oliphant was working on a translation of Montalembert's *Monks of the West,* and this work "soothed her" and brought her back to her "full strength," if not her full literary powers (*OA* 89).

The Turning Point and High Tide

I had not been doing well with my writing. I had sent several articles though of what nature I don't remember, to 'Blackwood,' and they had been rejected. Why, this being the case, I should have gone to them. . . to offer them, or rather to suggest to them that they should take a novel from me for serial publication, I can't tell,—they so jealous of the Magazine, and inclined to think nothing was good enough for it, and I just then so little successful. But I was in their debt, and very little to go on with. They shook their heads of course, and thought it would not be possible to take such a story,—both very kind and truly sorry for me, I have no doubt. (*OA* 90–91)

The "turning point" incident is familiar to all Oliphant readers. She begins the first substantial entry of her autobiography with the it (written sometime between 1861 and 1864)[51] and repeats it again in the 30 December 1894 entry, thirty years later. Oliphant recounts that she was "half desperate," "sore," "wounded," and "unsatisfied," "fighting to keep the tears within my eyes that time when they told me they did not want any story from me" (*OA* 3). It was at this juncture that she made the decision that set the course for the remainder of her life. She determined to move to Edinburgh, "to enter without any props upon my natural lonely life." The references to "natural lonely life" and "without any props" imply both a career and a personal decision. She would pursue her work alone, outside the sphere of literary society and without the support of a husband, this being the time when she rejected the marriage proposal of Rev. Robert Herbert Story.

Resolute in her intention to live the lonely life of a writer and determined not to be overcome by the Blackwood rejections, Oliphant then relates:

> I went home to my little ones, running to the door to meet me with 'flich-terin' noise and glee'; and that night, as soon as I had got them all to bed, I sat down and wrote a story which I think was something about a lawyer, John Brownlow, and which formed the first of the Carlingford series,—a series pretty well forgotten now, which made a considerable stir at the time. (*OA* 91)

As Oliphant remembers it, the creation of the *Carlingford* series was the "high tide" of her writing career (*OA* 103). The series was successful and profitable, with *Salem Chapel* making "a kind of commotion, the utmost I have ever attained to," and *The Perpetual Curate* earning her fifteen hundred pounds. Of these works she says, "I never got so much praise, and a not unfair share of pudding too" (*OA* 102). This was also the time that she finished the Edward Irving biography. The question of overproduction, for the moment, was insignificant.

Over the next thirty-five years Oliphant's literary reputation, as she relates it in the *Autobiography,* never reached the same heights. It was during these years that the question of overproduction was most plaguing. In the midst of caring for an ever-expanding family and maintaining a lifestyle of expensive schools for the boys and extensive travel for her entire entourage, she was troubled by the volume of work she must produce to sustain her household, often seeing herself as nothing more than a "production machine."

> When people comment upon the number of books I have written, and I say that I am so far from being proud of that fact that I should like at least half of them forgotten, they stare—and yet it is quite true; and even here I could no more go solemnly into them, and tell why I had done this or that, than I could fly. They are my work, which I like in the doing, which is my natural way of occupying myself, which are never so good as I meant them to be. And when I have said that, I have said all that it is in me to say. (*OA* 15)

While Oliphant resents the deluge of comments about her industry and the paucity of praise for the quality of her work, she is reluctant to speak in any detail about her writing. This serves two purposes: it "silences" the hated industrious characterization of her work, and it allows her to avoid the question of what her work is worth. But this was her public behavior toward her work. In her private thoughts she faced the question of production/overproduction squarely. Had she been less industrious, had she "taken the other way, which seemed the less noble, it might have been better for all of us. I might have done better work. I should in all probability have earned nearly as much for half the production had I done less" (*OA* 16).

Drying Up of the Imaginative Strain

This stage in Oliphant's literary career, the "drying up of the imaginative strain," was brief but painful. With the exception of the time in Rome just before Frank's death, the *Autobiography* records no break in her writing career. Throughout her life, amid all manner of economic crises, family trials, and sorrows, Oliphant wrote steadily. There was always a demand for her work—that is, until December 1887.[52]

> No work, that is the dreadful thing and the consciousness that I am old and that no spring of imagery is at all to be looked for, or that the public should change its always very mild approval into something more warm. That is never at all likely to come now. . . . And now I suspect the stream is ebbing away from me all together, and yet I have nothing before me but to work till I die. (*OA* 157)

This second low ebb in Oliphant's career soon passes and her writing picks up again. It is only when her last child, Cecco, dies at age thirty-four that her literary productivity comes to a full halt and she closes the actual autobiography with the wrenching statement, familiar by now, to all her readers:

> And now here I am all alone.
> I cannot write any more.

Return to Productive Work

But Oliphant did write again, and she continued to write—in her final days she could be found correcting proofs for a history of the Blackwood's Publishing House. While her day-to-day writing was plagued with constant interruptions, there were few major breaks in Oliphant's overall productivity. She wrote consistently for most of her life, yet the *Autobiography* records no steady progress toward a stellar success. Rather, her productivity comes full circle; the literary career that Oliphant traces in the *Autobiography* began as "evening entertainment" and ends in the same way. The final record[53] shows her writing another "baby story" for her own amusement—Cecco touching her shoulder and saying, "Poor Mamma" (*OA* 160).

The Writer Reading Herself: Oliphant's Ambivalence as Criticism

While Oliphant's ambivalence regarding her literary productivity may be attributed to others' criticism of her industry, the ambivalence can also be seen as the self-consciousness of the professional writer and critic. If we see Oliphant as critic—a writer who reads herself into existence and a critic who reads the writer—then her ambivalence may also be read as *criticism.*

Oliphant began her critical career for *Blackwood's* in the 1850s, reviewing the works of a range of authors from Hawthorne, Brontë, Dickens, Shelley, Eliot, and Hardy to de Maupassant, Balzac, and Turgenev. She was noted for her dislike of works that negated moral qualities; she objected to "monstrous, sickening, and nauseous scenes" and "frequently expressed her weariness with popular love stories."[54] It is not surprising that she, a critic for forty-five years, would review her own writing with a similar "cool appraisal."[55]

Much of the ambivalence over the quality of her work, then, may be traced to her own critical methods and these, in turn, to her creative processes. The *Autobiography* provides scant information on these subjects, but the entry marked "1894" offers some insight.

> I wrote as I read, with much the same sort of feeling. It seems to me that this is rather an original way of putting it (to disclose the privatest thought in my mind), and this gives me an absurd little sense of pleasure. (*OA* 118)

Here Oliphant seems to make an on-the-spot discovery about her methods. She describes the mode of her production, suggesting that she could tell a story with the same interest, feeling, and ease with which she read one—no mean feat in itself, as it implies a "natural" talent. But the statement entails much more. Oliphant recognized that the distinctions between reader and writer are blurred. She sensed what present-day theorists have gone to great lengths to document: that writing and reading are interdependent, that writers are their own first readers, and that writers construct their own writing as they read it. As Jane Tompkins argues, "Reading and writing join hands, change places, and finally become distinguishable only as two names for the same activity."[56] Unlike late theorists, however, Oliphant did not conclude that readers also construct the text along with the writer. The self-contained, objective text remained very much a part of her world.

The *Autobiography* is illustrative of Oliphant's mode of production. Her reader and writer selves blur into each other as she reads and writes herself into existence. Langbauer believes that this split within history making—do we simply read or also create the events as we write them?—does not much bother Oliphant: "The writing of her history in a sense comes to stand in for it; her reading of herself (re)creates and authorizes it."[57]

Margaret Oliphant inhabited a number of worlds and read herself from multiple perspectives. Her readings are displayed in a compendium of autobiographical forms she sees as appropriate to her many worlds. When she inhabits the world of the literary critic, she reads herself in terms of the critic's question, "Did I write too much?" She reminds her readers that both Trollope and Scott were prolific, yet they were considered good writers. Thus, readers (critics, in this case) should not count the volume of her writing against her.

For Oliphant ambivalence in the world of the everyday becomes criticism in the world of the professional writer and critic. At times the critic places herself on the best-seller list with *The Perpetual Curate,* and at others she begs her readers' forbearance for publishing works like *House on the Moor.* The various stages of her transformation—evening entertainment, low tides, turning points, high tides, the drying up of the imaginative strain, and the return once again to productive work—are interrupted by and constructed out of her experiences in the everyday. Thus, hers is an ordinary rather than an extraordinary transformation.

The *Autobiography* is Oliphant's way of reading the many worlds she inhabits—personal, social, and professional. She reads her various worlds by acknowledging, questioning, and subverting their many conventions and expectations. The *Autobiography* is also Oliphant's way of reading herself into the world. That hers is an ordinary life, with its ups and downs, its low ebbs and high tides, its fullness and its "awful blanks," means that Oliphant must subvert traditional forms of the autobiography. The "vicissitudes of human life," for her, "the most trite and common of subjects," requires a form that parallels life's uneven rhythms. It must detail the commonplaces; it must tell the human story; it must be "a prosaic little narrative."

That is why productivity works better than progress as figura for Oliphant's transformation.[58] The figurae of Newman's, Mill's, and Darwin's transformations imply myths of progress. Newman, within the figura of economy, progresses toward a fuller understanding of God. Mill, within the figura of reeducation, moves toward greater understanding of society and self. Darwin, within the figura of evolution, develops his scientific potential. In contrast, when Margaret Oliphant is transformed from bread-winner to a bigger me within the figura of literary productivity, she immediately overturns the bigger me persona with a "small," "obscure" me, which she then overturns with breadwinner. In making these reversals, she is doing her work as critic—being productive, even as she is thrusting her "little history" into the history of the world.

Progress implies movement toward the ideal; *productivity* has resonances of a struggle with the pragmatic, the practical. If we could imagine Oliphant constructing her transformation in terms of a myth of progress, hers might be a recounting of the humble beginnings of her writing career, the obstacles she overcame as she improved her artistry, till she arrives at the place at which she writes the "great book." Instead, Margaret Oliphant, within the figura of productivity, constructs a compendium of the ordinary interruptions to her "steady" writing life. Her readers might well say that she resolved the question of production/overproduction for herself: she kept writing.

The Dynamis of Economic Necessity or Artistic Fervor?

If Margaret Oliphant were in conflict over her identity, and if she were ambivalent about the nature of her transformation then, of necessity, she would have difficulty accounting for the force of her life changes. Was she to attribute her transformation to economic necessity or to "artistic fervour"? Had her life been ruled by the need to "keep the vultures off" or by a fuller conception?

The terms *economic necessity* and *artistic fervor* need clarification, since both encompass a range of attributions in the autobiography. What was economic necessity—the need to put food in her children's mouths and keep a roof over their heads—when Oliphant was first widowed with three small children was quite different in degree from the economic necessity she describes when she was sending her children to Eton and Oxford or traveling with them on the Continent. It is no different with artistic fervor; what began as delight in writing became at times artistic passion, at other times "artless art."

The tensions between the two motivating forces for Oliphant's writing may be found throughout the *Autobiography*. Phrases like "I am not unwilling to work," "I had my boys to bring up" (*OA* 56), "how little credit I feel due to me . . . how entirely a matter of daily labour" (*OA* 10), "this is for butter upon the daily bread" (*OA* 55), vie for motive attribution with "now and then the expression of my own heart" (*OA* 10), "a little stirring of ambition" (*OA* 16), writing "came natural to me, it was like talking or breathing" (*OA* 14), "I sat up all night in a passion of composition" (*OA* 91), "write a fine novel" (*OA* 16), and "labour with an artist's fervour" (*OA* 132). The Romantic dynamis of the genius artist empowered by the individual imagination was challenged by the Victorian dynamis of duty to one's community—in Oliphant's case, to her extended family. The Victorian dynamis of duty, by the same token, was beleaguered by her questions of artistry and literary reputation.

One is tempted to look for instances in which Oliphant resolves the dilemma of the dynamis; reviewing its shifts, however, a pattern counterposing artistic fervor with economic necessity emerges. Each time Oliphant settles on or designates the power behind her literary productivity, she overturns it with the opposing attribution. Artistic motivations result in the "great books"; economic motivations cause the writer to "write too much."

In the *Autobiography* Oliphant presents the opposing attributions in an array of permutations. We might compare her methods to Socrates' dialectic in the *Phaedrus* or to Aquinas' scholastic method—question, objection, reply—in the *Summa Theologica* or to what Montaigne identifies as "masking and unmasking" in the *Essays*. Or we might see them as similar to the method Oliphant employs in one of her novels, *Caleb Field* (1851), in which the Nonconformist minister "spoke in *antitheses* very carefully constructed" (*OA* 30; my emphasis). Each of the various terms shares the common quality of skepticism, and it is this skepticism that makes the *Autobiography* more than the "Victorian folly" her editors fabricated in the first editions. The first editions presented a simplistic dynamis: the motivating force for Oliphant's writing was a mother's need to support her children. The Jay edition allows Oliphant to ascribe a complex, ironic dynamis: a literary transformation empowered by artistic fervor *and* economic necessity.

Oliphant was never satisfied with easy explanations for the "what happens" in any realm: the public, the private, or the artistic. She viewed with equal skepticism the motive forces that account for change in politics, her personal life, autobiography, biography, and the lives of the characters in a novel. In what follows I consider how, in the *Autobiography*, this skepticism takes the form of a series of ironic stances constructed by Oliphant to explain the dynamis that accounts for her transformation. I begin with her earliest explanations (in terms of her writing history) and conclude with the position she held in the final days of her life. I do so not to suggest that Oliphant assumed a logical progression in her life and constructed an auto-biography out of that assumption but, instead, to highlight the various per-mutations of motive force that Oliphant constructs to explain her literary production.

"I had no liking then for needlework. . . so I took to writing." The initial impetus for Oliphant's writing was artistic in nature. While nursing her mother during an illness, she took up writing in lieu of needlework "to secure some amusement and occupation" for herself. Her first audience—her mother and her brother Frank—"were highly pleased" with her efforts. She was just sixteen when she wrote *Christian Melville* (*OA* 24–25). Oliphant's literary career began with a love of writing and continued, in its early years, because she wrote well and was encouraged by members of the literary community.

> And then Mr Colburn kindly . . . gave me £150 for 'Margaret Maitland.' I remember walking along the street with delightful elation, thinking that, after all, I was worth something—and not to be hustled aside. I remember, too getting the first review of my book in the twilight of a wintry dark afternoon, and reading it by the firelight—always half-amused at the thought that it was me who was being thus discussed in the newspapers. It was the 'Athenaeum,' and it was on the whole favourable. (*OA* 28–29)

Not only was the *Athenaeum* "favourable" toward her work, but Frances, Lord Jeffrey, critic for the *Edinburgh Review,* sent her "a letter of sweet praise which filled my mother with rapture and myself with an abashed gratitude" (*OA* 29). Oliphant had her first taste of artistic success, and, while she was "wonderfully little moved by the business altogether," she admitted to having "a great pleasure in writing."

"I was of course, writing steadily all the time." Oliphant soon shifts from a dynamis of artistic fervor to one of economic necessity. She recalls that when she married Frank Oliphant, in 1852, "neither of us, I suppose, knew anything about business—so long as we could get on and live." Frank was a stained glass artist and painter, and she wrote to add income to support the household, so that her husband could pursue *his* artistic career. When Frank became ill, Oliphant became the sole support of the family: "I had to

go on working all the time . . . our whole income . . . being £20 a-month, which Mr Blackwood had engaged to send me on the faith of articles. To think of the whole helpless family going to Italy, children and maid and all, upon that alone!" (*OA* 70). When Frank died, "quite conscious, kissing me when his lips were already cold, and quite, quite free from anxiety, though he left me with two helpless children and one unborn, and very little money, and no friends but the Macphersons," Oliphant's financial resources were very low. Her "fortune," when she began life as a widow and mother of three children, was a thousand pounds of debt, Frank's two hundred pound life insurance, her furniture in a warehouse, and "my own faculties, such as they were, to make our living and pay off our burdens by" (*OA* 78–79).

"I sat up all night in a passion of composition." The turning point, Oliphant's decision to lead a lonely life, locates the next dynamic shift in the *Autobiography*. Moving away from economic necessity as motive force for her writing, she returns to the dynamis of artistic fervor. The turning point occurred when (the Blackwoods having repeatedly rejected her literary submissions) an undaunted Oliphant resolved to make writing her career. She then wrote the first novel in her *Chronicles of Carlingford* series out of "passion, stirred to the very bottom of my mind." Her creative efforts won out, and the Blackwoods accepted the series for publication. Oliphant was clearly in financial straits at this time, but the dynamis identified here seems to have its basis in creativity, rather than financial exigency.

"With my head and my hands to provide for my children." Shifting yet again to economic necessity as motive force for her writing, Oliphant weighs her responsibilities against her assets. When asked by a friend, on one of her rare visits to London, "how she was 'left,'" Oliphant responded cheerfully that she was left with her "head" and her "hands" to provide for her children. The response implied that she must work to provide for her children and that writing—head and hands—would supply the means. It was during this same visit to London that Oliphant went to interview Thomas Carlyle regarding her work on Edward Irving's biography. She insists that, "shy as I always was, yet with courage that comes to one when one is about one's lawful work," her need to work was stronger than her fear of the "great" man (*OA* 96–97).

"It is my trade." When Oliphant turns to the explanation "it is my trade" as the motive force for her writing, her irony intensifies.

I have written because it gave me pleasure, because it came natural to me, because it was like talking or breathing, besides the big fact that it was necessary for me to work for my children. That, however, was not the first motive, so that when I laugh inquiries off and say that it is my trade, I do it only by way of eluding the question which I have neither time nor wish to enter into. (*OA* 14)

It is my trade was the dynamis Oliphant put out for public distribution. What appears as a somewhat detached response was, in fact, an ironic one. It allowed her to avoid both the economic and artistic questions posed by her literary and/or popular readership. She takes this ironic stance once again when she insists that "I know very well that for years past neither praise nor blame has quickened my pulse ten beats that I am aware of" (*OA* 10–11). These public assertions allowed Oliphant to move in society without calling attention to herself or her work—a fault she criticized in many.

In the private arena of her autobiography, however, the artistic fervor is brought to the fore once again. She writes that, although she never took her books "au grand serieux,"

I always took pleasure in a little bit of fine writing (afterwards called in the family language a 'trot'), which, to do myself justice, was only done when I got moved by my subject, and began to feel my heart beat, and perhaps a little water in my eyes, and ever more really satisfied by some little conscious felicity of words than by anything else. I have always had my singsong, guided by no sort of law, but by my ear, which was in its way fastidious to the cadence and measure that pleased me; but it is bewildering to me in my perfectly artless art, if I may use the word at all, to hear of the elaborate ways of forming and enhancing style, and all the studies for that end. (*OA* 104–5)

This is the most Oliphant has to say about her artistry, and here, as with her other explanations, she undercuts the whole notion of "grand art" with ordinary phrases such as trot, sing-song, and artless art. In some ways Oliphant's description of her artistry sounds like a private version of her public stance: "it is my trade." Readers must ask: "Is it restraint?" "Is it modesty?" "Is it one of her better fictive pieces?" And a final question, "Is the fact that her art is artless an explanation for Oliphant's dubious reputation?"

"To make a number of people comfortable at the cost of incessant work."

It being in reality easier to me to keep on with a flowing sail, to keep my household and make a number of people comfortable at the cost of incessant work, and an occasional great crisis of anxiety, than to live the self-restrained life which the greater artist imposes upon himself.

With this phrase Oliphant turns again to economic necessity as dynamis. At this point, however, necessity has taken a turn toward luxury—"butter for the bread." Oliphant's economic circumstances have changed. Whereas once she had only a large debt and a small insurance policy, now she is a successful author, earning as much as fifteen hundred pounds for a novel. The shift to economic necessity here has more to do with a higher standard of living than it does with survival. To finance Eton and Oxford for the "boys" and regular holidays for the entire family, not to mention a house-keeper and a secretary for herself, Oliphant worked for months nonstop, writing "twenty pages of an octavo book" a day (OA 55). In a passage that appears in a later entry, in 1895, Oliphant reveals her general attitude toward economics.

> I never had any expensive tastes, but loved the easy swing of life, without taking much thought for the morrow, with a faith in my own power to go on working, which up to this time has been wonderfully justified, but which has been a great temptation and danger to me all through in the way of economies. I had always a conviction that I could make up by a little exertion for any extra expense. Sickness, incapacity, want of health or ability to work, never occurred to me, I suppose. (OA 117)

Here Oliphant's fuller conception of life and its attendant expenses, rather than her fear of impoverishment, are the motive forces for her writing.

Oliphant's flock enlarged when she took on the care of her nephew and two nieces. Economic necessity now surpassed all other concerns. She recalls that she "had been obliged to work pretty hard before to meet all the too great expenses of the house," but now she must work even harder.

> I remember making a kind of pretence to myself that I had to think it over, to make a great decision, to give up what hopes I might have had of doing now my very best, and to set myself steadily to make as much money as I could, and do the best I could for the three boys. I think that in some pages of my old book I have put this down with a little half-sincere attempt at a heroical attitude. I don't think, however, that there was any reality in it. . . . It had to be done, and that was enough, and there is no doubt that it was much more congenial to me to drive on and keep everything going . . . than it ever would have been to labour with an artist's fervour and concentration to produce a masterpiece.

Shying away from a life governed by artistic fervor, Oliphant allows the dream of a "masterpiece" to be overshadowed by the practical dictum "it had to be done." The metaphors of sustenance overpower those of artistry in Oliphant's discourse during this period. Phrases such as "the price of the book was generally eaten up before it was printed," "troublesome debts and forestalling of money earned," "fed my flock," and "butter upon the daily bread" illustrate Oliphant's economic motives. They also suggest Oliphant's assurance that she can provide for her expanded family and provide well (*OA* 132–33).

"It is dreadful in the morning when I wake and try to keep the vultures off." Lest readers conclude that, once Oliphant "made her fortune" with the *Carlingford Chronicles* and the Irving biography and gained a favored position with *Blackwood's,* her economic worries were over, Oliphant sets the record straight. She overturns her "butter for bread" stance with a grim reminder that things did not always go so well. In 1887 she writes:

> This is a very dull Christmas day, nothing pleasant present, nothing to look forward to—my prospects very bad. The boys nil. . . . I want money. I want work, work that will pay, enough to keep this house going which there is no-one to provide for but me. . . . When I try another place it is always more expensive, and there are all the helpless young people, boys who ought to be earning their own living, girls who can't, but would somehow if I was out of the way, servants, dependents—all accustomed to have anything that is wanted and only me to supply all, and I will be sixty in a few months and my work is failing, whether my strength is or not. . . . It is dreadful in the morning when I wake and try to keep the vultures off. (*OA* 155)

It is with bitterness that Oliphant recalls her endless struggles "to supply all." "How vain is all this . . . their very birth, their careful education, my endless struggle that they should have every training, every enjoyment, all vain, vain, and they as if they had never been born" (*OA* 82). In a reflective footnote she admits that her casual attitude about economies and the hiding of her anxieties may have led the boys, especially Tiddy, to develop the attitude that hard work and serious exertion were unnecessary. Her "forlorn pleasure" in knowing that her children had wanted for nothing is turned to remorse (*OA* 117). The irony, for Oliphant, is that one can do "too much" for one's children, and, in her case, one can write too much.

"Success as measured by money never came to my share." Alternating between keeping the vultures off and more butter for the bread, Oliphant shifts to yet another permutation on the dynamis of economic necessity. If the motivation for her literary production (when she was able to keep the vultures off) was to provide butter for the bread, why was there not more butter? Why were her publishers never "very lavish" in their payment? What was the relation of money to literary reputation and artistry?

In posing these questions, Oliphant does a quick calculation of her contemporaries' earnings. George Eliot made ten times more than she, and Oliphant accepted this, but Trollope made three times as much, Miss Mulock a great deal more, while Miss Braddon's "books go on selling as well as ever now they say. Queer!—I don't understand it—not in all their cases at least" (*OA* 157). Money, she concludes, may or may not be a reliable "measure" of artistry. "I never could fight for a higher price or do anything but trust to the honour of those I had to deal with. Whether this was the reason why, though I did very well on the whole, I never did anything like so well as others, I can't tell, or whether it was really inferiority on my part" (*OA* 91). Like a number of plaguing issues, the relationship between income and and artistry remained unresolved in the *Autobiography*. Indeed, because writing was her livelihood and because Victorian editors, critics, and readers believed that success was measured in great part by earnings, Oliphant could not speak of one without the other.

"I am happy I am able to leave a safe little brother and sister home." Even as Oliphant grew older, providing for Cecco, Madge, and Denny (the last of her family) remained a powerful force in her literary productivity. She does not want to "enter into the competition and strain of life" again; she does not believe that "it should be required of her" at her age, but neither Cecco nor the girls are self-supporting. When she reviews the work that she has at hand—the *Autobiography* being one part of it—she notes that finishing it in eighteen months would allow her to leave Cecco with an annual income and a little house, where the girls could live until they married. Despite her weariness, she takes pleasure in being able to provide this "safe little brother and sister home" (*OA* 51).

"It has often carried me away from myself and quenched, or at least calmed the troubles of life." The economic dynamis, after holding sway over much of Oliphant's discourse in the *Autobiography*, is displaced by a tempered version of artistic fervor. The more fervent aspects of writing—"it has often carried me away from myself"—are restrained by its "calming" effects. In

a fairly significant shift of attribution Oliphant here suggests that involvement in the artistic enterprise moves her out of the pain of the everyday and moves her into the calming, soothing rhythms of her work.

"And now here I am all alone / I cannot write any more." Neither economic necessity nor artistic fervor were strong enough to overcome the paralyzing grief that Oliphant experienced at the death of her last child. The structure of the *Autobiography* mirrors this paralysis. When there were no children left to support Oliphant drew the curtain on her life narrative. The *Autobiography*, begun with a narrative about the death of her daughter, ends with the death of her last son and the end of her writing.

If we were left with only the evidence of the actual *Autobiography*, we might see the "end" of Oliphant's writing as permanent. But in the 1896 diary entry appended to the Jay edition, Oliphant writes: "Just a little note of this night. I had been working very hard and came to my room very late and tired" (*OA* 160). This statement appears two years after the "I cannot write any more" entry that ends the actual *Autobiography*. In addition to this "little note," we also learn from Oliphant's bibliography that she wrote a number of stories, novels, biographies, and criticism after 1894.[59] A dynamis beyond that of economic necessity must have empowered this work. Was it artistic fervor? A habit? Had writing become so much a part of her everyday life that "it is my trade," in its best sense, might be seen as Oliphant's final word on her writing? What does she mean when she says, "and now I suspect the stream is ebbing away from me all together, and yet I have nothing before me but to work till I die" (*OA* 157)? While this statement was written in 1887, several years before the statement of 1894 with which the *Autobiography* ends, it seems to ring more true to our sense of Margaret Oliphant. If we read "I cannot write any more" as closure to her *Autobiography*, rather than as an end to her writing altogether, we understand that Oliphant "cannot write any more" about her mother life because that life is over with the deaths of her sons. Therefore, "I have nothing before me but to work till I die" can then be taken as her "final word"; she is left with her working life—her writing. And readers are left with the sense that neither economic necessity nor artistic fervor are any longer at issue.

Keeping the Pot Boiling and the Reputation of a Circulating Library

Margaret Oliphant defends herself against charges of putting the mere necessities of living above the pursuit of the higher objects of art by contrasting the metaphors of "keeping the pot boiling" and the "reputation of a circulating library." Accused of being extravagant and taking "no thought for the morrow," she argued that she did, indeed, "in the way of constant work and constant undertaking of whatever kind of work came to my hand." Yet she admitted that it might have been better had she "added the grace of thrift, which is said to be the inheritance of the Scot, to the faculty of work." But Oliphant knew that she enjoyed getting past a crisis and that the "alternations of anxiety and deliverance were more congenial than the steady monotony of self-denial." She acknowledged, however, that there was another kind of self-denial that "should have made a truer artist than myself pursue the higher objects of art, instead of the mere necessities of living" and that this was wanting in her, too. Admitting that she will pay the penalty of leaving nothing behind "that will live," if she places necessity over art, she asks: "What does it matter? . . . What is the reputation of a circulating library to me?" She insists that, even in her most ambitious periods, "I would rather my children had remembered me as their mother than in any other way and my friends as their friend. I never cared for anything else. . . . it was good to have kept the pot boiling and maintained the cheerful household fire so long" (*OA* 136–37).

Oliphant follows this reflection on what was important to her with yet another twist on the assessment of her professional career. When a naive and thoughtless reader criticized one of her novels, she put her in her place (mentally, not actually) by snapping: "Indeed, my young woman! I should think something a good deal less than that *[Beleaguered City]* might be good enough for you." When she is angered by charges of "overproduction" and "industry," she declares emphatically, "I don't always think such small beer of myself" (*OA* 137).

We might conclude, then, that in the *Autobiography* Oliphant's conflicting personae, her ambivalence toward her transformation, and her inability to resolve the dilemma regarding the forces that drove her literary productivity were a reflection of the tensions that plagued a Victorian working woman tormented by guilt over her failures as mother and professional writer.[60] Oliphant's *Autobiography* goes beyond simple representation, however, in her treatment of these tensions. She posits what might be seen as a unique feature of Victorian women's life writing, her sense of a fuller conception of life *and* autobiography. Hers is a persona of amplitude rather than certitude, and she constructs her narrative around forms that are appropriate to the ordinary life rather than to a myth of progress. For all her success with plots and subplots in her fiction, Oliphant's life narrative has no plot. She does not allow the animus of her life to be shaped by the writer's art.[61]

For Oliphant art was situated in history, and history was predicated on everyday events and ordinary human beings. She was "always carrying a whole little world" with her wherever she went, insisting that both artistic fervor and economic necessity were parts of that world. Her fuller life was empowered by motive forces that ranged from survival-level economic necessity to aristocratic affluence, from the imaginative strain of creativity to artless art. The *Autobiography* confirms that she was breadwinner as well as a bigger me; she kept the pot boiling and maintained a reputation with the circulating library. She was sometimes a failure at both, sometimes not such small beer.

7

Autobiography's Contribution
to the Discourse

Having examined autobiography's functional elements—persona, figura, dynamis—we are now in a position to consider autobiography's unique place in and contributions to the world of discourse: first, to the discourse of a writer's corpus, then to the discourse of the writer's culture, and finally, to the discourse overall. Recognizing that critics are divided regarding the representations of discourse in these ways, I will show how autobiography is uniquely suited to the rethinking of these distinctions.

Autobiography Contributes Transformation to a Corpus

Just as my Accuser asks, "What, then, does Dr. Newman mean?"
. . . I reflected, and I saw a way out of my perplexity.
Yes, I said to myself, his very question is about my *meaning:*
"What does Dr. Newman mean?" (*Apol.* 102)

It is one of the major contentions of this text that autobiography adds the dimension of transformation to the body of texts that are signified by the persona that names a writer's corpus. What do *we* mean when we say "Newman" or "Newman says"? If we adopt a historical approach to this question, we would mean the actual Newman and his actions, his historically documentable activities and accomplishments. If we take a psychological approach, we would mean Newman as a complex psyche and speak of Newman's activities and attitudes in terms of their psychological causes. I suggest another, quite different sense; for the literary critic and the general reader *Newman* means a body of texts. Newman inserts himself into the world of discourse with his corpus. *Newman* stands metonymically for the corpus of his works, as shorthand for *Idea of a University, Essay in Aid of a Grammar of Assent, Apologia Pro Vita Sua,* and *An Essay on the Development of Christian Doctrine.* The name is, in this sense, the corpus.

Newman's autobiography provides an instance of what we mean when we say that Newman initiates a dialogue of transformation and establishes a place for himself in the discourse. We are not simply speaking of a historical Newman pleading for his reinstatement into the society of nineteenth-century Englishmen or his acceptance into the Roman Catholic community. Rather, the autobiographical persona, as it is an aspect of Newman (his corpus), serves to establish Newman's place in the discourse. The autobiography, or *Apologia,* is Newman's Newman, the rhetorically constituted and transformed persona of his corpus. Hence, the *Apologia* adds a dimension to our reading of Newman's corpus that is not available in the other texts. Without the autobiography his corpus consists mainly of theological or philosophical works, and the criteria that are applied to these works are generally the criteria of these disciplines. We do not apply such standards to the autobiography; the *Apologia* does not contribute disciplinary material, as such, to the corpus. It is neither theology, philosophy, sociology, nor history. Instead, in the *Apologia* the figura elaborates changes in Newman's Newman. It places his actions and the events of his life in a context configured as economy. The dynamis of living intelligence specifies the force that changes Newman, Mind and mind.

Thus, we can, because we have Newman's *Apologia,* understand the change that occurred between his *Via Media* and *An Essay on the Development of Christian Doctrine.* It offers a perspective that is not available in the other works of his corpus, and this may be one of the reasons that Newman insisted the *Apologia* always stand as volume 1 in any collected edition of his works. We can, on reading John Stuart Mill's autobiography, discover:

> The experiences of this period had two very marked effects on my opinions and character. In the first place, they led me to adopt a theory of life, very unlike that on which I had before acted, and having much in common with . . . the anti-self consciousness theory of Carlyle. . . . Those only are happy (I thought) who have their minds fixed on . . . the happiness of others. . . . The other important change which my opinions at this time underwent, was that I, for the first time, gave proper place, among the prime necessities of human well-being, to the internal culture of the individual. (*MA* 85–86)

Most of the texts in Mill's corpus are political philosophy: *Principles of Political Economy, On Liberty, The Subjection of Women, Thoughts on Parliamentary Reform.* On studying Mill's corpus, the reader can, and indeed must, infer that Mill changed his position, shifting from a Utilitarian philosophy of government to an organic one, from one paradigm of political philosophy to another. While the disciplinary texts illustrate that a change has occurred, they do not explicate the transformation experience. It is from his autobiography that we come to understand the "important change" that led to his "giving proper place . . . to the internal culture of the individual" in his political system. The persona of the *Autobiography* implies change in the before and after configurations of school-boy logician and philosopher of feeling, the figura elaborates the context for the transformation as reeducation, and the dynamis specifies the force of the change in the imagination, "thought coloured by feeling." The *Autobiography* is Mill's Mill. It is the change narrative in the corpus of an important political philosopher.

We can, on reading Darwin's *Autobiography*, understand how he came to change his practice of science from that described in his first paper to the Plinian Society on the "Ova of Flustra" in 1826 or in his *Beagle* journals of 1831–36 to that described in his monumental work on *The Origin of Species* in 1859. The *Autobiography* supplies the story behind the story of evolution and the long route Darwin took to get there. As explanation and validation of Darwin's changes, the *Autobiography* is Darwin's Darwin. It adds the dimension of how Darwin changed his practice of science from beetle collecting to serious research, from being a casual observer who on a tour with Sedgwick fails to see traces of "the wonderful glacial phenomena . . . the plainly scored rocks, the perched boulders, the lateral and terminal moraines," to a meticulous naturalist who carefully records the effects of cross-fertilization of orchids (*DA* 70, 133).

It is the same with Margaret Oliphant's *Autobiography*, we come to understand how the everyday, for her, was filled with a multitude of competing expectations—professional and personal—and how she continued to write in the midst of these conflicts and tensions. The novels, short stories, articles, travel books, histories, biographies, and translations give evidence of her literary productivity and her public appeal. These works do not tell us, however, how she changed from a young woman who wrote "for her own amusement" to a professional novelist, biographer, and critic. It is Oliphant's autobiography that contributes this transformation to her corpus.

Autobiographies are those texts that describe the transformations underlying writers' other works, as they name, identify, and characterize the personae and elaborate and specify the life change experiences through the figura and dynamis. Writers' other works appropriately do not explicate the processes of transformation or ascribe motivations for these new ways of thinking. It is their autobiographies that add this dimension to their corpora. Augustine's *Confessions*, for example, contributes explanation for the changes from his early works to his later writings, from the *Soliloquies* and *Contra Faustum Manichaeum* to *The City of God* or *Retractationes*. Montaigne's *Essays* record changes in his thinking from his first published work, in which he altered the prologue of his translation of Raymond Sebond's *Liber Creaturarum, sive Theologia Naturalis,* to his later letters, in which he pledges his person and his purse to the king of Navarre, Henry IV. Rousseau's autobiography supplies reasons for changes in his political philosophy from that expounded in *The Origins of Inequality* to those laid out in *Emile* and *The Social Contract.* Modern and postmodern autobiographies, such as Gertrude Stein's and Roland Barthes's, contribute instances of artistic and linguistic transformations to the works that constitute their oeuvres.

When no autobiography exists in the writer's corpus, biography sometimes supplies a version of the life change experience. Peter Ackroyd's biography of T. S. Eliot, for example, attempts to explain the differences evidenced between the *Wasteland* and *Four Quartets.* Biography functions, in place of the absent autobiography, to account for the transformation in Eliot's contributions to the discourse.[1]

Autobiography, then, speaks its meaning, actualizes its transformation—makes its contribution to a writer's corpus—through its rhetorical figuration. "Existing" in the text both implicitly and explicitly, persona, figura, and dynamis present unique and specific life change narratives that focus on the significance of the individual autobiographer's transformation rather than on events, dates, and facts.

Autobiography Contributes Transformation to a Culture

In addition to autobiography's contribution to an individual writer's corpus, autobiography also contributes a discourse of transformation to a particular culture, as it shapes and is shaped by a particular group or subgroup at a particular time and place in its history. Just as families collect tales about their histories, societies accrue autobiographies that provide them with inscriptions of human beings and how they change. Individual changes may be traced to changes in the culture, and, conversely, cultural changes occur in response to individual changes. This truism is manifested in the Victorian autobiographies in this study. Because each of the autobiographers belongs to the educated, professional, and, in Darwin's case, wealthy class, their narratives address particular segments of Victorian England. And, because each inhabits different worlds within this subgroup, their narratives make unique contributions to the various subcultures. Newman addresses certain theological and academic segments of the culture; Mill, liberal elements of the political sector; Darwin, the scientific community; and Oliphant, the literary. Each inserts her or his narrative of transformation into the culture by means of the persona, figura, and dynamis as the autobiographies are taken up and read by their contemporary audiences.

Victorian Personae

John Henry Cardinal Newman, characterized as Anglican turned Catholic, John Stuart Mill, characterized as reasoning machine turned philosopher of feeling, Charles Darwin, characterized as beetle collector turned naturalist, and Margaret Oliphant, characterized as artist turned breadwinner turned artist, along with Carlyle's fictive persona, tailor and retailored tailor, mark out very different Victorian personae. Beyond their individual uniquenesses, however, they allow us to identify some of the representative persona types that can be found in certain segments of Victorian culture.

Newman, like many other Victorian Anglican theologians, is enmeshed in controversy over the liberalization of the Church of England. With Newman we discover that he infuses the Anglican persona in all its forms (Evangelical, Noetic, Tractarian, Layman) with Catholic features so as to defend his position against charges of contradiction or "lies." He attempts to reestablish his credibility with a theological community that is shocked by his transformation.

As liberal political philosopher, Mill finds that he is very much in tune with a certain political subgroup in Victorian England, the Utilitarians. The before and after characteristics (boy dedicated to logic, philosopher concerned with feelings) reveal, however, a sharp dissonance between the two terms and thus imply that Mill may be out of tune with the general public. To design a political system that is not based on material need, that will work for human beings, Mill must take the larger English population into account; he must listen to the entire Victorian community—the populace, the poet, and the political theorist. Mill represents a political element of the Victorian population that is committed to the overall welfare of the Victorian citizenry.

Because Charles Darwin is such a prominent figure in the history of science and because his *Autobiography* is anecdotal, direct, and unassuming, its unique place in the history of autobiography regularly goes unnoticed. Its uniqueness is due, in part, to the introduction of a new type of persona not encountered in prior autobiographies. Unlike the tension between the terms of the Newman and Mill personae, with the Darwin persona both beetle collector and acclaimed naturalist encompass the notion of scientist, the first naive, the latter mature. What distinguishes Darwin's persona type in the Victorian culture is that, in the continuum of terms that mark out his persona, the potential for the latter is present in the former—"young" scientist and "old" scientist. It is what Darwin himself characterizes as "innate capacity." Innate capacity became a popular term among Victorian scientists, but it resonated throughout Victorian society. Victorian poets, political economists, liberal theologians, and eugenicists blithely took up his metaphor while rejecting the radical ideas of the man of science.

The names that Margaret Oliphant gives herself indicate, among other things, a confusion over gender roles. She discovers that she is neither the perfect Victorian mother—all the members of her extended family die or come to nothing—nor is she as prominent a novelist as her female contemporaries George Eliot, George Sand, and Charlotte Brontë. She is, however, a writer who reads herself into autobiography, rather than focusing on the characters and plots of her novels. In so doing, she introduces a new type of autobiography into the literary culture of Victorian England. Its forms are appropriate to the "ordinary" life of a "fat, little commonplace woman, rather tongue-tied."

Due to a variety of factors—the writers' professions, purposes in writing, their ages, their audiences—we can see the *was* and *is* configurations of the personae as highly individualistic or unique. On the other hand, these configurations share attitudes, values, and qualities that are integral to certain segments of Victorian culture. National apostasy and liberalization of the Church of England, Utilitarianism, mechanistic political economy, the origin of species, and the production and distribution of literature were concerns for many Victorians. The names the four autobiographers give themselves embody these concerns. These Victorians, like the Romantics before them, were concerned with the potential of the individual; in contrast to the Romantics, however, they valued the contribution of the individual to the society. They were committed to duty; they valued change, productivity, and progress. They saw themselves as changing, but they also saw themselves as change agents in religion, politics, science, and literature.

Like Carlyle's tailor, they saw themselves as integral to the "reweaving" of society.

Are these sets of characteristics or persona types—Anglican / Catholic, reasoning machine / philosopher of feeling, beetle collector / acclaimed naturalist, breadwinner/artist—the only ones that can be discovered in the autobiographies? While they are some of the more obvious, they should not be considered as "final words" for the selves. Rather, these characterizations or names may be seen as starting places for further study of the narrative selves inscribed in the autobiographies. They offer basic rhetorical terms out of which other critical approaches to the genre may be developed.

Victorian Figurae

The figura, as it encapsulates, summarizes, and grounds the notion of change in autobiography must be a metaphor that names the transformation. That is why economy works as a suitable figura for John Henry Cardinal Newman's transformation in the *Apologia Pro Vita Sua,* as does reeducation for Mill, evolution for Darwin, and productivity for Oliphant. While these figurae encapsulate or summarize individual transformations, they also participate in (share in and shape) the metaphors, images, and figures that serve as grounds, limits, and modes of transformation in certain segments of Victorian culture. These are not working-class metaphors, nor are they images and figures that were operative among the servant classes. The figurae in this study are terms available in the discourse of the educated, professional classes.

"Economies or Dispensations of the Eternal," "gradual assent," "slow course of change," "first one disclosure then another," "assemblage of concurring and converging possibilities"—these are images that Newman draws upon to express the nature and mode of his religious transformation. In an individual, specific sense we could say that Newman's conversion is unique to him alone; clearly, for instance, it is different from the spontaneous conversions of the Evangelicals. But it is very much akin to political change in Victorian England. While some Victorians, such as the Chartists, socialists, and anarchists, promoted radical change, these groups were offset by conservative elements, and, thus, revolutionary or precipitous change was avoided. Newman's figura of a gradual, economical transformation spoke to these more conservative elements in the Victorian citizenry.

As with Newman, the network of images that define the mode and limits of John Stuart Mill's transformation from reasoning machine to humanistic political philosopher suggest a conversion experience. Unlike Newman's transformation, however, Mill's is the conversion of reeducation. References to the unusual and rigorous intellectual training provided by Mill's father are displaced by images that suggest a new sort of education. These sets of images clash against each other, old mentality and new—father and son. In an individual sense we could say that the son is saving himself from the father. In terms of Victorian politics we could say that Mill is displacing a mechanistic political philosophy for a more humanistic one. The figura of Mill's transformation draws its shape and substance from the political philosophers who were concerned with mechanization and its destructive consequences. A reeducated Mill attempts to reeducate his society in the kind of government befitting the English people. He attempts to teach them the benefits of Victorian industry and technology. In this way Mill not only joins the Victorian political community; he becomes a member of a Continental community. Like the Saint-Simonians, he believes that progress—political, industrial, technological—can be beneficial, if human beings are taken into account in society's development.

Survival of the fittest, struggle for existence, and evolution are metaphors that Charles Darwin uses to explain both his theory of species and his own development as a scientist. Taken together, they describe his transformation as gradual, evolving. Evolution, the figura of Darwin's unique transformation, may also be seen as indicative of progress in the society at large. The Victorian period was a time of order *and* turmoil. As Asa Briggs tells us, "the stability of the period can be overemphasized." Orderly, gradual change ran alongside other, less balanced tendencies. "Although there was a belief in the superiority of English representative institutions, at particular moments as in 1854 and 1855, they were more vigorously attacked than at any other period in the nineteenth century."² Rowdyism reached its peak at election times; there was a growth in militant radicalism in the cities, which led, in 1867, to the second Reform Bill. Economic stability was interrupted by economic crises in 1857 and 1866, and war scares threatened the peace. All things considered, however, Darwin's metaphor holds. The Victorians took the crises in stride; they adapted to changes. Carlyle's forecast of the end of our "poor old England" when the vote was granted to urban workers failed to come to pass. The country survived one more evolving.

Incessant work, industry, and infinite labour are the network of images that are tied to the figura of productivity in Margaret Oliphant's autobiography. From an individual standpoint these images depict her day-to-day existence. In terms of Victorian culture they suggest a certain mind-set. While there were significant disagreements among the Victorians over how to define labor, how to reward it, and who should benefit from it—and "trade" was viewed with contempt by the upper classes—"work," "production," and "labor" were lauded in periodicals, sermons, and political speeches. While "hard work was considered the foundation of all material advancement; and both clear thinking and hard work were deemed essential to continued national progress,"[3] for Oliphant such productivity contributed to her ambivalence over her status as an artist.

This seems to suggest that the transformations of Newman, Mill, Darwin, and Oliphant fit neatly and easily into the cultural and linguistic frameworks of Victorian England. We know that this is far from the truth; the work they did—Newman's rejection of the Church of England, Mill's liberal politics, Darwin's scientific theories, and Oliphant's literary reviews—often set them at odds with the English public. While the metaphors, network of images, and figures that the four Victorians chose to summarize their transformations were available in the culture, each of the four also used them to argue for change: theological, political, scientific, and literary. Oliphant uses the notions of production and overproduction to critique the practice of formulaic novel writing—her own and others. Darwin uses evolution, with its "being more sagacious than man," to forestall charges of unorthodoxy directed toward his scientific theories. Newman uses economy to argue for membership in the Catholic Church. Mill uses reeducation to reexamine his own political philosophy and to call for a reexamination of government practices. Like Teufelsdröckh, who was encouraged by his English editor to write his "Auto-Biography" so that his plan for the reconstruction of society laid out in the "Philosophy of Clothes" could be carried forward, the four Victorians chose figures that called for change in the various Victorian worlds they inhabited.

Economy, reeducation, evolution, productivity—the concept of *figura* encompasses both the figure of speech and the visual image that stands behind it as generative and aggregate. As with the personae, the *figurae* are heuristic; they are ways of understanding *some* of the transformation types evident in Victorian culture. We could, just as readily, explore Newman's autobiography from the *figura* of development, Mill's autobiography from the *figura* of conversion, Darwin's from the *figura* of growth, Oliphant's from the *figura* of professionalism. There is, then, no one right *figura* for an autobiography. As heuristic, *figura* may be seen as a distinct, individual "mark" on the culture and as a way that the culture marks the individual as she or he participates in those understandings derived from a culture's language and stories. Autobiography contributes a discourse of transformation to the culture through its figurations.

Victorian Dynamis

The dynamis for the transformations in the four autobiographies—"living intelligence, "thought coloured by feeling," "zeal and environment," "economic necessity or artistic fervour?"—are motives of change implied by the personae and the figurae. While they are unique and specific to the individual autobiographer, they also allow us to draw some interesting conclusions about the motive forces to which some Victorians attributed change in their culture. They share in a general dynamis that is Romantic in character: human potential. This Romantic motive force, however, is tempered by a Victorian dynamis; human potential is directed toward cultural concerns.

Notice that the dynamis of Newman's transformation, the living intelligence, has aspects of the potential of the individual, the mind of God as illuminated in scripture and dogma, and a concern for English Christians. Unlike Teufelsdröckh's absentee God, Newman's God was very much present for a large portion of the Victorian population, who "still called God into the reckoning whenever they needed Him. . . . Thousands of sermons of every denomination proclaimed that the whole English social system rested not only on divine sanction but on the particular operations of Providence."[4] Newman was being responsible to his country when he asked his fellow citizens to understand how an English Anglican could turn Catholic.

Similarly, Mill attributes his transformation to mind, but he adds the imagination and characterizes the dynamis as thought colored by feeling. "Thought coloured by feeling" shares in a Romantic dynamis—the potential of the individual—but as it is directed toward the political needs of his society, Mill, as a new sort of English political philosopher, constructs a political philosophy that takes into account both the human and material well-being of England's citizens. *On Liberty* is one expression of Mill's commitment to Victorian society.

The motive force of Darwin's transformation, zeal and environment, shares in this same idea. The zeal of the individual operates in concert with the environment to bring about the development of the scientist and science. Darwin's motive force zeal can be seen as Romantic in character; it is a devotion to or a passion for science. Yet nature is all-important in a transformation that is configured as evolution, and Darwin must attribute his change to zeal *and* environment. Unlike Teufelsdröckh's mechanized universe that stultifies and grinds him to pieces, Darwin's world is alive; it abounds in "wonderfully complex and changing circumstances." In his efforts to push the boundaries of science Darwin joins other Victorian scientists, both professional and amateur, who are dedicated to the improvement of society through scientific research.

Margaret Oliphant's novels, literary reviews, histories, and biographies attest to her productivity. Transformed from a young woman who wrote for her own amusement to a productive artist, she does not attribute her transformation to God, as does Newman, but she does point to God (blame Him) as cause of her grief and her widowed condition. Because she maintained an extended household and pursued a career in writing, she was forced to "carry a whole little world" with her wherever she moved. Her creativity was often interrupted or displaced by her need to be productive. A Victorian dynamis, commitment to duty, continually vies for place with a Romantic dynamis, the creative potential of the individual. Oliphant counters the criticism that she wrote too much by showing how productivity was her duty; it was tied to her need to provide for her children. It is worth recalling, however, that Oliphant's novels did much more than feed her family ("the price of a book was generally eaten up before it was printed"); she used her heroines to subvert Victorian stereotypes and to flaunt Victorian conventions.

We could say, then, that a Romantic dynamis is at work in each of the four transformations but that this motive power has as part of its force a Victorian dynamis. In simplest terms we could say that the potential of the individual is shaped by duty to society. These Victorian autobiographers believed in the individual, but they also believed in progress and productivity. They wanted to correct the abuses of unrestrained individualism by instilling in their fellow citizens a sense of responsibility for social well-being. They are thus in sync with a prevailing belief, articulated by Samuel Smiles in his book *Self-Help,* that

> steady application to work is the healthiest training for every individual, so is it the best discipline of a state. Honorable industry travels the same road with duty; and Providence has closely linked both with happiness.[5]

Preaching the "gospel of work" through homilies and prophecies, Smiles agrees with Mill that "the principal industrial excellence of the English people [lay] in their capacity of present exertion for a distant object."[6] The Victorian dynamis, then, must go beyond the Romantic dynamis of the individual to take into account the values of work and duty to England called for by Smiles and Carlyle and exemplified in the autobiographies of Newman, Mill, Darwin, and Oliphant.

When we characterize the motive forces of the four autobiographies as Victorian, then, we are examining them in cultural terms, or as dynamis types, that were operative during the period: the power of the individual mind and imagination, responsible to both self and society. Thus we can see dynamis types, like metaphors of the self and patterns of experience, as tied to the culture and the texts of the times.

Autobiography Contributes Transformation to the Discourse

As particular autobiographies image forth transformation in an individual writer's corpus and culture, autobiography, as genre, stands as a text of transformation in the larger universe of discourse. As genre, autobiography makes its contribution to the discourse as those texts that provide us with an understanding of how change is rhetorically constituted. Autobiography, like all forms of communication through inscribed discourse, is a human institution: someone telling someone else *something*. Autobiography is a unique kind of human institution, however, in that it tells how something happened to a *me*. While readers acknowledge that this *me* is a construct, they also see the *me* of autobiography as standing in a different (not privileged) relationship to the world and reader than do, for example, the characters Madame Bovary or Stephen Dedalus. "The taking up of one's life in language that adumbrates the autobiographical perspective testifies to the autobiographer's particular involvement in the world, a landing rather than a hovering."[7] Autobiography constructs a coherent story from the tattered remains of our experience. For Eakin autobiography is a counter to death. Speaking of Sartre's *Words,* he surmises, "As long as the engine of plot 'purrs,' the heart beats, for life as a structure of meaning and literature are one; the alternative to narrative motion is death."[8] Gunn sees the autobiography as characterizing our actual experience in two ways: first, in its manifest representation of temporal succession, the surface level of day-after-day temporality that is most immediately available to reading; and, second, in its latent dimension of depth that constitutes the more significant grounding for the *fittingness* between narrative and being in the world.⁹ Starobinski sees autobiography as opposition to oblivion:

> The life of an individual does not become fully determinate until it exhibits itself; but as we come under the scrutiny of others, we pay for the support we derive from them by undergoing, even in our own lifetime, the ordeal of death, or negativity; and it is by way of this ordeal that we acquire our full personal identity. Indeed, by showing ourselves we lose a part of what we are, we expose ourselves to risk, we entrust ourselves to the safekeeping of others, we "mortgage" our lives. . . . To write is to behold oneself in a second body created by deliberate alienation of the self; it is to produce a verbal tissue—the text—offered to the comprehension of the virtual reader. The text is that strange object that draws its life from the disappearance of the craftsman who made it. The written work, a vicarious form of life, a likeness destined to survive its original, externalizes life and internalizes death.¹⁰

Autobiography as narrative of transformation contributes "involvement," "reconciliation," "fittingness," and "survival" to the discourse. To return to the example of Newman, if we accept Michael Ryan's deconstructive contention that the *Apologia* is only a "speaking away" of Newman's self, then we have no Newman at all (or Mill, or Darwin, or Oliphant).¹¹ If, on the other hand, we see autobiography as "fittingness between narrative and being in the world," or as heartbeat and plot "purr" then the *Apologia* Newman is both his Newman and ours, alive to himself as he reconstructs a "coherent story" from his experiences and alive ("mortgaged") to us as the book that "survives" him, that lives in his stead. No literary theory can obliterate entirely the reader's expectation that autobiography is "life discursive," about an actual person, and that the events inscribed in the text have some relationship to actual events in the world of the everyday.

As autobiography is life discursive, it stands as the universal *word* for human transformation. Autobiography is about transformation, and yet *transformation* is a perverse term that will not itself stand still. Autobiography declares that change itself changes. If we briefly survey autobiography from antiquity to postmodern times, we discover that the rhetorical aspects of persona, figura, and dynamis give evidence of their own transformations and, in turn, display just how much the narratives of change have changed across the periods of its history.

And It Moves

Autobiographies from antiquity take the forms of defense of one's actions, praise of one's deeds, or declaration of one's loyalty to the gods or the polis. Autobiographies from the medieval period, like the *Confessions* of Saint Augustine, take the form of prayers of confession and reject pagan values for the Christian. Michel Montaigne's *Essays* replace conversion narratives with essays that explore the humanist values of the Renaissance. Jean-Jacques Rousseau's *Confessions* explore not only Enlightenment ideas and human manifestations of them but, also, internal feelings and motives. With his autobiography we could say that Rousseau *invents* the Romantic period. The autobiographies of Newman, Mill, Darwin, and Oliphant take the values of the Romantics, with their emphases on the unlimited potential of the individual, and extend them to include duty to one's country, one's church, one's scientific community, and one's family. Gertrude Stein's autobiography rejects the values of Romantic narrative altogether, opting, instead, for autobiography as surface manifestation, trading a narrative of feelings for narrative as a work of art. We see these values as tied to what we now call the Modernist period. Roland Barthes's autobiography displaces the Modernist view with the postmodern. He attempts to construct the way in which a text (autobiography) displaces both the self and the work of art. Whereas Stein's narrative collapses the boundaries between self and work of art, Barthes insists that all we have is text—a language self that continues to be transformed with each new reading (misreading, deviate reading) and each new reader.

Through the aspects of persona, figura, and dynamis autobiography contributes a discourse of transformation to an individual writer's corpus, to a culture, and to the larger discourse. Taken together, the transformations of the persona from antiquity to the present show how the inscribed self of autobiography has changed from a self secure in the presence of the gods or God to the total absence of self. Antiphon, secure in his relationship to Athens' gods, is first "Athenian citizen accused" then "virtuous citizen without motive for revolution." Augustine is first "pagan" then "Christian"; Montaigne is first "essayist" then "essayist changed by his *Essays*." Rousseau is first "innocent child of nature" then "persecuted social reformer," "victim." Newman is first Anglican then Catholic; Mill is first school-boy logician, then philosopher of feeling; Darwin is beetle collector then "acclaimed naturalist; Margaret Oliphant is breadwinner then artist; Gertrude Stein is first Alice B. Toklas's Gertrude Stein then "everybody's"

Gertrude Stein; Roland Barthes is first old "image-repertoire"—language images of the body—then "text."

The transformations of the personae taken across this set of autobiographies give evidence that the ways of inscribing the self in autobiography have changed from a model self to a Christian or spiritual self to a secular or public self to a Romantic self of feelings and to a Victorian self of duty. Overturning Rousseau's self of feelings and ignoring the Victorian sense of duty, Stein's self of surface manifestations becomes a work of art. Roland Barthes's self as language displaces the self altogether. Transformation shows its perversity, its predilection to change through the persona. With each new depiction of the self an old way of viewing the self and inscribing it is overturned. This suggests that in the autobiography we have a history of *deviating personae*.

Taken together, the transformations of the figura show how the types for inscribing transformation have changed. Figuration itself is transformed by the misreading of prior figures. Autobiographers in antiquity inscribed their transformations in terms of model selves actualized through voyages, battles, observations, or restorations. Augustine describes his transformation in terms of a spiritual "confession," a prayerful dialogue between a sinful man and his God. Montaigne inscribes his transformation as "essaying," a dialogue between the man and his book. Rousseau characterizes his transformation as "a chain of misfortunes" of a man at odds with his culture. The four Victorians construct the figures of their transformations to show concern for society. Stein's *Autobiography of Alice B. Toklas* is a "misprision" of earlier autobiographies, with their excessive expressions of internal feelings and subconscious motives. Stein gives us a new type of figura, that of "transactions," believing that only that which is visible, conscious, at the surface, can or should be conveyed by the autobiographer. Barthes presents his transformation as displacements or "zig-zags"; self-images are displaced by text. The autobiographical figurae give evidence that modes of change change.

Dynamis, taken across these autobiographies, also gives evidence of change. The motive force for Antiphon's change is attributed to the Athenian gods; the power of Augustine's transformation is attributed to God; Montaigne sees the dynamis of his transformation arising from questioning, humanist skepticism, and detachment. Rousseau sees *himself* as the force of transformation; it is only the circumstances of life and the deceitfulness of those around him that keep him from realizing his full potential. The Victorians attribute change to the potential of the individual and a commitment to duty. Gertrude Stein sees the artist's genius as the power of her transformation. She enlarges or transforms the self by juxtaposing surface portrait after surface portrait in the creation of her own multifaceted (and "multifaced") portraiture. Roland Barthes attributes his transformation to the dynamis of "the hand that writes"; writing is the power of displacement; it becomes for Barthes a dynamis of "deviance."

These various attributions of dynamis suggest that the ways of explaining the power of transformation have changed: from the gods or God to an enlightened skepticism and, subsequently, to an individual ego, to artistic genius, to the "hand that writes," a new kind of writing, absent of images— chirography. Taken together, the transformations of the dynamis show how the power of transformation in autobiography has changed from the power of the gods or God, the Logos, to the power of writing, logology, or to the perversity of word games *(dissoi logoi)*.

Persona, figura, and dynamis, then, give summary evidence that change, as it is inscribed in autobiography, has itself changed. The transformation of a self, central to autobiographical discourse in earlier times, has changed to textual transformation—from the self speaking language to language speaking the self. More recent autobiographers, tired of word games and dissatisfied with absence of self, have refused to write the self out of existence (over and over again). They have begun to write the self in innovative modes and have grounded the transformations of the self in the imagination as it keeps the self alive in the world of autobiography.[12] My example is Maxine Hong Kingston.

In *The Woman Warrior: Memoirs of a Girlhood among Ghosts* Kingston attests that she is unwilling to allow the self to be displaced by language. She makes language her servant by "retelling" old "talk-stories" in her autobiography—a series of new talk-stories. She reinvests her self with a life that language, her Chinese mother's talk-stories, had stripped from her. *The Woman Warrior* can be seen as Kingston's revenge on language and its power to terrify or scare away the self. She screams at her mother:

> And I don't want to listen to any more of your stories; they have no logic. They scramble me up. You lie with stories. You won't tell me a story and then say, 'This is a true story,' or, 'This is just a story.' I can't tell the difference. I don't even know what your real names are. I can't tell what's real and what you make up. Ha! You can't stop me from talking. You tried to cut off my tongue, but it didn't work." So I told the hardest ten or twelve things on my list all in one outburst.[13]

Kingston "masters" language with her own words. Forbidden by her mother to speak of her aunt, the "No Name Woman," because the aunt has violated the community's code prohibiting adultery and has stained the family honor, Kingston deliberately retells the aunt's story. In so doing, Kingston makes a place for the aunt and for herself that has been denied them by the traditions of Chinese discourse. Kingston tells of the mighty woman warrior who, with family oaths carved on her back, avenges her people. She tells of the captured poetess Ts'ai Yen, whose songs rose high and clear above the barbarian reed pipes and, when brought back from savage lands, were sung with Chinese instruments.

Contrast this fully integrated persona—characterized as courageous and creative, with ornate back and beautiful voice, warrior and a poet—to Barthes's disappearing self, only "the hand that writes." Contrast Barthes's narrative of transformation—zig zag, mere marks, writing motion—to Kingston's talk-stories. Constructing a text of a life that draws on and mimics an oral tradition in opposition to one that displays itself through the means of marks and letters, Kingston's stories are revisions, or retellings, of earlier oral narratives; the *Memoirs* becomes a tale of a woman retelling tales. Kingston's autobiography demonstrates what Barthes's, with its narrowed, distanced, and disappearing self (hand), does not; the displacement of the postmodern "no-self" with a self of *plenitude*—a self that fully integrates the old and new, the Chinese and American, male and female, the oral and inscribed. It is a talk-written self, a self of continuity *and* change.

Language sabotages Kingston no longer. Telling her own truth, constructing her own talk-stories, making language serve her, Kingston continues to wrestle the "ghosts that sit on her head." Within the figura of talk-story the Chinese girl with the "dried-duck voice" has changed to woman warrior—poet avenger—"speak-writing" of living, sorting, and changing.

> The throat pain always returns, though, unless I tell what I really think. . . . I continue to sort out what's just my childhood, just my imagination, just my family, just the village, just movies, just living.[14]

Autobiography, then, is the "literature of transformation." Spoken, written, or sung, autobiographies are that set of texts that provide us with an understanding of how change occurs and how that change, once performed, presented, or inscribed, finds its place, or meaning, in the larger discourse. As Samuel Taylor Coleridge (the poet read by each of the four Victorian autobiographers) reminds us:

Every man's language has, first, its *individualities;* secondly, the common properties of the *class* to which he belongs; and thirdly, words and phrases of *universal* use.[15]

The autobiographical transformation, as it is a reflection on experience, is at first individual. As it is constituted by language and directed toward its contemporary audience, it speaks through metaphors that are held in common, that are shared by the texts that surround it. As it is taken up into the ongoing discourse, autobiography establishes its place as universal word for transformation. As Gertrude Stein reminds us,

"It moves, but it also stays."

Appendix: The Elisabeth Jay Chronology of Margaret Oliphant's Life

[To this I have added the chronology of Oliphant's autobiographical entries. Oliphant's original headings for the entries in the *Autobiography* are italicized. My brief summary of each entry and additional comments appear in brackets.]

1828   4 April: Margaret Oliphant Wilson born at Wallyford, Midlothian, youngest child of Francis W. Wilson (c. 1788–1858), clerk, and Margaret Oliphant (c. 1789–1854). Her two elder brothers are Francis (Frank) and William (Willie). During her first ten years the family move first to Lasswade, near Edinburgh, and then to Glasgow.

1838   Family move to Liverpool.

1845   Margaret suffers broken engagement.

1849   Publication of Margaret's first novel. She spends three months in London as housekeeper for Willie and there meets her cousin, Francis Wilson Oliphant (Frank).

1851   Margaret and her mother visit Edinburgh.

1852   Willie leaves his first ministerial post in Etal, Northumberland, and returns home, disgraced.

        4 May: Margaret marries her cousin Frank (1818–59), artist and stained-glass window designer, and moves to London. In August her parents and Willie move to London to be near her.

1853   21 May: Birth of daughter, Margaret Wilson Oliphant (Maggie).

1854   22 May: Birth of second daughter, Marjorie Isabella.

        17 September: Death of Margaret's mother.

1855   8 February: Death of Marjorie Isabella. [Jay lists this under 1854.]

        November: Death of third child, a son, after only one day.

1856   16 November: Birth of fourth child, Cyril Francis (Tiddy or Tids).

1857   First signs of Frank Oliphant's tubercular condition.

1858   28 May: Death of fifth child, Stephen Thomas, aged nine weeks.

1859   Margaret, Frank, and the children leave for Italy hoping to improve Frank's health. Margaret's regular contributions to *Blackwood's Magazine* provide the family income.

20 October: Frank dies in Rome.

12 December: Birth of last child, Francis Romano (Cecco).

1860   February: Margaret and her children return to England to stay with her brother Frank and his family in Birkenhead. Summer spent in Fife. In October Margaret and her children move to Edinburgh.

1861   Begins *Chronicles of Carlingford* series. Moves to Ealing in October to be close to friends.

N.D.   *No heading.* [First substantial entry of the *Autobiography;* describes Oliphant's "turning point." Must have been written between the writing of the early stories in the *Chronicles of Carlingford* series in the early 1860s and daughter Maggie's death in 1864] (*OA* 3–4).

1863   Margaret and her children accompany friends to Italy.

1864   27 January: Eldest child, Maggie, dies in Rome; remainder of the year spent in Italy, Switzerland, and France.

Rome, 1864. [Oliphant details the "dreadful moment when my firstborn was taken from me"] (*OA* 4–9).

Albano, March 13. [Oliphant upbraids and reproaches God for her losses] (*OA* 9–11).

Capri. [Oliphant continues her mourning for Maggie] (*OA* 11–13).

[Major break in the manuscript of the *Autobiography;* Oliphant makes no entries from 1864 until 1885.]

1865   September: Returns from France to London. In December moves to Windsor for boys' schooling at Eton.

1866   Annie Louisa Walker (future Mrs. H. Coghill, editor of *Autobiography*) becomes Margaret's housekeeper and secretary.

1868   Brother Frank suffers financial ruin. Margaret takes in his two eldest children and sends Frank junior to Eton when his parents go abroad.

1870   Margaret's recently widowed brother Frank returns to England, apparently having suffered a nervous breakdown. He and his two youngest children, Margaret Oliphant (Madge) and Janet Mary (Denny) become wholly dependent upon Oliphant.

1875   July: Margaret's brother Frank dies.

August: Madge and Denny sent to school in Germany.

October: Tiddy goes up to Balliol College, Oxford, and Margaret's nephew Frank, a qualified engineer, sails for India.

1879   Madge and Denny return from Germany in the spring, Madge to train as a wood-engraver and Denny to attend boarding-school in Windsor. In October their brother Frank dies in India.

1884   Tiddy leaves for Ceylon to be private secretary to the Governor, but soon returns in poor health. In the summer Margaret enjoys her first mystical experience, in St. Andrews.

1885   Margaret's brother Willie dies in Rome where he had been supported by her for quarter of a century.

[A note Oliphant wrote some time after 1894 when both her sons were dead is inserted between the 1864 and the 1885 entries: "Whether anything should be taken from the preliminary pages, Denny, with the help of perhaps Cousin Annie, or some other friend (none so capable) whom she can trust, must decide."]

[1885]   *Windsor, 1st February 1885.* [Twenty-one years have passed since the last entry, which Oliphant has just been reading; she is now fifty-seven but feels not "quite grown up." This is the first extended chronological narrative; it discusses her birth, her growing up years, her marriage, the birth of her two daughters, the deaths of her mother and her second daughter and the brief but happy days in London] (*OA* 13–44).

[1887]   *No heading.* APPENDIX A: Diary entry for Christmas night, 1887 [This entry is written three years before Tiddy dies and seven years before Cecco's death. This would mean that Tiddy was thirty-one and Cecco was twenty-eight, some of the worst times for them. Oliphant concludes the entry: "Very sad ending to the year. All these hopes gone"] (*OA* 155–58). [Jay places this and the other two diary entries ("B" and "C") at the end of the *Autobiography.*]

[1888]   *No heading.* APPENDIX B: 1888 Diary [Written two years before Tiddy's death and six years before Cecco's, Oliphant records that the year began in great anxiety. Cecco is in the Riviera for his health and Oliphant is in great financial trouble. She claims to be doing more writing to clear off debts. Things are "good and bad." She finishes the biography of Principal Tulloch but refuses to do a second edition because the profit is too small] (*OA* 159).

1890   Margaret, accompanied by her sons and Madge, travel to Jerusalem in the spring for research purposes.

[Oliphant breaks the chronological story here, jumping from "married life in London" (1852 to 1859) to Tiddy's death (November 1890) forty years later. In actuality the entry is made only five years later.]

> *Sunday 9 November 1890.* [Tiddy Memorial. Margaret Oliphant is sixty-two when her son dies and she writes this memorial] (*OA* 44–46).
> [November 16] *Davos.* [Tiddy's thirty-fourth birthday, a week after his death. Oliphant writes of traveling through Davos and the dark mountains with Cecco and Denny. At lunch Cecco tells how, "if all had been well," they would have been drinking to Tiddy's health. Since they could not, he asks them to drink to meeting him in heaven] (*OA* 46).
> *November 19.* [Oliphant relates how "this day last week we laid him [Tiddy] in the grave"] (*OA* 46–47).
> *Saturday 22.* [Three days later. Oliphant hopes that it will be "a little comfort" to her if she writes down the history "of the week that ended everything for this world." She tells how Tiddy became ill, his hallucinations, a brief reprieve, severe coughing spasms, and, finally, his childlike death] (*OA* 47–50).
> *December 9th.* [Twenty days later. The first segment of this entry details some of the delightful scenes in Tiddy's life. The second segment deals with Oliphant's work in progress and how it will provide a "safe little brother and sister home" for Cecco, Denny, and Madge] (*OA* 50–54).
> [1891]   *1st Jan 1891.* [Nearly two months after Tiddy's death. Oliphant takes account of her family, "three above and three below": Tiddy (singing in the "heavenly choir"), Frank (nephew), and Maggie—above; Cecco, Denny, and Madge (nieces)—below] (*OA* 54–57).

[At this point in the manuscript editor Jay inserts two inner dialogues with Tiddy that Oliphant must have found when she resumed her chronological narrative on 4 September 1892. This suggests that the 18 January 1891 entry was written over a period of the next three years and concluded with Cecco's death on 1 October 1894.]

February 13, 1891. [Inner dialogue with Tiddy. Oliphant discusses Tiddy's sins and her anguish. She remarks on finding today (4 September 1892) the inner dialogue (below) from August 1892. She had placed them together because their moods were so similar] (*OA* 58–59).

August 1892. [Inner dialogue on dreams of Tiddy. Oliphant records two dreams of Tiddy] (*OA* 60).

1891   *January 18, 1891.* [Written over a period of three years, Oliphant picks up the chronological thread of her life-narrative where she left off talking about her married life in London. In fact, she repeats information provided in the earlier chronological narrative: housekeeping in Harrington Square; Maggie's birth, the deaths of her mother and a second daughter. She ends this chronological section with their trip to Italy for Frank's health and his death in Rome] (*OA* 60–79).

1893   July: Madge marries William Valentine, jute manufacturer.

1894   In October Margaret's last surviving child, Cecco, dies. Denny changes her name by Deed Poll to Oliphant.

2nd October 1894. [A Memorial to Cecco. The information in this section suggests that it was written over the entire three-year period from 1891 to 1894. At this point Oliphant again breaks her chronological narrative to write a memorial to Cecco] (*OA* 79–83).

6th October. [Cecco's funeral day, four days later. Oliphant decides to remain in London to be near the graves of her two sons] (*OA* 83–85).

Monday 8 October. [The "day week" of Cecco's "death day"; two days after his funeral. Oliphant's carries on an internal dialogue with Cecco and God] (*OA* 85–86).

Christmas Night, 1894. [Three months after Cecco's death Oliphant again picks up the thread of her chronological narrative. She begins with Cecco's birth after Frank's death and concludes this section with her return to England, as a widow with three small children] (*OA* 86–89).

[The first volume ends here. Volume 2 begins five days after the last entry. Oliphant continues her chronological narrative. Editor Jay notes that "the date 1860 appears at the top of the first page, presumably to remind Mrs. Oliphant of the point she had reached in her story."]

December 30, 1894. [Cecco has been dead for three months. Oliphant resumes her narrative with her return from Rome, a stay with her brother in Birkenhead, then to a small cottage in Elie, Scotland, and a repeat of the "turning point" incident and the writing of the *Carlingford Chronicles* recorded in the first entry] (*OA* 89–99).

[1895]   *January 22.* [Oliphant continues her narrative about the events of 1861, when she moves her family to Ealing, to a tiny house on Uxbridge Road. She begins to recover from her grief and her writing is going well. She concludes this entry with the trip to Rome she took with the children and her women friends. She hints at the sorrow that was to come] (*OA* 99–108).

[Oliphant ends the 22 January, 1895 entry regarding the events of 1863. The date of the next entry is problematic. She dates it 1894, but it must be a slip, given that the year has just turned.]

1894 [5?]. [Oliphant begins this entry with mourning for Maggie who died of gastric fever on 27 January 1864. She continues the chronological narrative with the misfortunes of her brother Frank and her responsibility for his son and two daughters after his death. She tells of her problems with her own sons and concludes the chronological section with an account of all the children—the girls are sent to school in Germany and the boys to India, Oxford, and Eton—ending at 1875. She jumps to a final reckoning of her sons and one last passage of mourning over their deaths] (*OA* 108–54).

1896   *Janvier 14 Mardi.* APPENDIX C: 1896 Diary [This entry comes two years after Cecco's death and a year and a half before Oliphant's own. Following a note to "Go to London Library," Oliphant's last diary entry records a final dialogue with Cecco] (*OA* 160).

April: Final move to Wimbledon.

1897   25 June: Margaret Oliphant Wilson Oliphant dies.

Notes

Preface

1. To Barbara Herrnstein Smith's definition of narrative as "someone telling someone else something happened," I have added, for autobiography, "to *me*" (Herrnstein Smith, "Afterthoughts on Narrative III: Narrative Versions, Narrative Theories," in *On Narrative*, ed. W. J. T. Mitchell, Chicago and London: University of Chicago Press, 1981): 228.

2. Arnaldo Momigliano, *The Development of Greek Biography: Four Lectures* (Cambridge: Harvard University Press, 1971). With regard to the history of the term *autobiography*, Momigliano tells us that "according to the O.E.D. it first appeared in English in 1809 with Robert Southey. The facts known to me seem to point to a more interesting origin. In 1796 Isaac D'Israeli devoted a chapter of his *Miscellanies or Literary Recreations* to 'Some observations on diaries, self-biography and self-characters' (pages 95–110). The reviewer of D'Israeli's book in the *Monthly Review* 24 (1797): 375 noticed the word *self-biography* and commented: 'We are doubtful whether the latter word be legitimate . . . yet *autobiography* would have seemed pedantic.' The anonymous writer in the *Monthly Review* seems to have invented the word *autobiography*. Though pedantic it proved to be preferable to *self-biography*, which D'Israeli had favoured" (14).

Chapter 1

1. Jean Starobinski, *Montaigne in Motion*, trans. Arthur Goldhammer (Chicago and London: University of Chicago Press, 1985), xi.

2. Harriet Jacobs, *Incidents in the Life of a Slave Girl Written by Herself* (Cambridge, Mass., and London: Harvard University Press, 1987), 1.

3. Edmund Gosse, *Father and Son* (New York: W. W. Norton, 1963), 9.

4. Harriet Martineau, *Autobiography*, 2 vols. (Boston: Haughton, Osgood and Company, 1879).

5. See Carolyn A. Barros: "Figura, Persona, and Dynamis: Autobiography and Change," *Biography* 15, no. 1 (Winter 1992): 1–28.

6. Three outstanding historical works must be mentioned: a history of early biography and autobiography by Arnaldo Momigliano, *The Development of Greek Biography: Four Lectures* (Cambridge: Harvard University Press, 1971); Karl J. Weintraub, *The Value of the Individual: Self and Circumstance*

in Autobiography (Chicago: University of Chicago Press, 1978); and William C. Spengemann, *The Forms of Autobiography: Episodes in the History of a Literary Genre* (New Haven: Yale University Press, 1980). Georg Misch's extensive work, treating the history of autobiography up through Dante, is available in German; the two early volumes, *A History of Autobiography in Antiquity,* trans. E. W. Dickes (Cambridge: Harvard University Press, 1971), are out of print.

7. Working from Jacques Lacan, Peter Brooks's essay "Fictions of the Wolfman: Freud and Narrative Understanding," *Diacritics,* 9, no. 1 (March 1979): 72–81, is a fine example of this perspective.

8. For a discussion of these patterns in autobiography, see the "Figura" section.

9. Jean Starobinski, "The Style of Autobiography," in *Autobiography: Essays Theoretical and Critical,* ed. James Olney (Princeton: Princeton University Press, 1980), 78.

10. Tzvetan Todorov, *The Poetics of Prose* (Ithaca: Cornell University Press, 1977), 219–33.

11. Ibid., 230.

12. Ibid., 232.

13. Ibid., 233.

14. Hayden White, "The Value of Narrativity in the Representation of Reality," in Mitchell, *On Narrative,* 1.

15. Ibid., 17.

16. Gerard Genette, *Narrative Discourse,* trans. Jane E. Lewin (Ithaca: Cornell University Press, 1980), 28–29.

17. Herrnstein Smith, "Afterthoughts on Narrative III," 228–29.

18. Paul Ricoeur, "Narrative Time," in Mitchell, *On Narrative,* 170. "Story following" is not a passive activity for Ricoeur; readers are "following" the story in terms of "understanding the successive actions, thoughts, and feelings in question insofar as they present a certain directedness. . . . with expectations concerning the outcome. . . . the story's conclusion is the pole of attraction of the entire development."

19. Michel de Montaigne, *Essays and Selected Writings,* ed. and trans. Donald M. Frame (New York: St. Martin's Press, 1963), 316–17.

20. Or, if writers are employing autobiography to speak theory, we might say that the subject of the discourse is *disguised* as self.

21. Philippe Lejeune, *L'Autobiographie en France* (Paris: A. Colin, 1971), 33.

22. White, "Value of Narrativity," 12.

23. Saint Augustine, *The Confessions,* trans. Rex Warner (New York: New American Library, 1963), 213.

24. Jean-Jacques Rousseau, *The Confessions,* trans. J. M. Cohen (New York: Penguin Classics, 1952), 262.

25. Vladimir Nabokov, *Speak, Memory* (New York: G. P. Putnam's Sons, 1966), 12.

26. Susanna Egan, *Patterns of Experience in Autobiography* (Chapel Hill and London: University of North Carolina Press, 1984). Egan tells us that Newman began keeping journals in 1820, that he transcribed and added to them

from 1823 to 1828, that he retranscribed them with omissions in 1840, and that "on 31 December 1872 (the end of the year is, of course, to the autobiographic mind another significant point at which to end and begin things), he began recopying, this time with even more omissions. All the superseded copies were carefully burned in 1874" (52).

27. Cynthia Huff, "Jane and Thomas Carlyle's Letters as Autobiography," NEH Summer Seminar on Autobiography, Louisiana State University, June 1988.

28. White, "Value of Narrativity," 5.

29. Mary DeJong, "Hymns as Autobiography," NEH Summer Seminar on Autobiography, Louisiana State University, June 1988.

30. Georges Gusdorf, "Scripture of the Self: 'Prologue in Heaven,'" *Studies in Autobiography, Southern Review* 22, no. 2 (April 1986): 280–95.

31. Starobinski, *Montaigne in Motion,* x.

32. Emile Benveniste, *Problems in General Linguistics,* trans. Mary Elizabeth Meek (Coral Gables: University of Miami Press, 1971), 209.

33. See Richard E. Young, Alton L. Becker, and Kenneth L. Pike, *Rhetoric: Discovery and Change* (New York: Harcourt Brace Jovanovich, 1970), 120–21. A heuristic approach serves three functions: (1) it aids the investigator in retrieving relevant information that is stored in the mind; (2) it draws attention to important information that the investigator does not possess but can acquire by direct observation, reading, and experimentation; and (3) it prepares the investigator's mind for the intuition of a hypothesis, insight, or a new understanding. "Heuristic search, although systematic, is never a purely conscious, mechanical activity; intuition is indispensable and some trial and error inevitable" (121).

34. Genette, *Narrative Discourse,* 27.

35. Herrnstein Smith, "Afterthoughts on Narrative III," 222.

36. White, "Value of Narrativity," 7.

37. Paul John Eakin, *Fictions in Autobiography: Studies in the Art of Self-Invention* (Princeton: Princeton University Press, 1985), 186.

38. Genette, *Narrative Discourse,* 28.

39. See Georges Gusdorf, "Conditions and Limits of Autobiography," *Autobiography: Essays, Theoretical and Critical,* trans. James Olney (Princeton: Princeton University Press, 1980), 28–48. Many believe that, when this essay first appeared, in 1956, in *Formen der Selbstdarstellung: Analekten zu einer Geschichte des literarischen Selbstportraits,* autobiography became a legitimate genre for study by literary scholars.

40. Saint Augustine, *Confessions,* 258.

41. Ingmar Bergman, *The Magic Lantern,* trans. Joan Tate (New York: Viking Penguin, 1988).

42. Sor Juana Inés de la Cruz, *A Woman of Genius,* trans. Margaret Sayers Peden (Salisbury, Conn.: Lime Rock Press, 1982), 43.

43. Bergman, *Magic Lantern,* 13.

44. Jean-Paul Sartre, *The Words,* trans. Bernard Frechtman (New York: Vintage Books, 1981), 49–50.

45. Nelson Goodman tells us: "Our first impulse with any tale when the order of

telling is clear is to take the order of occurrence to be the same as the order of telling; we then make any needed corrections in accord with temporal indications given in the narrative and with our antecedent knowledge both of what happened and of causal processes in general. But discrepancy between order of telling and order of occurrence cannot always be discovered instantaneously—or at all. . . . A little time is needed to make the correction" ("Twisted Tales; or, Story, Study, and Symphony,"in Mitchell, *On Narrative,* 100–101).

46. Ibid., 107–10.

47. Herrnstein Smith tells us that readers will generally construe some chronology ("rough" or "precise," depending on the level of engagement) for the narrative events on the basis of some combination of the following: (1) "prior knowledge or beliefs concerning the chronology of those implied events as derived from other sources including other narratives"; (2) "familiarity with the relevant conventions of the language in which that narrative is presented"; (3) "familiarity with the relevant conventions and traditions of the style and genre of that narrative"; (4) "knowledge and beliefs, including cultural assumptions, with respect to how things in general, and the particular kinds of things with which that narrative is concerned, happen and 'follow from' each other," a sense of the logic of "temporal and causal sequence"; and (5) "certain more or less universal perceptual and cognitive tendencies involved in this processing—apprehending and organizing—information in any form" ("Afterthoughts on Narrative III," 226).

48. Ibid., 223. Also see Genette, *Narrative Discourse,* 36.

Chapter 2

1. Elizabeth Bruss, "Eye for I: Making and Unmaking Autobiography in Film," 296–320; Louis Renza, "The Veto of the Imagination," 268–95; and Michael Sprinker, "Fictions of the Self: The End of Autobiography," 321–42—all in Olney, *Autobiography.* See also Philippe Lejeune, "Autobiography in the Third Person," *NLH* 9 (1977): 27–50.

2. Jerome Hamilton Buckley, *The Turning Key: Autobiography and the Subjective Impulse since 1800* (Cambridge, Mass., and London: Harvard University Press, 1984); Robert Sayre, *The Examined Self: Benjamin Franklin, Henry Adams, Henry James* (Princeton: Princeton University Press, 1964); Paul Jay, *Being in the Text: Self-Representation from Wordsworth to Roland Barthes* (Ithaca and London: Cornell University Press, 1984); Heather Henderson, *The Victorian Self: Autobiography and Bibical Narrative* (Ithaca and London: Cornell University Press, 1989); Robert Elbaz, *The Changing Nature of the Self: A Critical Study of the Autobiographic Discourse* (Iowa City: University of Iowa Press, 1987); John Morris, *Versions of the Self: Studies in English Autobiography from John Bunyan to John Stuart Mill* (New York: Basic

Books, 1966); Patricia Spacks, *Imagining a Self: Autobiography and Novel in Eighteenth Century England* (Cambridge: Harvard University Press, 1976); James Olney, *Metaphors of Self: The Meaning of Autobiography* (Princeton: Princeton University Press, 1972).

3. Sprinker, "Fictions of the Self," 325.

4. I am indebted to Thomas E. Porter, *Myth and Modern American Drama* (Detroit: Wayne State University Press, 1969), for this discussion on persona.

5. Paul Jay, "What's the Use? Critical Theory and the Study of Autobiography," *Biography* 10, no. 1 (Winter 1987): 39–54. See also Eugene Vance, "Augustine's *Confessions* and the Grammar of Selfhood," *Genre*, no. 6 (1973): 3; and Paul de Man, "Autobiography as De-facement," *MLN* 94 (December 1979): 930.

6. Thomas Carlyle, *Sartor Resartus* (New York: Holt, Rinehart and Winston, 1970), hereafter cited in the text as *SR*.

7. I am playing off Georges Gusdorf's notion that "an autobiography cannot be a pure and simple record of existence, an account or a logbook. . . . A record of this kind, no matter how minutely exact, would be no more than a caricature of real life" ("Conditions and Limits of Autobiography," in Olney, *Autobiography*, 42).

8. Barros, "Autobiography and Change," 8.

9. John Bunyan, *The Pilgrim's Progress and Grace Abounding to the Chief of Sinners,* ed. James Thorpe (Boston: Houghton Mifflin, 1969), para. 49.

10. Brooks, "Wolfmann," 72.

11. Starobinski, "Style of Autobiography," 75–79.

12. Barbara Herrnstein Smith, *On the Margins of Discourse* (Chicago: University of Chicago Press, 1978), ix.

13. Kenneth Burke, *A Grammar of Motives* (Berkeley, Los Angeles, and London: University of California Press, 1969), 60.

14. Hayden White, *Tropics of Discourse: Essays in Cultural Criticism.* (Baltimore: Johns Hopkins University Press, 1978), 5.

15. M. Katherine Hayles, *Chaos Bound: Orderly Disorder in Contemporary Literature and Science* (Ithaca and London: Cornell University Press, 1990).

16. Ibid., xiv, 209.

17. Egan, *Patterns of Experience in Autobiography,* 5. Egan sees the four narrative patterns—paradise, journey, conversion, and confession—as "effective tools for the autobiographer." "Each of these 'myths' is capable of describing the quality of his secret and inner experience both because it acts as an emotionally and generally accurate description of that experience and because it means much the same thing to him as it does to his reader."

18. Mikhail Mikhailovich Bakhtin, *The Dialogic Imagination,* ed. Michael Holquist, trans. Caryl Emerson and Michael Holquist (Austin and London: University of Texas Press, 1981), 315.

19. John Barrett Mandel, "Bunyan and the Autobiographer's Artistic Purpose," *Criticism* 10 (1963): 225–43.

Chapter 3

1. Charles Frederick Harrold and William D. Templeman, *English Prose of the Victoria Era* (New York: Oxford University Press, 1954), xxxvi.
2. John Henry Cardinal Newman, *Apologia Pro Vita Sua*, ed. David J. DeLaura (New York: W. W. Norton, 1968), 78–79; hereafter cited as *Apol.*
3. Jonathan Edwards, *Personal Narrative*, ed. Ola Elizabeth Winslow (New York: Signet Books, 1966), 94.
4. Linda H. Peterson, *Victorian Autobiography: The Tradition of Self-Interpretation* (New Haven: Yale University Press, 1986), 96, 98. I concur with Peterson's reading of Newman's conversion. It is a conversion by interpretation of texts, rather than emotional experience. "Newman felt compelled to record three times that the evangelical pattern of experience did not represent his own." For Newman "experimental knowledge" was superseded by "the language of books." Like Thomas Scott, Newman did not wrestle with "angelic messengers or demonic voices"; rather, he struggled with "biblical and ecclesiastical texts."
5. Newman's coat of arms when he became cardinal bore the inscription "Cor ad cor loguitur" (heart speaks to heart).
6. J. N. D. Kelly, *Early Christian Doctrines* (New York: Harper and Row, 1978), 104, 110–11.
7. Newman, *Apologia,* "Note F., The Economy," 259.
8. Ibid.
9. Ibid., 257.
10. Ibid., 259.
11. Michael Ryan, "The Question of Autobiography in Cardinal Newman's *Apologia Pro Vita Sua*," *Georgia Review* 31 (1977): 698.
12. "Not by means of logic was God pleased to save his people" (*Apol. 136*).

Chapter 4

1. John Stuart Mill, *Autobiography and Other Writings,* ed. Jack Stillinger (Boston: Houghton Mifflin, 1969), 93; hereafter cited as *MA* (Mill's *Autobiography*).
2. John Stuart Mill, *The Earlier Letters of John Stuart Mill,* in *Collected Works of John Stuart Mill,* ed. Frances E. Mineka (Toronto: University of Toronto Press, 1963), 12:205.
3. Though Mill would later come to lose respect for Utilitarian reform, he never gives up his admiration for Bentham's innovative application of the inductive method (John Stuart Mill, "Bentham," *Autobiography and Other Writings,* 213–56).
4. Carlyle, *Sartor Resartus,* 207.
5. This was, of course, a fairly standard criticism used by conservatives against

trade unions and other nineteenth-century political groups that were working toward better wages.

6. Mill, "Bentham," 237.

7. The reading of the romantic poet does not make Mill a romantic; rather, a social romantic. Mill is beginning, at this point, to shape a political philosophy that shares values with Wordsworth, a concern for "the common feelings and common destiny of human beings," and with Claude Henri Saint-Simon, an evolutionary organicism, a return to a primitive Christian view of love combined with the scientific development of industry and technology. Persons who ascribed to these principles were often referred to as social romantics. See the discussion of the Saint Simonians in the "Figura" section.

An interesting aside: Saint-Simon's great uncle, Louis de Rouvroy Saint-Simon, is best known for his autobiography, *Memories,* a forty-three-volume work of his intriguing career as a diplomat during the reign of Louis XIV.

8. Mill, "Bentham," 237–38.

9. Ibid., 238.

10. Ibid., 229.

11. Ibid., 221–23. Note that C. K. Ogden in Bentham's *Theory of Fictions* (Paterson, N.J.: Littlefield, Adams, 1969) provides a thorough study of Bentham's theory. He stresses the point that Mill did not fully understand the import of Bentham's linguistic investigations of political philosophy. Nor perhaps did Bentham himself. Bentham, in an attempt to rid the legal system of its generalizations and impressionistic terminology, inadvertently showed just how much of practical political philosophy is dependent on the ambiguity of language for its flexibility in interpretation and implementation. Also see Kenneth Burke, *A Rhetoric of Motives* (Berkeley, Los Angeles, and London: University of California Press, 1950), in which he discusses Bentham's attempt to "transcend the suggestiveness of imagery" in the *Table of the Springs of Action* (90); he notes that Bentham saw Coleridge's archetypal design behind the imperfect institutions as "allegorical idols" (91).

12. William Wordsworth, "The Tables Turned," *Lyrical Ballads,* in *English Romantic Writers,* ed. David Perkins (New York: Harcourt, Brace and World, 1967), 209.

13. John Stuart Mill, "Coleridge," *Autobiography and Other Writings,* 260, 262.

14. Ibid., 260.

15. Ibid., 304.

16. Ibid., 263.

17. Carlyle, *Sartor Resartus,* 184.

18. Wolfgang von Goethe, *The Autobiography,* trans. John Oxenford (Chicago: University of Chicago Press, 1974). Goethe, in his autobiography (the title literally translated is *Poetry and Truth*), makes much of mature and imaginative commitment to the improvement of society and disdains self-aggrandizement and deterministic manipulation of external surroundings. Carlyle's *Sartor Resartus* calls on its hero Teufelsdröckh to "see his duty and do it."

19. Mill, "Bentham," 230.

20. Ibid.
21. William Wordsworth, "Preface, Second Edition of the Lyrical Ballads," in Perkins, *English Romantic Writers,* 321.
22. Mill, "Bentham," 230.
23. Ibid., 230–31.
24. John Stuart Mill, *On Liberty,* ed. David Spitz (New York: W. W. Norton, 1975), 60.
25. Ibid., 12.
26. Ibid., 44.
27. Asa Briggs, in *Victorian People: A Reassessment of Persons and Themes 1851–67* (Chicago: University of Chicago Press, 1970), suggests that the failure of the Utilitarians was due in large part to the English deference for the aristocracy. Mill himself believed that the "time was unpropitious, the reform fervor being in its period of ebb." The Tory forces were rallying, and the Radical forces were small (*MA* 128).

Chapter 5   ·

1. The Enlightenment citizen of the seventeenth and eighteenth centuries had believed that the world was governed by rational principles. The familiar metaphors characterized God as cosmic clockmaker and the universe as a gigantic mechanical clock wound up and let run. Humanity, by the aid of reason and science, was standing at the threshold of perfection. The Lisbon earthquake overturned all these notions.
2. Charles Darwin, *The Autobiography of Charles Darwin, 1809–1882,* with original omissions restored and edited by Nora Barlow (New York: W. W. Norton, 1958), 82; hereafter cited as *DA (Darwin's Autobiography).*
3. Bunyan, *Pilgrim's Progress and Grace Abounding to the Chief of Sinners,* para. 49.
4. "Possibility" and "proof" are Darwin's method of scientific practice; he hypothesizes along lines of possibility and then gathers evidence or proof from his observations.
5. Nora Barlow reports that Coleridge, in his later years, coined the word *darwinising* to describe Erasmus's "wild theorizing." "He stigmatised Dr. Darwin's philosophy in *Zoonomia* as the "State of Nature or the Orang Outang theology of the human race, substituted for the first chapters of the Book of Genesis";—a strange foreshadowing of the outraged protests that followed on the publication of *The Origin of Species* two generations later (*DA,* "Appendix," 150).
6. This statement needs qualification: men like Alfred Bussel Wallace and Jean Bastiste Lamarck were hard at work to discover a mechanism for transformation of the species.
7. Charles Darwin, *The Origin of Species,* variorum text edited by Morse Peckham (Philadelphia: University of Pennsylvania Press, 1959), 3:129.

8. Edward Manier, *The Young Darwin and His Cultural Circle* (Dordrecht, Neth.: D. Reidel, 1978), 173; Mary Hesse, *The Structure of Scientific Inference* (Berkeley: University of California Press, 1974).

9. Manier, *The Young Darwin*, 177.

10. Robert K. Merton, *Science, Technology and Society in Seventeenth-Century England* (New Jersey: Humanities Press, 1978), 216.

11. Darwin, *Origin of Species* (New York: New American Library, 1958), 75.

12. Loren Eisley, *Darwin's Century* (Garden City, N.Y.: Anchor/Doubleday, 1961), 168.

13. Gosse, *Father and Son,* 85.

14. Ibid., 86.

15. Ibid.

16. Ibid.

17. Ibid., 86–87.

Chapter 6

1. Margaret Oliphant, *The Autobiography and Letters of Mrs M. O. W. Oliphant Arranged and Edited by Mrs Harry Coghill* (Edinburgh and London: William Blackwood and Sons, 1899). Two other editions were published in 1899. Minor corrections were made for the second edition. The third edition abbreviated both the text and letters and omitted the Oliphant bibliography. The 1974 edition included an introduction by Q. D. Leavis; the 1988 edition reprinted only the *Autobiography,* with a foreword by Laurie Langbauer.

2. Margaret Oliphant, *The Autobiography of Margaret Oliphant: The Complete Text,* edited and introduced by Elisabeth Jay (Oxford: Oxford University Press, 1990). See Jay's "Note on the Text" for a full discussion on the history of the five earlier editions. Jay's edition is based upon the original manuscripts, two volumes, "the first in a small hardbound book . . . the second in a red morocco binding." Jay also includes passages from three of Oliphant's surviving diaries "whose content and form seem closely related to the disclosures of the autobiographical volumes proper" (xx). I have constructed a chronology of the *Autobiography's* composition and inserted it in Jay's chronology of Oliphant's life (See app.).

3. Margaret Oliphant's reputation as a literary figure is cloudy. In the "Figura" section of this chapter I attempt to clear up some of the confusion by detailing the reasons for the critical ambivalence regarding her stature. While I am both interested and involved in a reappraisal of Oliphant's work, in this essay I am neither arguing for or against her place in the Victorian canon.

4. Newman does make an oblique reference to the death of his sister as causing a temporary mental breakdown.

5. D. J. Trela, ed., *Margaret Oliphant: Critical Essays on a Gentle Subversive*

(London: Associated University Presses, 1995), 15. Trela argues that Oliphant's "fictional representation of women was more radical than her public political views."

6. Merryn Williams, "Feminist or Antifeminist? Oliphant and the Woman Question," in Trela, *Margaret Oliphant,* 165–80.

7. Oliphant criticizes her beloved friend Trollope, in particular, for making his autobiography an "intimate chat" about the characters in his fiction, rather than a narrative of his own life (*OA* 14).

8. Laurie Langbauer, "Absolute Commonplaces: Oliphant's Theory of Autobiography," in Trela, *Margaret Oliphant,* 124–34.

9. Ibid., 124–25.

10. Ibid., 125.

11. For a discussion of Carlyle's views on the way that the ordinary resides in the extraordinary and the extraordinary in the ordinary, I refer readers back to the Carlyle chapter.

12. J. W. Cross, ed., *George Eliot's Life as Related in her Letters and Journals,* 3 vols. (Edinburgh and London: William Blackwood and Sons, 1883).

13. Jay, "Freed by Necessity, Trapped by the Market: The Editing of Oliphant's *Autobiography*" in Trela, *Margaret Oliphant,* 142–43.

14. Jay, intro., *Autobiography,* xv.

15. Ibid., vii.

16. Avrom Fleishman, "Personal Myth: Three Victorian Autobiographies," in *Approaches to Victorian Autobiography,* ed. George P. Landow (Athens: University of Ohio Press, 1979): 215–34. Fleishman, in discussing John Stuart Mill's autobiography, writes: "the one [myth] he grasps to give shape to his own career is a synecdoche of the myth prevailing in his society. The myth holds that life is progress, in accordance with the liberal faith in human progress through educational enlightenment and utilitarian reform" (218).

17. Jay, intro., *Autobiography,* xv.

18. Langbauer, "Absolute Commonplaces," 127

19. Margaret Oliphant, "The Fancies of a Believer," *Blackwood's* 132 (July 1882): 243.

20. "Oliphant felt herself precluded from the domestic and professional advantages accorded to male writers, whose sense of progress and achievement could be measured in attaining such public goals as secure editorial positions. Yet when she compared herself with women writers she constantly stressed the burden of business and domestic decisions, traditionally assumed to be male prerogatives that had been pressed upon her" (Jay, intro., *Autobiography,* xiii).

21. For an in-depth discussion of Oliphant's role as mother, see Linda H. Peterson, "Audience and the Autobiographer's Art: An Approach to the *Autobiography* of Mrs. M. O. W. Oliphant," in Landow, *Approaches to Victorian Autobiography,* 158–74.

22. Linda Peterson, "The Female *Bildungsroman*," in Trela, *Margaret Oliphant,* 84. Peterson notes that Oliphant was critical of any writer whose books

"depicted motherhood as anything less than 'sacred.'" Oliphant finds Annie Thackery Ritchie's *Story of Elizabeth* and Harriet Martineau's *Autobiography* as particularly offensive.

23. This entry appears as appendix A of the Jay edition of the *Autobiography* (*OA* 155–58).

24. Oliphant did not mourn equally for all her losses. She does not mention, in the *Autobiography*, the birth of Stephen Thomas in 1858 and his death nine days later. She does speak of her father "going off by himself" in his last days but fails to mention his death and views the passing of her brother Frank as benevolent, his release from suffering. Oliphant leaves us, instead, with intense accounts of the losses of her mother, two of her three babies, her husband, her daughter Maggie, and her sons Tiddy and Cecco.

25. Jay, intro., *Autobiography*, x. The major portions of the unpublished material in the Oliphant autobiography were written immediately after the deaths in 1864, 1890, and 1894 of her three surviving children, Maggie at age ten, Tiddy at thirty-three, and Cecco at thirty-four.

26. Jay, appendix C, *Autobiography*, 160.

27. Virginia Woolf, *Three Guineas* (London: Hogarth Press, 1938).

28. Jay, intro., *Autobiography*, x.

29. Ibid., xi. Jay tells us that Oliphant maintained friendship or had acquaintances with many of the literary, political, and religious giants of her day. She wrote a poem for the queen, translations and biographies of major political and religious figures, and critical reviews on all of England's leading writers. "Her repeated assertions of social awkwardness neglect her considerable gifts as a hostess capable, for instance, of organizing an open-air party on the island of Runnymede . . . to celebrate the twenty-fifth anniversary of her connection with the publishing firm of Blackwoods', an event which in itself suggests a sense of her own worth in the creative partnership."

30. See Trela, intro., *Margaret Oliphant*, 15–16, for a discussion of the misrepresentation of Oliphant's work.

31. While Oliphant describes herself as "amused" by this treatment, in *Effie Ogilvie* she displays the ordinary trait of vindictiveness by making an "unflattering reference" to Grace Greenwood (see Jay, "Note to Page 41," *Autobiography*, 167).

32. Oliphant reviewed Symonds's book *Life*, prepared from his private memoirs and letters by H. F. Brown in 1895, in "Men and Women," *Blackwood's* (April 1895).

33. Jay, intro., *Autobiography*, viii.

34. Peterson, "Audience and the Autobiographer's Art," 172.

35. Jay, "Freed by Necessity," 139.

36. Trela suggests that to the casual observer Oliphant was seen as a "borderline penny-a liner" (Trela, intro., *Margaret Oliphant*, 16).

37. This particular charge Trela credits to Trevor Royle in *Precipitous City: The Story of Literary Edinburgh*.

38. Jay, intro., *Autobiography*, xvi.

39. John Stock Clarke, "The Paradoxes of Oliphant's Reputation," in Trela, *Margaret Oliphant,* 34–35.
40. Jay, intro., *Autobiography,* xvi.
41. Writing in the *Scottish Review* in 1897, William Wallace acknowledged that George Eliot achieved much that was beyond Oliphant's powers, and yet he insisted that the comparison is sometimes in the latter's favor: "Mrs. Oliphant grasped the realities of Carlingford as George Eliot never grasped the realities of Middlemarch." Clarke adds that, while Wallace praises Oliphant highly, in the end he "uses the overproduction myth to deny her major status" (Clarke, "Paradoxes," 45–46).
42. Among others, Trela lists Robert and Vineta Colby, Q. D. Leavis, John Stock Clarke, Margaret [Rubik] Holubetz, J. A. Haythornethwaite, Gaye Tuchman and Nina Fortin, Merryn Williams, Joseph H. O'Mealy, Jennifer Uglow, Penelope Fitzgerald, and Elisabeth Jay (Trela, intro., *Margaret Oliphant,* 25–26).
43. Margarete Rubik, "The Subversion of Literary Clichés in Oliphant's Fiction," in Ibid., 50.
44. Ibid., 51, 53, 57, 61.
45. Clarke, "Paradoxes," 34–35.
46. George Saintsbury, *History of Nineteenth-Century Literature,* 3d ed. (London: Macmillan, 1901); and Hugh Walker, *Literature of the Victorian Era* (Cambridge: Cambridge University Press, 1910).
47. Clarke, "Paradoxes," 46.
48. Peterson, "Female *Bildungsroman,*" 87.
49. I am indebted to Trela for this passage taken from Oliphant's obituary of Anthony Trollope (*Margaret Oliphant,* 11).
50. Jay, "Note to Page 73," 170.
51. Jay tells us that "a number of false starts" precede the first substantial entry in the first of the two autobiographical volumes. She believes that the pages, some of which have been torn out, "some half-erased," "some heavily scored through," have to do with Oliphant's brother Willie and the "very doubtful experiment" of allowing him to assume the authorship of four of her early novels (Jay, intro., *Autobiography,* xix).
52. Jay, appendix A, *Autobiography,* 155–58.
53. "1896, APPENDIX C," *Autobiography,* 160.
54. Dale Kramer, "The Cry That Binds: Oliphant's Theory of Domestic Tragedy"; and Rubik, "Subversion of Literary Clichés in Oliphant's Fiction," both in Trela, *Margaret Oliphant,* 153, 158, 57.
55. Kramer, "Cry That Binds," 149.
56. Jane P. Tompkins, ed., *Reader-Response Criticism: From Formalism to Post-Structuralism* (Baltimore: Johns Hopkins University Press, 1980), x.
57. Langbauer, "Absolute Commonplaces," 128.
58. Margaret Oliphant, "The Fancies of a Believer," *Blackwood's* 157 (February 1895): 243.
59. At present we have only a few incomplete bibliographies of Oliphant's work,

the first by her original editors, Denny Wilson and Annie Coghill, and another, confined to Oliphant's fiction, completed by John S. Clarke.

60. Jay, Williams, and Rubik treat this issue in their essays in Trela *Margaret Oliphant.* Also see: J. A. Haythornethwaite, "The Wages of Success: *Miss Marjoribanks*, Margaret Oliphant and the House of Blackwood," *Publishing History* 15 (1984): 91–107; Gaye Tuchman with Nina Fortin, *Edging Women Out: Victorian Novelists, Publishers, and Social Change* (New Haven: Yale University Press, 1989); Jenni Calder, *Women and Marriage in Victorian Fiction* (New York: Oxford University Press, 1976); and Judith Lowder Newton, *Women, Power, and Subversion: Social Strategies in British Fiction, 1778–1860* (Athens: University of Georgia Press, 1981).

61. Jay, intro., *Autobiography,* xiii.

Chapter 7

1. Peter Ackroyd, *T. S. Eliot—A Life* (New York: Simon and Schuster, 1984).
2. Briggs, *Victorian People,* 4–5.
3. Ibid., 1.
4. Ibid., 12.
5. Samuel Smiles, *Self-Help* (London: John Murray, 1859).
6. Briggs, *Victorian People,* 117.
7. Janet Varner Gunn, *Autobiography: Toward a Poetics of Experience* (Philadelphia: University of Pennsylvania Press, 1982), 17.
8. Paul John Eakin, *Fictions in Autobiography: Studies in the Art of Self-Invention* (Princeton: Princeton University Press, 1985), 179.
9. Gunn, *Autobiography: Toward a Poetics of Experience,* 38.
10. Starobinski, *Montaigne in Motion,* 33–34.
11. Ryan, "Question of Autobiography in Cardinal Newman's *Apologia Pro Vita Sua,*" 698.
12. See Philippe Lejeune, "Pent-on Innover en Autobiographie," *L'Autobiographie* (Aix-en-Provence: VIes Recontres psychanalytiques, 1987).
13. Maxine Hong Kingston, *The Woman Warrior: Memories of a Girlhood among Ghosts* (New York: Vintage Books, 1977), 235.
14. Ibid., 239.
15. Samuel Taylor Coleridge, *Biographia Literaria,* in *The Norton Anthology of English Literature,* ed. M. H. Abrams (New York: W. W. Norton, 1968), 281.

Bibliography

Ackroyd, Peter. *T. S. Eliot—A Life*. New York: Simon and Schuster, 1984.

Adams, Timothy Dow. *Telling Lies in Modern American Autobiography*. Chapel Hill: University of North Carolina Press, 1990.

Augustine, Saint. *The Confessions*. Trans. Rex Warner. New York: New American Library, 1963.

Bakhtin, Mikhail Mikhailovich. *The Dialogic Imagination*. Ed. Michael Holquist. Trans. Caryl Emerson and Michael Holquist. Austin: University of Texas Press, 1981.

Barlow, Nora. "On Charles Darwin and His Grandfather." *The Autobiography of Charles Darwin, 1809–1882*. New York: W. W. Norton, 1969.

Barros, Carolyn A. "Figura, Persona, and Dynamis: Autobiography and Change." *Biography* 15, no. 1 (Winter 1992): 1–28.

Barthes, Roland. *Roland Barthes by Roland Barthes*. Trans. Richard Howard. New York: Hill and Wang, 1977.

Benveniste, Emile. *Problems in General Linguistics*. Trans. Mary Elizabeth Meek. Coral Gables: University of Miami Press, 1971.

Bergman, Ingmar. *The Magic Lantern*. Trans. Joan Tate. New York: Viking Penguin, 1988.

Briggs, Asa. *Victorian People: A Reassessment of Persons and Themes, 1851–67*. Chicago: University of Chicago Press, 1970.

Brooks, Peter. "Fictions of the Wolfman: Freud and Narrative Understanding." *Diacritics* 9, no. 1 (March 1979): 72–81.

Bruss, Elizabeth. "Eye for I: Making and Unmaking Autobiography in Film." In *Autobiography: Essays Theoretical and Critical*, ed. James Olney, 296–320. Princeton: Princeton University Press, 1980.

Buckley, Jerome Hamilton. *The Turning Key: Autobiography and the Subjective Impulse since 1800*. Cambridge: Harvard University Press, 1984.

Bunyan, John. *The Pilgrim's Progress and Grace Abounding to the Chief of Sinners*. Ed. James Thorpe. Boston: Houghton Mifflin, 1969.

Burke, Kenneth. *A Grammar of Motives*. Berkeley: University of California Press, 1969.

———. *A Rhetoric of Motives*. Berkeley: University of California Press, 1950.

Calder, Jenni. *Women and Marriage in Victorian Fiction*. New York: Oxford University Press, 1976.

Carlyle, Thomas. *Sartor Resartus*. New York: Holt, Rinehart and Winston, 1970.

Cellini, Benvenuto. *Autobiography*. Trans. John Addington Symonds. New York: Dolphin, 1961.

Clarke, John Stock. "The Paradoxes of Oliphant's Reputation." In *Margaret*

Oliphant: Critical Essays on a Gentle Subversive, ed. D. J. Trela, 33–48. London: Associated University Presses, 1995.

Coleridge, Samuel Taylor. *Biographia Literaria* in *Norton Anthology of English Literature*, vol. 2. Ed. M. H. Abrams. New York: W. W. Norton, 1968.

Cross, J. W., ed. *George Eliot's Life as Related in her Letters and Journals.* 3 vols. Edinburgh and London: William Blackwood and Sons, 1883.

Darwin, Charles. *The Autobiography of Charles Darwin, 1809–1882.* With original omissions restored and edited by Nora Barlow. New York: W. W. Norton, 1969.

———. *The Origin of Species.* New York: New American Library, 1958.

———. *The Origin of Species.* Variorum text. Ed. Morse Peckham. Philadelphia: University of Pennsylvania Press, 1959.

DeJong, Mary. "Hymns as Autobiography." NEH Summer Seminar on Autobiography. Louisiana State University, June 1988.

De la Cruz, Sor Juana Inés. *La Respuesta / A Woman of Genius.* Trans. Margaret Sayers Peden. Salisbury, Conn.: Lime Rock Press, 1982.

De Man, Paul. "Autobiography as De-facement." *MLN* 94 (December 1979): 930.

Eakin, Paul John. *Fictions in Autobiography: Studies in the Art of Self-Invention.* Princeton: Princeton University Press, 1985.

Edwards, Jonathan. *Personal Narrative.* Ed. Ola Elizabeth Winslow. New York: Signet, 1966.

Egan, Susanna. *Patterns of Experience in Autobiography.* Chapel Hill: University of North Carolina Press, 1984.

Eisley, Loren. *Darwin's Century.* Garden City, N.Y.: Anchor/Doubleday, 1961.

Elbaz, Robert. *The Changing Nature of the Self: A Critical Study of Autobiographical Discourse.* Iowa City: University of Iowa Press, 1987.

Eliot, T. S. *Four Quartets.* San Diego: Harcourt Brace Jovanovich, 1943.

Fleishman, Avrom. *Figures of Autobiography: The Language of Self-Writing in Victorian and Modern England.* Berkeley: University of California Press, 1983.

———. "Personal Myth: Three Victorian Autobiographies." In *Approaches to Victorian Autobiography*, ed. George P. Landow, 215–34. Athens: University of Ohio Press, 1979.

Genet, Jean. *The Thief's Journal.* Trans. Bernard Frectman. New York: Grove Press, 1964.

Genette, Gerard. *Narrative Discourse.* Trans. Jane E. Lewin. Ithaca: Cornell University Press, 1980.

Gibbon, Edward. *The Autobiography of Edward Gibbon.* Ed. Dedro A. Saunders. New York: Meridian Books, 1961.

Goethe, Johann Wolfgang. *The Autobiography.* Trans. John Oxenford. Chicago: University of Chicago Press, 1974.

Goodman, Nelson. "Twisted Tales; or, Story, Study, and Symphony." In *On Narrative*, ed. W. J. T. Mitchell, 99–115. Chicago: University of Chicago Press, 1981.

Gosse, Edmund. *Father and Son. A Study of Two Temperaments.* New York: W. W. Norton, 1963.

Gunn, Janet Varner. *Autobiography: Toward a Poetics of Experience.* Philadelphia: University of Pennsylvania Press, 1982.

Gusdorf, Georges. "Conditions and Limits of Autobiography." In *Autobiography: Essays Theoretical and Critical,* ed. James Olney, 28–48. Princeton: Princeton University Press, 1980.

———. "Scripture of the Self: 'Prologue in Heaven.'" *Studies in Autobiography. Southern Review* 22, no. 2 (April 1986): 280–95.

Harrold, Charles Frederick, and William D. Templeman. *English Prose of the Victorian Period.* New York: Oxford University Press, 1954.

Hayles, M. Katherine. *Chaos Bound: Orderly Disorder in Contemporary Literature and Science.* Ithaca: Cornell University Press, 1990.

Haythornethwaite, J. A. "The Wages of Success: *Miss Marjoribanks,* Margaret Oliphant and the House of Blackwood." *Publishing History* 15 (1984): 91–107.

Henderson, Heather. *The Victorian Self: Autobiography and Biblical Narrative.* Ithaca: Cornell University Press, 1989.

Herrnstein Smith, Barbara. "Afterthoughts on Narrative III: Narrative Versions, Narrative Theories." In *On Narrative,* ed. W. J. T. Mitchell, 209–32. Chicago: University of Chicago Press, 1981).

———. *On the Margins of Discourse.* Chicago: University of Chicago Press, 1978.

Hesse, Mary. *The Structure of Scientific Inference.* Berkeley: University of California Press, 1974.

Huff, Cynthia. "Jane and Thomas Carlyle's Letters as Autobiography." NEH Summer Seminar, Lousiana State University, June 1988.

Jacobs, Harriet A. *Incidents in the Life of a Slave Girl Written by Herself.* Cambridge: Harvard University Press, 1987.

Jay, Elisabeth. "Freed by Necessity, Trapped by the Market: The Editing of Oliphant's *Autobiography.*" In *Margaret Oliphant: Critical Essays on a Gentle Subversive,* ed. D. J. Trela, 135–46. London: Associated University Presses, 1995.

Jay, Paul. *Being in the Text: Self-Representation from Wordsworth to Roland Barthes.* Ithaca: Cornell University Press, 1984.

———. "What's the Use? Critical Theory and the Study of Autobiography." *Biography* 10, no. 1 (Winter 1987): 39–54.

Kelly, J. N. D. *Early Christian Doctrines.* New York: Harper and Row, 1978.

Kingston, Maxine Hong. *The Woman Warrior: Memoirs of a Girlhood among Ghosts.* New York: Vintage, 1977.

Kramer, Dale. "The Cry That Binds: Oliphant's Theory of Domestic Tragedy." In *Margaret Oliphant: Critical Essays on a Gentle Subversive,* ed. D. J. Trela, 147–64. London: Associated University Presses, 1995.

Landow, George P., ed. *Approaches to Victorian Autobiography.* Athens: University of Ohio Press, 1979.

Langbauer, Laurie. "Absolute Commonplaces: Oliphant's Theory of Autobiography." In *Margaret Oliphant: Critical Essays on a Gentle Subversive,* ed. D. J. Trela, 124–34. London: Associated University Presses, 1995.

Laye, Camara. *The Dark Child.* New York: Farrar, Straus and Giroux, 1954.

Lejeune, Philippe. "Autobiography in the Third Person." *NLH* 9 (1977): 27–50.

———. *On Autobiography.* Trans. Katherine Leary. Minneapolis: University of Minnesota Press, 1989.

Mandel, John Barrett. "Bunyan and the Autobiographer's Artistic Purpose." *Criticism* 10 (1968): 225–43.

Manier, Edward. *The Young Darwin and His Cultural Circle.* Dordrecht, Neth.: D. Reidel, 1978.

Martineau, Harriet. *Harriet Martineau's Autobiography.* 2 vols. Boston: Houghton, Osgood, 1879.

Merton, Robert K. *Science, Technology and Society in Seventeenth-Century England.* New Jersey: Humanities Press, 1978.

Mill, John Stuart. *Autobiography and Other Writings.* Ed. Jack Stillinger. Boston: Houghton Mifflin, 1969.

———. *The Earlier Letters of John Stuart Mill.* Vol. 12 of *The Collected Works of John Stuart Mill.* Ed. Frances E. Mineka. Toronto: University of Toronto Press, 1963.

———. *On Liberty.* Ed. David Spitz. New York: W. W. Norton, 1975.

Misch, Georg. *A History of Autobiography in Antiquity.* Trans. E. W. Dickes. 2 vols. Cambridge: Harvard University Press, 1951.

Mitchell, W. J. T., ed. *On Narrative.* Chicago: University of Chicago Press, 1981.

Momigliano, Arnaldo. *The Development of Greek Biography: Four Lectures.* Cambridge: Harvard University Press, 1971.

Montaigne, Michel de. *Essays and Selected Writings.* Ed. and trans. Donald M. Frame. New York: St. Martin's Press, 1963.

Morris, John N. *Versions of the Self: Studies in Autobiography from John Bunyan to John Stuart Mill.* New York: Basic Books, 1966.

Morrison, J. S. "Antiphon." In *The Older Sophists,* ed. Rosamond Kent Sprague, 106–240. Columbia: University of South Carolina Press, 1972.

Nabokov, Vladimir. *Speak, Memory.* New York: G. P. Putnam's Sons, 1966.

Newman, John Henry Cardinal. *Apologia Pro Vita Sua.* Ed. David De Laura. New York: W. W. Norton, 1968.

———. *Essay in Aid of a Grammar of Assent.* London: Burns and Oates, 1881.

———. *An Essay on the Development of Christian Doctrine.* London: Longmans, 1888.

———. *Idea of a University.* London: B. M. Pickering, 1873.

Newton, Judith Lowder. *Women, Power, and Subversion: Social Strategies in British Fiction, 1778–1860.* Athens: University of Georgia Press, 1981.

Ogden, C. K. *Bentham's Theory of Fictions.* Paterson, N.J.: Littlefield, Adams, 1969.

Oliphant, Margaret. *The Autobiography and Letters of Mrs M. O. W. Oliphant, Arranged and Edited by Mrs Harry Coghill.* Edinburgh and London: William Blackwood and Sons, 1899.

———. *The Autobiography of Margaret Oliphant: The Complete Text.* Ed. Elisabeth Jay. Oxford: Oxford University Press, 1990.

———. "The Fancies of a Believer." *Blackwood's* 132 (July 1882): 237–47.

Olney, James, ed. *Autobiography: Essays Theoretical and Critical.* Princeton: Princeton University Press, 1980.

———. *Metaphors of Self: The Meaning of Autobiography.* Princeton: Princeton University Press, 1972.

Peterson, Linda H. "Audience and the Autobiographer's Art: An Approach to the *Autobiography* of Mrs. M. O. W. Oliphant." In *Approaches to Victorian Autobiography,* ed. George P. Landow, 158–74. Athens: University of Ohio Press, 1979.

———. *Victorian Autobiography: The Tradition of Self-Interpretation.* New Haven: Yale University Press, 1986.

———. "The Female *Bildungsroman:* Tradition and Revision in Oliphant's Fiction." In *Margaret Oliphant: Critical Essays on a Gentle Subversive,* ed. D. J. Trela, 66–89. London: Associated University Presses, 1995.

Porter, Thomas E. *Myth and Modern American Drama.* Detroit: Wayne State University Press, 1969.

Renza, Louis. "The Veto of the Imagination." In *Autobiography: Essays Theoretical and Critical,* ed. James Olney, 268–95. Princeton: Princeton University Press, 1980.

Ricoeur, Paul. "Narrative Time." In *On Narrative,* ed. W. J. T. Mitchell, 165–86. Chicago: University of Chicago Press, 1981.

Rousseau, Jean-Jacques. *The Confessions.* Trans. J. M. Cohen. New York: Penguin, 1952.

Rubik, Margarete. "The Subversion of Literary Clichés in Oliphant's Fiction." In *Margaret Oliphant: Critical Essays on a Gentle Subversive,* ed. D. J. Trela, 49–65. London: Associated University Presses, 1995.

Ruskin, John. *Praeterita.* New York: Merrill and Baker, 1885.

Russell, Bertrand. *The Autobiography of Bertrand Russell.* Boston: Little, Brown, 1951.

Ryan, Michael. "The Question of Autobiography in Cardinal Newman's *Apologia Pro Vita Sua.*" *Georgia Reveiw* 31 (1977): 672–99.

Saintsbury, George. *History of Nineteenth-Century Literature,* 3d ed. London: Macmillan, 1901.

Sartre, Jean Paul. *The Words.* Trans. Bernard Frechtman. New York: Vintage, 1981.

Sayre, Robert F. *The Examined Self: Benjamin Franklin, Henry Adams, Henry James.* Princeton: Princeton University Press, 1964.

Smiles, Samuel. *Self-Help.* London: John Murray, 1859.

Soyinka, Wole. *Aké: The Years of Childhood.* New York: Vintage, 1983.

Spacks, Patricia. *Imagining a Self: Autobiography and Novel in Eighteenth-Century England.* Cambridge: Harvard University Press, 1976.

Spengemann, William C. *The Forms of Autobiography: Episodes in the History of a Literary Genre.* New Haven: Yale University Press, 1980.

Sprinker, Michael. "Fictions of the Self: The End of Autobiography." In *Autobiography: Essays Theoretical and Critical,* ed. James Olney, 321–42. Princeton: Princeton University Press, 1980.

Starobinski, Jean. *Montaigne in Motion*. Trans. Arthur Goldhammer. Chicago: University of Chicago Press, 1985.

———. "The Style of Autobiography." In *Autobiography: Essays Theoretical and Critical*, ed. James Olney, 73–83. Princeton: Princeton University Press, 1980.

Stein, Gertrude. *The Autobiography of Alice B. Toklas*. New York: Vintage Books, 1933.

———. *Everybody's Autobiography*. New York: Random House, 1937.

Teresa, Saint. *The Life of Saint Teresa of Avila*. Trans. David Lewis. London: Burns and Oates, 1962.

Todorov, Tzvetan. *The Poetics of Prose*. Ithaca: Cornell University Press, 1977.

Tompkins, Jane P., ed. *Reader-Response Criticism: From Formalism to Post-Structuralism*. Baltimore: Johns Hopkins University Press, 1980.

Trela, D. J., ed. *Margaret Oliphant: Critical Essays on a Gentle Subversive*. London: Associated University Presses, 1995.

Tuchman, Gaye, with Nina Fortin. *Edging Women Out: Victorian Novelists, Publishers, and Social Change*. New Haven: Yale University Press, 1989.

Vance, Eugene. "Augustine's *Confessions* and the Grammar of Selfhood." *Genre* 6 (1973): 3.

Vico, Giambattista. *The Autobiography of Giambattista Vico*. Trans. Max H. Fisch and Thomas Bergin. Ithaca: Cornell University Press, 1944.

Walker, Hugh. *Literature of the Victorian Era*. Cambridge: Cambridge University Press, 1910.

Weintraub, Karl Joachim. *The Value of the Individual: Self and Circumstance in Autobiography*. Chicago: University of Chicago Press, 1978.

White, Hayden. *Tropics of Discourse: Essays in Cultural Criticism*. Baltimore: Johns Hopkins University Press, 1978.

———. "The Value of Narrativity in the Representation of Reality." In *On Narrative*, ed. W. J. T. Mitchell, 1–23. Chicago: University of Chicago Press, 1981.

Williams, Merryn. "Feminist or Antifeminist? Oliphant and the Woman Question." In *Margaret Oliphant: Critical Essays on a Gentle Subversive*, ed. D. J. Trela, 165–80. London: Associated University Presses, 1995.

Woolf, Virginia. *Three Guineas*. London: Hogarth Press, 1938.

Wordsworth, William. "Preface, Second Edition of the *Lyrical Ballads*." In *English Romantic Writers*, ed. David Perkins, 320–33. New York: Harcourt, Brace and World, 1967.

———. "The Tables Turned." *Lyrical Ballads*. In *English Romantic Writers*, ed. David Perkins, 209. New York: Harcourt, Brace and World, 1967.

Young, Richard E., Alton L. Becker, and Kenneth L. Pike. *Rhetoric: Discovery and Change*. New York: Harcourt Brace Jovanovich, 1970.

Index